MICHAEL JOSEPH

Published by the Penguin Group
Penguin Books Ltd, 80 Strand, London WC2R 0RL, England
Penguin Group (USA) Inc., 375 Hudson Street, New York, New York 10014, USA
Penguin Group (Canada), 90 Eglinton Avenue East, Suite 700, Toronto, Ontario,
Canada M4P 2Y3 (a division of Pearson Penguin Canada Inc.)
Penguin Ireland, 25 St Stephen's Green, Dublin 2, Ireland (a division of Penguin Books Ltd)
Penguin Group (Australia), 250 Camberwell Road, Camberwell, Victoria 3124, Australia
(a division of Pearson Australia Group Pty Ltd)
Penguin Books India Pvt Ltd, 11 Community Centre, Panchsheel Park,
New Delhi – 110 017, India
Penguin Group (NZ), 67 Apollo Drive, Rosedale, North Shore 0632,
New Zealand (a division of Pearson New Zealand Ltd)
Penguin Books (South Africa) (Pty) Ltd, 24 Sturdee Avenue, Rosebank,
Johannesburg 2196, South Africa
Penguin Books Ltd, Registered Offices: 80 Strand, London WC2R 0RL, England

www.penguin.com

First published 2010
1

Printed in China

Colour reproduction by Altaimage Ltd

A CIP catalogue record for this book is available from the British Library

This edition produced for The Book People Ltd, Hall Wood Avenue, Haydock, St Helens, WA11 9UL

ISBN: 978–0–718–15747–0

AT ELIZABETH DAVID'S TABLE

Her very best everyday recipes

Elizabeth David

Compiled by Jill Norman

Photography by David Loftus

Illustrations by Jon Gray

MICHAEL JOSEPH
an imprint of
PENGUIN BOOKS

Sans souci sans chagrin
Bonne table et bon vin.

CONTENTS

A FOREWORD IN TRIBUTES 7

INTRODUCTION 12

Fast and Fresh 18

STARTERS & LIGHT DISHES 22

Fresh Herbs 42

SOUPS 46

Confort Anglais, French Fare 66

EGGS 70

Pasta Asciutta 94

PASTA 98

The Markets of France: Cavaillon 118

VEGETABLES 122

My Dream Kitchen 156

RICE 158

Italian Fish Markets 172

FISH, SHELLFISH & CRUSTACEA 176

Dishes for Collectors 204

MEAT 208

Wine in the Kitchen 256

POULTRY & GAME BIRDS 258

Para Navidad 288

SAUCES 292

Banketting Stuffe 306

SWEET DISHES & CAKES 310

The Baking of an English Loaf 344

BREAD & YEAST BAKING 348

The Italian Pizza and the French Pissaladière 362

BOOKS BY ELIZABETH DAVID 372

INDEX 374

A FOREWORD *in* TRIBUTES

It's a real honour to be asked to write a few words about the late Elizabeth David. I never had the opportunity to meet her; I so wish I had. But even so, her work has really influenced my own career in a powerful but indirect way. Ours is a tough industry to be a part of, male or female, and it just so happens that many of the greatest cooks I know are women. Like her, they're amazing: strong, confident, incredibly creative, with an intuitive understanding of what people want to eat. Two of the very best cooks, Rose Gray and Ruth Rogers, are big fans of her work and even had the privilege of serving her at The River Café. They drilled many of the ideas pioneered by Elizabeth David into my head as a young chef coming up in their kitchen. In my mind, they are her modern-day equivalents.

Elizabeth David's travels and adventures around the Mediterranean were, without question, a massive reference point in her life and work. She soaked up the local food, historic recipes and traditions of the countries she visited and gained a huge respect for simple, natural cooking. The food, people and ingredients she wrote about opened up new and exciting worlds to British readers.

What Elizabeth David really excelled at was taking the recipes or traditions of the places she visited and making them accessible to the country she was from. For me, that's where the genius of her food writing lies. I've definitely been inspired by her books and think that her work was about more than food; it was about bringing common sense and simplicity to cooking at a time when we needed it most. Britain was worn down by war rations and she gave people hope, optimism and the know-how to turn a few good ingredients into something authentic and special with a continental twist.

What Penguin has done with this wonderful edition is cherry-pick her greatest hits. Hopefully this will introduce her to a new generation of food lovers. Her work proves that if you have a genuine passion, confidence to push the boundaries, and what you're doing is simple and logical, there's no limit to what you can achieve. She was a true trailblazer, a woman who has inspired the finest cooks in this country, whether they realize it or not.

Jamie Oliver

From the age of five, when I recall Liza teaching me and my brother Rupert to cook a chicken in her Chelsea kitchen, I looked forward to my encounters with her – with a mixture of trepidation and excitement. Both terrifying and quick-witted, in a way that demanded your complete attention, she waited keenly for your answers before responding in either a gently quizzical manner or with pauses and a potential missile. When you pressed the front doorbell, you left Chelsea and entered a fully bohemian world. The smell of Gauloises cigarettes wafted up to the hallway, becoming stronger as you descended into the kitchen. Her detectably upper-class but husky voice complemented her elegant black pencil skirts and men's white shirts. She rarely wore colour and had a style which was more French chic than bohemian, and was totally unlike my mother. Liza defined herself as metropolitan, internationalist and fiercely independent. A distant cry from her family background of country houses and Tory shire politics.

The kitchen décor was in contrast to her stylish modernity, a treasury of ephemera and found furniture. Things were piled up on all available surfaces, from books and papers crowding out the cat on the chaise longue to exotic foods in bowls, their contents providing kitchen context with their aromas, colours and shapes. Clunky spotlights threw shadows on the furniture, and a converted Victorian brass chandelier hovered over the hastily made pine table where she sat on a rush ladder-back chair, working or preparing food, as there was no other surface in the kitchen. There was little circulation space, so the table was the destination and did for everything. I never saw her either in a hurry or rushing the business of cooking, or much else for that matter. Her selection of an enticing menu came without visible effort, giving me the impression of it being a special occasion but without the fuss, where the process was almost as pleasurable as the final result.
Johnny Grey, Elizabeth's nephew

Elizabeth David spread the colour and sun of the Mediterranean in her writing at a crucial time for English cooking. At the end of the 1940s, a generation of cooks had been compromised by rationing. My mother's rice pudding, cooked in the bottom oven of the Aga with nutmeg, one of Elizabeth David's favourite spices, was exotic for an eight-year-old interested in food. When her first book was published in 1950, I read it from cover to cover, thrilled at the explanations of how to cook the ingredients and spices I had been intrigued by in the food shops in Soho.

Elizabeth came to The River Café once during our first two years, kindly brought by Simon Hopkinson. It was a very gusty day and she nearly got blown away as we met her at the entrance. She was frail at the time, but everything became calm after she had perused our eclectic red wine list and the menu which that day had 'Elizabeth David's chocolate and almond cake' on it. Our day was made for us and it remains one of the vivid memories of early times at our restaurant. *Rose Gray*

Some of the happiest memories of my early years, are my adventures in the family kitchen, with a cook's knife in one hand and a well-used copy of Elizabeth David's *Mediterranean Food* in the other. Aged twenty-two, naïvely thinking that I knew almost everything there was to know about food, I decided that I was to become a writer and, in order to do that, I felt I needed advice. I wrote to dozens of famous people, asking the ridiculous question 'How do I become a writer?' Not surprisingly, I received very few responses, but one day the phone rang and my mother called up the stairs, 'Elizabeth David is on the phone for you.' I remember sitting on the bed shaking with nervous excitement, listening to her speak. She was so kind and generous with her advice, and very patient. I hardly spoke at all during those few minutes, but the focus of her advice was to keep writing until you receive an acceptance.

Soon after I had opened my restaurant in 1984, Mrs David arrived unannounced for lunch. I approached the table and told her how flattered and pleased I was that she had chosen to visit Clarke's. Thereafter, she came frequently to visit us. Towards the end of her life I was invited to visit her at home, where she would receive guests in her bedroom, sitting up in bed surrounded with books, papers, pens and notes – and this is how I will remember her – working, researching and writing to the end. *Sally Clarke*

Times spent at table with Elizabeth David were the most treasured of times. Sometimes they were brief, such as a snatched moment or two with a swift glass of wine at the closing stages of a Bibendum lunch, me still dressed in my work whites. On other occasions, friends of hers had kindly invited me to join them for the entirety, which could be a pleasure with mixed blessings. Actually watching Elizabeth eat my dishes – albeit as very small servings – nudged my natural insecurity and I would become that curious thing: the nervous guest at his own table. Elizabeth remained eternally courteous to me, however, and would proclaim that the 'spiced aubergine salad was as delicious as ever'. (It was of course based on one of her own recipes, via Joyce Molyneux.)

The one occasion I will for ever recall most dear was early one Boxing Day evening (her birthday), sitting at table in the basement of her Chelsea home with Jill Norman. We drank Dom Perignon, munched on a seemingly endless supply of Roka cheese biscuits and simply gossiped. Easy listening. Shouting laughter. Just right.

Although knowing Elizabeth David was a pleasure and a privilege indeed, it is her recipes and inspired writing that continue to give me the greatest joy. So obviously authentic and correct, together with almost poetic memoir and a perfect sense of place, she embodies all there is for the reader to whom cooking is not simply a chore – although the commonplace cook should also fare well – but an enlightening experience. Some of her recipes I know I shall continue to cook till the day I die. *Simon Hopkinson*

I met Elizabeth David in the spring of 1989 while working at The River Café. I was doing puddings at the time and when I came into work Rose Gray said to me, 'Elizabeth David's coming to lunch, and I want you to put her chocolate cake on the menu.' Fair enough. She meant the famous one from *French Provincial Cooking*, with ground almonds instead of flour, and a dash of strong coffee, and I was cooking it once or twice a week at the time. But what Rose didn't know, and ED certainly didn't know, was that I'd slowly been upping the amount of chocolate in the recipe, to the point where it was nearly double the original quantity. I felt that made it a richer, more indulgent cake, not better than the original, but more suitable for pudding. Dilemma! Go back to the original recipe? Or present my bastardized version to the great lady herself . . . Well, I guess it's a mark of my youthful arrogance that I chose the latter option.

No great surprise that when it came to pudding she ordered the cake which had her name on it. I watched from the wings nervously as she worked her way through it, a modest spoonful at a time, while chatting to her companion, until all that was left on her plate were a few chocolatey crumbs and an untouched blob of *crème fraîche*, which we always served with the cake. She clearly didn't approve of that. But the cake, at least, seemed to pass muster. Well, I thought to myself, she's getting on a bit, probably hasn't even made the cake for a couple of decades . . . I went back to work, smiling to myself.

A few minutes later, Rose tapped me on the shoulder. 'Elizabeth would like a word with you . . . '

My legs turned to jelly and, as I stumbled over to her table, my mouth went peanut-butter dry . . .

'You cooked this cake?' She fixed me with her bright all-seeing eyes. I wanted to run and I wanted to lie, but I knew I couldn't do either.

'Er, yes, I did . . . '

'But it's different from the one in the book, isn't it . . . ?'

'Er, just a bit. I've . . . er . . . bit more chocolate . . . ' I mumbled. She held her look and I realized a deeper explanation was required. 'Bit . . . richer . . . more puddingy . . . '

She let me ramble on, reddening, for a few seconds, then stopped me with a slight but firm raising of her scant eyebrows. 'Well . . . ' she said, 'whatever you've done to it . . . it's good.' She turned back to her companion and, realizing the discussion was over, I nodded my thanks and sloped away.

I have never received a more thrilling compliment for anything I have ever cooked. And I never will. *Hugh Fearnley-Whittingstall*

INTRODUCTION

Elizabeth David was born in 1913, one of four daughters of Rupert and Stella Gwynne. Her father was Conservative MP for Eastbourne and she had a conventional middle-class upbringing, with nanny and governess. She later went to a girls' school where the food was decidedly inferior – 'nothing will surely ever taste so hateful as nursery tapioca, or the appalling boiled cod of schooldays'. At sixteen, she was sent to live with a French family in Passy, and if her studies at the Sorbonne did not leave a lasting impression, 'what stuck was the taste for a kind of food quite ideally unlike anything I had known before'. On her return to England she had a spell at the Oxford repertory theatre and a brief acting career at the Open Air Theatre in Regent's Park.

In the late 1930s she went off with a lover to France, where she met the writer Norman Douglas – the two became firm friends in spite of the disparity in their ages (she was twenty-four and he seventy-two), and Douglas had a great influence on Elizabeth both as a writer and through his approach to life. At the beginning of the Second World War, she was living on the Greek island of Syros and was evacuated to Egypt, where she ran a reference library for the Ministry of Information in Cairo. Here she met and married Anthony David, an officer in the Indian army. At the end of 1945 she went to join him in New Delhi, but became ill and after some months returned to Britain.

Elizabeth David's first published work, *A Book of Mediterranean Food*, appeared in 1950, but her writing career had begun in the winter of 1946–7, in a hotel in Ross-on-Wye. She had returned to the deprivations of post-war Britain after years of relative plenty in the Middle East and, although the hotel was at least warm, she wrote that the food was 'produced with a kind of bleak triumph which amounted almost to a hatred of humanity and humanity's needs'. She started to write down her memories of Middle Eastern and Mediterranean cooking, creating a private refuge from the cheerless reality of rationing. In 1949 a friend in the literary world offered to show her collection of notes and recipes to publishers. Most of them thought the idea of a cookery book when there was little food to cook at best absurd, but John Lehmann liked the material and agreed to publish it.

The introduction to *Mediterranean Food* paints a vibrant picture: 'The cooking of the Mediterranean shores, endowed with all the natural resources, the colour and flavour of the south, is a blend of tradition and brilliant improvisation. The Latin genius flashes from the kitchen pans. It is honest cooking.' At that time the ingredients of the Mediterranean lands – olive oil, saffron, garlic, basil, aubergines, figs, pistachio nuts –

were hardly to be found in central London, and readers had to rely on memory or imagination to savour Elizabeth's recipes.

These were honest recipes too, collected in Provence, Italy, Corsica, Malta and Greece. *Mediterranean Food* was acclaimed as a serious work, with reviewers expressing their belief that once the shortages in Britain were lifted the book would become practical as well as inspirational. The first Penguin edition, published in 1955, brought the book to a wide audience at the right time. Rationing had ended in 1954 and Mediterranean imports were beginning to arrive. Many of Elizabeth's dishes were unknown in the Britain of the 1950s, but in a few years foods like paella, moussaka, ratatouille, hummus and gazpacho had become familiar in home kitchens, restaurants and supermarkets throughout the country.

The success of *A Book of Mediterranean Food* was followed in 1951 by *French Country Cooking*, a small book of robust, rustic dishes. In 1960 appeared the more substantial, classic work *French Provincial Cooking*, which dealt with 'sober, well-balanced, middle-class French cookery, carried out with care and skill, with due regard to the quality of the materials, but without extravagance or pretension' – a phrase which sums up neatly Elizabeth's own standards. The two French books drew many enthusiasts to France to explore the foods of the countryside 'at the riverside inns, the hospitable farmhouses of the Loire and the Dordogne, of Normandy and the Auvergne, in sea-port bistros, and occasionally also in *cafés routiers*'. Pâtés and terrines, soups enriched with bacon and garlic, meat and poultry stews simmered in wine, and open tarts both savoury and sweet found their way into the repertoire of enterprising and creative British cooks. In the 1960s, dinner parties, whether cheap and cheerful or stylish and sophisticated, were often drawn straight from her books.

Meanwhile, Elizabeth had returned to live in Italy for a year, to research and collect material for her third book, *Italian Food*, which came out in 1954. She was one of the first writers to emphasize the importance of regional differences in Italian food. The country was not unified until the later part of the nineteenth century, so to an Italian there was, and is, no such thing as Italian food: 'there is Florentine cooking, Venetian cooking, there are the dishes of Genoa, Piedmont, Romagna; of Rome, Naples and the Abruzzi; of Sardinia and Sicily; of Lombardy, Umbria and the Adriatic coast'. These provincial differences are clear to every discerning traveller, but at that time found no reflection in the Italian restaurants in Britain; they served up the spaghetti, veal and

chicken dishes the British had come to regard as Italian food. Elizabeth then started work on *Summer Cooking*, a smaller and less demanding collection of recipes for simple summer meals, cold buffets and picnics, drawn from old English dishes as well as those of the countries she had travelled in. She concentrated on herbs, fruits and vegetables in season, and on light dishes of poultry or fish.

By 1964 all five books were available in paperback, and they have remained in print to the present day, with sales into the millions. They found, and continue to find, a large and enthusiastic audience. During the years spent writing the books, Elizabeth also contributed to a variety of newspapers and magazines, having first been commissioned to write a piece entitled 'Rice Again' for *Harper's Bazaar* in 1949. At different times she was a regular contributor to *Vogue*, *House and Garden*, the *Sunday Times*, *Wine and Food*, *The Spectator* and *Nova*. Writing for *The Spectator* pleased her most, for there she was allowed to write a column about food, getting away from the standard formula of an introductory paragraph and a clutch of recipes. Her subjects were wide-ranging but topical, with occasional 'harmless fun at the expense of restaurant guides or the baiting of public relations persons who made imbecile suggestions'.

Elizabeth had a passionate interest in English cooking, and owned a large collection of old English cookery books which she read avidly. From this enthusiasm came the idea for *Spices, Salt and Aromatics in the English Kitchen*, published in 1971. A fine collection of English spiced and aromatic dishes, it revived old treats such as salt duck and spiced beef.

English Bread and Yeast Cookery took five years to write and is the most comprehensive book on English baking. At the time of publication (1977) it had an immense influence. Eighty per cent of the bread sold in Britain came from factories – soft, white and sliced. A revolt against bland, flabby industrial bread was gathering momentum and people were starting to bake their own bread. They seized Elizabeth's bread book and created a demand for flour from small millers, for supplies of yeast, for good bread tins. The industrial loaf is still with us, but look at the wide variety of other breads on sale in supermarkets, delicatessens and from independent bakers, and thank Elizabeth.

Writing was never easy for Elizabeth, yet there is a directness and warmth and an unfailing integrity always present in her work. Her polished style came from writing and rewriting, always by hand, until she was satisfied with the result. She was constantly curious, a stickler for accuracy and the acknowledgement of sources. She had high standards and expected them of others. She detested fuss and anything pretentious or sham. She spoke out about the poor quality of many 'factory' foods, about bad restaurants, and condemned writers who published recipes for travesties of traditional dishes.

Elizabeth's recipes make you want to cook; the aroma of a dish and its vibrant colours spring from the page. The instructions may be brief and sometimes sketchy, and were not written in the formulaic style that is considered appropriate today, but they do not let you down. She assumes her readers are intelligent, curious and able to think for themselves. Her writing is clear and authoritative; she tells you the correct way to make a risotto or a pilaff, *ossi buchi* or *bœf à la bourguignonne*. She wrote as she cooked: with respect for tradition and provenance, with passion and knowledge. She celebrated the pleasures of the table in simple, authentic recipes and evocative essays on the markets of France or Italy, on dishes discovered on her travels, or describing the food of the past.

On both sides of the Atlantic many chefs took up the demand for good-quality ingredients and used her recipes. They continue to acknowledge the debt they owe to Elizabeth David. Many people who do not know her name or her writing have been affected by her influence on chefs and other food writers. Elizabeth was not a public figure, and did not want to be. She chose writing as her means of communicating, and this she did with elegance, erudition, wit and humour. She remains an essential presence in the food world; her writing made it possible for today's celebrity chefs and television supercooks to find a receptive audience.

At Elizabeth David's Table contains a combination of easy, quick recipes that fit well into today's busy schedules, and classic dishes that may take longer but once put together are often left to cook slowly and can be prepared well before the meal. Some recipes are kept in the narrative style, but where there are many ingredients they have been listed at the head of the recipe. Between the recipe chapters are essays on different topics, written over the course of her life. For the first time, the dishes have been photographed, keeping to the same muted colours, earthenware pots and plain white china that Elizabeth describes in her 'Dream Kitchen' essay on page 156-7.

I hope you will enjoy this illustrated collection of recipes from the greatest food writer of our times.

Jill Norman, March 2010

FAST *and* FRESH

It isn't only the expense, the monotony and the false tastes of the food inside most tins and jars and packages which turn me every day more against them. The amount of space they take up, the clutter they make and the performance of opening the things also seem to me quite unnecessarily exasperating. However, even cookery journalists who spend most of their lives with a saucepan in one hand and a pen in the other can't dispense entirely with the kind of stores from which a meal can every now and again be improvised. What I personally require of such things is that there shall be no question whatever of their letting me down or giving me any unwelcome surprise. Out with any product which plays tricks or deteriorates easily. And out also with all the things of which one might say they'll do for an emergency. If something isn't good enough for every day, then it isn't good enough to offer friends, even if they have turned up demanding a meal without notice.

Twenty years ago, during the war years, which I spent in the Eastern Mediterranean, I became accustomed to planning meals from a fairly restricted range of provisions. Now I find myself returning more and more to the same sort of rather ancient and basic foods. They suit my taste and they are the kind of stores which will always produce a coherent and more or less complete meal, which is just what haphazardly bought tins and packages won't do. What happens when you have to open four tins, two jars and three packets in order to make one hasty cook-up is that you get a thoroughly unsatisfactory meal; and the contents of half-used tins and jars have got to be dealt with next day – or left to moulder in the fridge. The only stores I had to bother about when I lived for a time in a small seashore village on an Ægean island were bread, olive oil, olives, salt fish, hard white cheese, dried figs, tomato paste, rice, dried beans, sugar, coffee and wine.

With fresh fish – mostly small fry or squid, but occasionally a treat such as red mullet or a langouste to be obtained from one of the fisher boys, with vegetables and fruit from the garden of the tavern-owner, eggs at about twopence a dozen, and meat – usually kid, lamb or pork – available only for feast days, the diet was certainly limited, but at least presented none of the meal-planning problems which, as I have learned from readers' letters, daily plague the better-off English housewife.

Subsequently, in war-time Egypt, I found, in spite of the comparative plenty and variety and the fact that in Greece I had often grumbled about the food, that the basic commodities of the Eastern Mediterranean shores were the ones which had begun to seem essential. Alexandrians, not surprisingly, knew how to prepare these commodities in a more civilized way than did the Greek islanders. The old-established merchant families of the city – Greek, Syrian, Jewish, English – appeared to have evolved a most delicious and unique blend of Levantine and European cookery and were at the same time most marvellously hospitable. I have seldom seen such wonderfully glamorous-looking, and tasting, food as the Levantine cooks of Alexandria could produce for a party. And yet when you got down to analysing it, you would find that much the same ingredients had been used in dish after dish – only they were so differently treated, so skilfully blended and seasoned and spiced that each one had its own perfectly individual character and flavour.

In Cairo the dividing line between European and Eastern food was much sharper. It was uphill work trying to make English-trained Sudanese cooks produce interesting food. Most of them held a firm belief that the proper meal to set before English people consisted of roast or fried chicken, boiled vegetables and a pudding known to one and all as grème garamel.

My own cook, Suleiman, was a Sudanese who had previously worked only for Italian and Jewish families. He was erratic and forgetful, but singularly sweet-natured, devoted to his cooking pots and above all knew absolutely nothing of good, clean, English schoolroom food.

I used occasionally to try to teach him some French or English dish for which I had a nostalgic craving, but time for cooking was very limited, my kitchen facilities even more so, and on the whole I left him to his own devices.

So it came about that for three or four more years I lived mainly on rather rough but highly flavoured, colourful shining vegetable dishes, lentil or fresh tomato soups, delicious spiced pilaffs, lamb kebabs grilled over charcoal, salads with cool mint-flavoured yoghurt dressings, the Egyptian fellahin dish of black beans with olive oil and lemon and hard-boiled eggs – these things were not only attractive but also cheap and this was important because although Egypt was a land of fantastic plenty compared with war-time Europe, a lot of the better-class food was far beyond the means of young persons living on British Civil Service pay without foreign allowances, and tinned stores were out of the question because there was no room for them in the cave which my landlord was pleased to describe as a furnished flat.

What I found out when I returned to England to another five or six years of the awful dreary foods of rationing was that while my own standard of living in Egypt had perhaps not been very high, my food had always had some sort of life, colour, guts, stimulus; there had always been bite, flavour and inviting smells. Those elements were totally absent from English meals.

As imports came slowly back, I found once more, and still find, that it is the basic foods of the Mediterranean world which produce them in the highest degree. And it is curious how much more true variety can be extracted from a few of these basic commodities than from a whole supermarketful of products, none of which really taste of anything in particular.

So long as I have a supply of elementary fresh things like eggs, onions, parsley, lemons, oranges and bread and tomatoes – and I keep tinned tomatoes too – I find that my store cupboard will always provide the main part of an improvised meal. If this has to be made quickly it may be just a salad of anchovy fillets and black olives, hard-boiled eggs and olive oil, with bread and a bottle of wine. If it is a question of not being able to leave the house to go shopping, or of being too otherwise occupied to stand over the cooking pots, then there are white beans or brown lentils for slow cooking, and usually a piece of cured sausage or bacon to add to them, with onions and oil and possibly tomato. Apricots or other dried fruit can be baked in the oven at the same time, or I may have oranges for a fruit salad, and if it comes to the worst there'll at least be bread and butter and honey and jam. Or if I am given, say, forty-five minutes to get an unplanned meal ready – well, I have Italian and Patna rice and Parmesan, spices, herbs, currants, almonds, walnuts, to make a risotto or a pilaff. And perhaps tuna, with eggs to make mayonnaise, for an easy first dish. The countless number of permutations to be devised is part of the entertainment.

from The Spectator, *9 December 1960*

STARTERS *and* LIGHT DISHES

It is very easy to make an attractive first course from vegetables, eggs, prawns, rice and simple sauces; it is only a question of imagination, and the most elementary knowledge of cooking. The simplest starters are the best, looking clean and fresh. One of the nicest of all is the Genoese one of raw broad beans, rough salame sausage and salty sheep's milk Sardo cheese; each of these things is served on a separate dish, and each person peels his own beans and cuts his own cheese; if the same ingredients were all mixed up together in a bowl the point would be quite lost. In the same way, a salad of tuna piled up on haricot or French beans dressed with oil has two quite contrasting but compatible flavours, whereas if the tuna is mashed up among the beans, the flavours and textures of both are sacrificed, and the appearance of the dish messy as well.

Apart from all the little dishes which can be cheaply made at home, there are now so many products on the market which make delicious starters. All the smoked fish – trout, mackerel, buckling, salmon, sturgeon, eel – need no accompaniment other than lemon, and bread and butter; smoked cod's roe pounded into a paste with olive oil and lemon juice is excellent served with hot toast (eaten straight it is good but disconcertingly sticky).

Among Italian antipasti are to be found some of the most successful culinary achievements in European cooking. The most common antipasti are some kind of salame sausage, olives, anchovies, ham, small artichokes in oil, peppers in oil, raw fennel and raw broad beans. Of varieties of salame there is seemingly no end. Some are garlicky, some not; some are eaten very fresh, others are considered best when they have matured. Prosciutto di Parma and prosciutto San Daniele are at their best perhaps the most delicious hams in the world and the most perfect antipasti. Whose was the brilliant idea of combining fine slices of these hams with fresh figs? Or melon? (Though melons are very much a second best.)

Antipasti of fish, all kinds of small fry served in oil and vinegar sauces, as well as anchovies and the inevitable tuna, are at their best in Italy. Prawns, scampi, shrimps, seppie, calamaretti, totani, moscadini (the last four are of the squid family), mussels, clams, sea dates, sea truffles, oysters, crabs, cold sturgeon in oil, all appear as starters.

Vegetables are presented in a number of ways, and there are plenty of ideas from which we could borrow. It is the unexpected which makes the charm of many of these little dishes: papery slices of raw artichokes; anchovies garnishing a salad of raw mushrooms; slices of Gruyère cheese with crisp fennel or rounds of uncooked peppers; cooked artichoke hearts mixed into a salad of green peas, broad beans and potatoes; tuna encased in rolled-up peppers. To the enterprising there is no limit to the number of dishes with which, without overdoing the mixtures, a promising start to a meal may be contrived.

PIEDMONTESE PEPPERS

Peperoni alla Piemontese

Cut some *red, yellow* or *green peppers* in half lengthways. Take out all the seeds and wash the peppers. If they are large, cut each half in half again. Into each piece put 2 or 3 slices of *garlic*, 2 small sections of raw *tomato*, about half a fillet of *anchovy* cut into pieces, a small nut of *butter*, a dessertspoon of *olive oil*, a very little *salt*. Arrange these peppers on a flat baking dish and cook them in a moderate oven at 180°C/gas 4, for about 30 minutes. They are not to be completely cooked; they should in fact be al dente, the stuffing inside deliciously oily and garlicky.

Serve them cold, each garnished with a little parsley.

Allow ½ or 1 pepper per person.

CORIANDER MUSHROOMS

This is a quickly cooked little dish which makes a delicious cold hors d'œuvre. The aromatics used are similar to those which go into the well-known *champignons à la grecque*, but the method is simpler, and the result even better. In larger quantities the same dish can be made as a hot vegetable to be eaten with veal or chicken.

175g/6oz firm, white, round and very fresh mushrooms, lemon juice, 2 tablespoons olive oil, a teaspoon of crushed coriander seeds, and 1 or 2 bay leaves, salt, freshly ground pepper.

Rinse the mushrooms, wipe them dry with a clean cloth, slice them (but do not peel them) into quarters, or if they are large into eighths. The stalks should be neatly trimmed. Squeeze over them a little lemon juice.

In a heavy frying pan or sauté pan, warm the olive oil. Into it put the coriander seeds. Let them heat for a few seconds. Keep the heat low. Put in the mushrooms and the bay leaves. Add the seasoning. Let the mushrooms cook gently for a minute, cover the pan and leave them, still over very low heat, for another 3 to 5 minutes. Cultivated mushrooms should not be cooked for longer than the time specified.

Uncover the pan. Decant the mushrooms – with all their juices – into a shallow serving dish and sprinkle them with fresh olive oil and lemon juice.

Whether the mushrooms are to be served hot or cold do not forget to put the bay leaf which has cooked with them into the serving dish. The combined scents of coriander and bay go to make up part of the true essence of the dish.

Cooked mushrooms do not keep well, but a day or two in the refrigerator does not harm this coriander-spiced dish. It is also worth remembering that uncooked cultivated mushrooms can be stored in a plastic box in the refrigerator and will keep fresh for a couple of days.

Enough for three people.

PROVENÇAL TOMATO SALAD

Tomates provençales en salade

Take the stalks off a large bunch of *parsley*; pound the leaves with a little *salt*, in a mortar, with 2 cloves of *garlic* and a little *olive oil*.

Cut the tops off good raw *tomatoes*; with a teaspoon soften the pulp inside, sprinkle with *salt*, and turn them upside down so that the water drains out. Fill the tomatoes up with the parsley and garlic mixture. Serve them after an hour or two, when the flavour of the garlic and parsley has permeated the salad.

TOMATOES *with* CREAM

Put the required number of whole *tomatoes* into boiling water to remove the skins. Arrange them in a shallow salad bowl.

Pour over them a dressing consisting simply of thick fresh *cream* into which is stirred a little *salt* and a tablespoon of chopped *tarragon* or fresh sweet *basil*.

A splendid accompaniment for a cold or, for that matter, a hot chicken.

Allow 1–2 tomatoes per person.

AUBERGINE PURÉE

This is a Middle Eastern dish which is intended to be served as an hors d'œuvre with bread, or with meat, in the same manner as a chutney.

Grill or bake 4 *aubergines* until their skins crack and will peel easily. Mash the peeled aubergines, mix them with 2 or 3 tablespoons of *yoghurt*, the same of *olive oil*, *salt*, *pepper*, *lemon juice*. Garnish with a few very thin slices of raw *onion* and chopped *mint* leaves.

Enough for four people.

AUBERGINE CHUTNEY

Boil 2 *aubergines* in their skins; leave them to get cold. Peel them and put the pulp through a food processor. Stir a crushed clove of *garlic* into the purée, add a little minced *onion*, *green chilli* and grated *ginger*, and season with *salt*, *pepper* and *lemon juice*.

Enough for three to four people.

CHICKEN LIVER PÂTÉ

With the exception of the incomparable *pâté de foie gras*, bought pâtés in England are seldom very satisfactory, and it is not difficult to make your own. If you have no earthenware or ovenproof porcelain terrines in which to cook them, this need be no deterrent. For a very small cost enamelled baking tins in all sizes, fireproof glass dishes, or even oblong loaf tins can be bought, and these serve just as well. They don't look quite so nice on the table, but the pâtés can be turned out on to a dish and sliced for serving.

250–500g/½–1lb chicken livers, or duck, turkey, chicken and goose liver mixed, pork, duck or goose fat or butter, brandy, port or Madeira, ½ a clove of garlic, salt and pepper, a small pinch of thyme leaves.

Clean the livers carefully and pare off any parts of them which look greenish, as they will give a bitter taste to the pâté. Melt 30g/1oz of butter in a frying pan; put in the livers, whole, and let them cook gently for about 5 minutes. They must remain pink inside. Take them from the pan and put them into a mortar or blender. To the butter in the pan add 2 tablespoons of brandy and let it bubble; then 2 tablespoons of port or madeira, and cook another minute. Add half a clove of garlic, salt, ground black pepper and a small pinch of thyme to the livers and pound or blend them to a paste; pour in the butter mixture from the pan, and 60g/2oz of fresh butter. When all is thoroughly amalgamated and reduced to a paste, put it into an earthenware terrine in which it will come to within 1cm/½ inch of the top.

In a clean pan melt some pure pork, duck or goose fat, or butter. Pour it through a strainer on to the pâté; there should be enough to form a covering about ½cm/¼ inch thick, so that the pâté is completely sealed. When the fat has set, cover with a piece of foil and the lid of the terrine. Store in the larder or refrigerator. The pâté should not be eaten until two or three days after it has been made, and as long as it is airtight will keep a week or two in the larder and several weeks in a refrigerator. Serve it very cold, in the terrine, with toast.

This is a rich pâté, and butter is not necessary with it.

500g/1lb of chicken livers makes enough pâté for eight to ten people.

PORK *and* LIVER PÂTÉ

Terrine de campagne

This is the sort of pâté you get in French restaurants under the alternative names of *pâté maison* or *terrine du chef*. Serve this pâté as a first course, with toast or French bread. Some people like butter as well, although it is quite rich enough without. An obliging butcher will usually mince for you the pork, veal and liver, provided he is given due notice. It saves a great deal of time, and I always believe in making my dealers work for me if they will.

500g/1lb pork belly, minced, 500g/1lb lean veal, minced, 250g/½lb pig's liver, minced, 125g/4oz streaky bacon or pork back fat, 1 clove of garlic, crushed, 6 black peppercorns, crushed, 6 juniper berries, crushed, 1–2 teaspoon salt, ¼ teaspoon ground mace, 3–4 tablespoons dry white wine, 2 tablespoons brandy.

To the minced meats, all thoroughly blended, add 60g/2oz of the streaky bacon or pork fat cut in thin, irregular little dice, the garlic and seasonings, and the wine and brandy. Mix very thoroughly and, if there is time, leave to stand for an hour or two before cooking, so that the flavours penetrate the meat. Turn into one large 1.25-litre/2-pint capacity terrine, or into 2 or 3 smaller ones, about 5–6cm/2½ inches deep. Cut the remaining fat or bacon into thin strips and arrange it across the top of the pâté. Place the terrines in a baking tin filled with water and cook, uncovered, in a slow oven, 160°C/gas 3, for 1¼ to 1½ hours. The pâtés are cooked when they begin to come away from the sides of the dish.

Take them from the oven, being careful not to spill any of the fat, and leave them to cool. They will cut better if, when the fat has all but set, they are weighted. To do this, cover with greaseproof paper and a board or plate which fits inside the terrine and put a weight on top. However, if this proves impractical, it is not of very great importance. If the terrines are to be kept longer than a week, cover them completely, once they are cold, with a sealing layer of just-melted pure pork lard.

When cooking any pâté remember that it is the depth of the terrine rather than its surface area which determines the cooking time. The seasonings of garlic and juniper berries are optional.

The proportions of meat, liver and seasonings making up a pâté can be altered to suit individual tastes, but always with due regard to the finished texture of the product. A good pâté is moist and fat without being greasy, and it should be faintly pink inside, not grey or brown. A dry pâté is either the result of overcooking, or of too small a proportion of fat meat having been used.

Enough for eight to ten people.

RILLETTES

Rillettes will keep for weeks, and make an excellent standby for an hors d'œuvre. Serve them with bread and white wine.

750g–1kg/1½–2lb belly of pork, with a good proportion of lean to fat, 1 clove of garlic, a sprig of fresh thyme or marjoram, salt, pepper, a pinch of ground mace.

Remove bones and rind from the meat, and cut it into small cubes. Put these into a thick pan with the chopped garlic, the herbs and seasoning. Cook on a very low flame, or in the slowest possible oven at 140°C/gas 1 for 1½ hours, until the pieces of pork are quite soft without being fried, and swimming in their own fat. Place a wide sieve over a bowl, and pour the meat into the sieve so that the fat drips through into the basin. When the meat has cooled, pull it into shreds, using two forks. If you cannot manage this, chop the meat. But unless you are making rillettes in a large quantity, try to avoid using the electric blender. It gives the meat too compact and smooth a texture. Pack the rillettes into small earthenware or china pots, and seal them with their own fat. Cover with greaseproof paper or foil.

Enough for four to six people.

PORK *and* SPINACH TERRINE

This pâté can be eaten hot as a main course, but I prefer it cold, as a first dish, and with bread or toast just as a pâté is always served in France.

The interesting points about this dish are its appearance, its fresh, uncloying flavour and its comparative lightness, which should appeal to those who find the better-known type of pork pâté rather heavy. You could, for example, serve a quite rich or creamy dish after this without overloading anybody's stomach.

At Orange, that splendid town they call the gateway to Provence, I once tasted a pâté which was more fresh green herbs than meat. I was told that this was made according to a venerable country recipe of Upper Provence. The pâté was interesting but rather heavy. I have tried to make it a little less filling. Here is the result of my experiments.

500g/1lb uncooked spinach, spinach beet or chard, 500g/1lb freshly minced fat pork, seasonings of salt, freshly ground pepper, mixed spices.

Wash, cook and drain the spinach. When cool, squeeze it as dry as you can. There is only one way to do this – with your hands. Chop it roughly.

Season the meat with about 3 teaspoons of salt, a generous amount of freshly ground black pepper, and about a ¼ teaspoon of mixed ground spices (mace, allspice, cloves).

Mix the meat and spinach together. Turn into a 600-ml/1-pint earthenware terrine or loaf tin. On top put a piece of buttered greaseproof paper. Stand the terrine or tin in a baking dish half filled with water.

Cook in a low oven at 160°C/gas 3 for 45 minutes to an hour. Do not let it get overcooked or it will be dry.

Enough for six to eight people.

depuis
CARBONE

Caillettes de l'Ardèche
Teyssier Salaisons 07320 St.

FRESH HERBS

The use of herbs in cooking is so much a matter of tradition, almost of superstition, that the fact that it is also a question of personal taste is overlooked, and experiments are seldom tried; in fact the restriction of this herb to that dish is usually quite arbitrary, and because somebody long ago discovered that basil works some sort of spell with tomatoes, fennel with fish, and rosemary with pork, it occurs to few people to reverse the traditional usage; to take an example, fennel is an excellent complement to pork, adding the sharpness which is supplied in English cookery by apple sauce, while basil enhances almost anything with which it is cooked; for ideas one has only to look to the cooking of other countries to see how much the use of herbs as a flavouring can be varied.

In England mint is considered to have an affinity for lamb, new potatoes, and green peas; the French regard the use of mint as a flavouring as yet another sign of English barbarism, and scarcely ever employ it, while all over the Middle East, where the cooking is far from uncivilized, mint is one of the most commonly used of herbs; it goes into soups, sauces, omelettes, salads, purées of dried vegetables and into the sweet cooling mint tea drunk by the Persians and Arabs. In Spain, where the cooking has been much influenced by the Arabs, it is also used in stews and soups; it is usually one of the ingredients of the sweet sour sauces which the Italians like, and which are a legacy from the Romans, and in modern Roman cooking wild mint gives a characteristic flavour to stewed mushrooms and to vegetable soups. The Indians make a fresh chutney from pounded mint, mangoes, onion and chillies, which is an excellent accompaniment to fish and cold meat as well as to curries. Mint is one of the cleanest tasting of herbs and will give a lively tang to many vegetables, carrots, tomatoes, mushrooms, lentils; a little finely chopped mint is good in fish soups and stews, and with braised duck; a cold roast duck served on a bed of freshly picked mint makes a lovely, fresh-smelling summer dish; a few leaves can be added to the orange salad to serve with it.

With its highly aromatic scent, basil is one of the most delicious of all herbs, best known for bringing out the flavour of tomato salads and sauces. In Provence, in Italy, in Greece, basil grows and is used in great quantities. The Genoese could scarcely exist without their pesto, a thick compound of pounded basil, pine nuts, garlic, cheese and olive oil which is used as a sauce for every kind of pasta, for fish, particularly red mullet, and as a flavouring for soups and minestrones. Once you have become a basil addict it is hard to do without it; Mediterranean vegetables such as peppers and aubergines, garlicky soups and wine-flavoured dishes of beef, salads dressed with the fruity olive oil of Provence or Liguria and all the dishes with tomato sauces need basil as a fish needs water, and there is no substitute.

Of that very English herb sage I have little to say except that, and this is where the question of personal taste comes in, it seems to me to be altogether too blatant, and used far too much; its all-pervading presence in stuffings and sausages is perhaps responsible for the distaste for herbs which many English people feel. The Italians are also very fond of sage, and use it a great deal with veal and with liver; it seems to give a musty rather than a fresh flavour, and I would always substitute mint or basil for sage in any recipe. The same applies to rosemary, which when fresh gives out a powerful oil which penetrates anything cooked with it; in southern France it is used to flavour roast lamb, pork and veal, but should be removed from the dish before it is served, as it is disagreeable to find those spiky little leaves in one's mouth; in Italy rosemary is stuffed in formidable quantities into roast sucking pig, and in the butchers' shops you see joints of pork tied up ready for roasting wreathed round and threaded with rosemary; it looks entrancing, but if you want to taste the meat, use only the smallest quantity, and never put it into stock destined for a consommé or for a sauce.

Thyme, marjoram and wild marjoram are all good and strong-flavoured herbs which can be used separately or together for robust stews of beef in red wine, for those aromatic country soups in which there are onions, garlic, bacon, wine, cabbage; one or other of these herbs should go into stuffings for chicken, goose and turkey, for peppers and aubergines, into meat croquettes (accompanied by grated lemon peel), terrines of game, and stews of hare and rabbit; either thyme or marjoram is almost essential to strew in small quantities on mutton, pork and lamb chops and liver to be fried or grilled; wild marjoram is called *origano* in Italy and Spain and is used for any and every dish of veal and pork, for fish and fish soups, and is an essential ingredient of the Neapolitan pizza, that colourful, filling, peasant dish of bread dough baked with tomatoes, anchovies and cheese.

Fennel has many uses besides the sauce for mackerel which is found in all old English cookery books. For the famous Provençal *grillade au fenouil* the sundried, brittle stalks of the fennel are used as a bed on which to grill sea bass (*loup de mer*) or red mullet; there is a Tuscan chicken dish in which the bird is stuffed with thick strips of ham and pieces of fennel bulb and pot-roasted; in Perugia they stuff their sucking pig and pork with fennel leaves and garlic instead of the rosemary prevalent elsewhere in Italy; one of the best of Italian sausages is *finocchiona*, a Florentine pork salame flavoured with fennel seeds; if you like the aniseed taste of fennel, use it chopped up raw in soups, particularly iced soups, and in vinaigrette sauces, in rice salads to give the crisp element so necessary to soft foods, in mixed vegetable salads, in fish mayonnaises, in the court-bouillon in which fish is to be poached, in stuffings for baked fish, in chicken salads, and mixed with parsley and juniper berries for a marinade for pork chops which are to be grilled.

Tarragon is essentially a herb of French cookery; *poulet à l'estragon* and *œufs en gelée à l'estragon* are classics of the French kitchen; without tarragon there is no true Sauce Béarnaise; with chives and chervil or parsley it is one of the *fines herbes* for omelettes, sauces, butters, and many dishes of grilled meat and fish. It is a herb to be used with care for its charm lies in its very distinct and odd flavour and too much of it spoils the effect, but a few leaves will give character to many dishes and particularly to smooth foods such as sole cooked in cream, *œufs en cocotte*, cream soups, bisques of shell fish, stewed scallops, potato purées and also to tomato salads. In Italy, tarragon is to be found only in and around Siena, where it is used in the stuffing for globe artichokes, and to flavour green salads.

The quantity in which any given herb is to be used is a matter of taste rather than of rule. Cookery books are full of exhortations to discretion in this matter, but much depends on the herb with which you happen to be dealing, what food it is to flavour, whether the dish in question is to be a long-simmered one in which it is the sauce which will be ultimately flavoured with the herbs, or whether the herbs are to go into a stuffing for a bird or meat to be roasted, in which case the aromas will be more concentrated, or again whether the herbs will be cooked only a minute or two, as in egg dishes, or not cooked at all, as when they are used to flavour a salad or a herb butter. Whether the herbs are fresh or dried is an important point. The oils in some herbs (rosemary, wild marjoram, sage) are very strong, and when these dry out the flavour is very much less powerful. But in the drying process nearly all herbs (mint is an exception) acquire a certain mustiness, so that although in theory one should be able to use dried herbs more freely than fresh ones, the opposite is in fact generally the case.

Some fresh herbs disperse their aromatic scent very quickly when in contact with heat; a few leaves of fresh tarragon steeped in a hot consommé for 20 minutes will give it a strong flavour, whereas if the tarragon is to flavour a salad considerably more will be necessary. Lemon thyme and marjoram are at their best raw, or only slightly cooked, as in an omelette; the flavour of fennel stalks is brought out by slow cooking; basil has a particular affinity with all dishes in which olive oil is an ingredient, whether cooked or in salads. Knowledge of the right quantities, and of interesting combinations of herbs, can be acquired by using egg dishes, salads and soups as a background. Even if the herbs have been dispensed with a less cautious hand than is usually advised the result will not be a disaster, as it can be when some musty dried herb has completely permeated a roast bird or an expensive piece of meat. You may, on the contrary, have discovered some delicious new combination of tastes, and certainly the use of fresh herbs will be a startling revelation to all those people who know herbs only as something bought in a packet called 'mixed dried herbs', and for which you might just as well substitute sawdust.

from Summer Cooking, *1955*

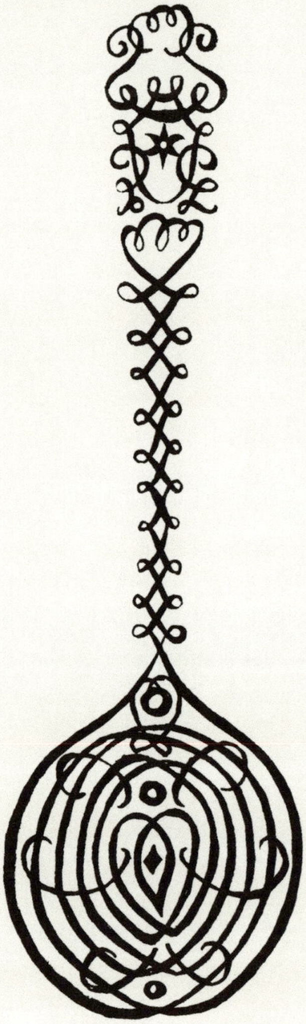

SOUPS

> The making of a good soup is quite an art, and many otherwise clever cooks do not possess the *tour de main* necessary to its successful preparation. Either they over-complicate the composition of the dish, or they attach only minor importance to it, reserving their talents for the meal itself, and so it frequently happens that the soup does not correspond in quality to the rest of the dishes; nevertheless, the quality of the soup should foretell that of the entire meal.

Madame Seignobos, who wrote these words some fifty years ago in a book called *Comment on forme une cuisinière*, was probably referring to trained cooks, and does not mention those other happy-go-lucky ones who tell you, not without pride, 'of course I never follow a recipe, I just improvise as I go along. A little bit of this, a spoonful of that . . . it's much more fun really.' Well, it may be more fun for the cook, but is seldom so diverting for the people who have to eat his products, because those people who have a sure enough touch to invent successfully in the kitchen without years of experience behind them are very rare indeed. The fortunate ones gifted with that touch are those who will also probably have the restraint to leave well alone when they have hit on something good; the ones who can't resist a different little piece of embroidery every time they cook a dish will end by inducing a mood of gloomy apprehension in their families and guests. The domain of soup-making is one which comes in for more than its fair share of attention from the 'creative' cook, a saucepan of innocent-looking soup being a natural magnet to the inventive, and to those who pride themselves on their gifts for inspired improvisation.

I remember when I was very young being advised by the gastronomic authority among my contemporaries to take pretty well everything in the larder, including the remains of the salad (if I remember rightly, some left-over soused herring was also included), tip it into a pan, add some water, and in due course, he said, some soup would emerge. I very soon learned, from the results obtained by this method, that the soup pot cannot be treated as though it were a dustbin. That lesson was elementary enough. The ones that are harder to assimilate are, first, in regard to the wisdom or otherwise of mixing too many ingredients, however good, to make one soup; the likelihood is that they will cancel each other out, so that although your soup may be a concentrated essence of good and nourishing ingredients, it will not taste of anything in particular. Secondly, one has to learn in the end that the creative urge in the matter of embellishments is best kept under control. If your soup is already very good of its kind, possessed of its own true taste, will it not perhaps be spoilt by the addition of a few chopped olives, of a little piece of diced sausage, of a spoonful of paprika pepper? These are matters which everyone must decide for himself.

GAZPACHO

Gazpacho, the popular iced Spanish soup, was described, somewhat disparagingly, by the novelist Théophile Gautier in his *Un Voyage en Espagne* (translated by Catherine Alison Phillips) after a journey to Spain in 1840; like all good Frenchmen he was apt to be suspicious of foreign food.

> Our supper was of the simplest kind; all the serving men and maids of the hostelry had gone to the dance, and we had to be content with a mere gaspacho. This gaspacho is worthy of a special description, and we shall here give the recipe. You pour some water into a soup tureen, and to this water you add a dash of vinegar, some cloves of garlic, some onions cut into quarters, some slices of cucumber, a few pieces of pimento, a pinch of salt; then one cuts some bread and sets it to soak in this pleasing mixture, serving it cold. It is the favourite dish of the Andalusians, and the prettiest women do not shrink from swallowing bowlfuls of this hell-broth of an evening. Gaspacho is considered highly refreshing, an opinion which strikes me as rather rash, but, strange as it may seem the first time one tastes it, one ends by getting used to it and even liking it.

Modern versions of gazpacho appear to be very different from the hell-broth described by Gautier. The basis of them is chopped tomato, olive oil, and garlic, and there may be additions of cucumber, black olives, raw onion, red pepper, herbs, a couple of coarsely chopped hard-boiled eggs, and bread. Sometimes a selection of the vegetables – the cucumber, olives, peppers, onions – and the bread, are finely chopped and handed round separately in small dishes instead of being incorporated in the basic soup.

Chop 500g/1lb raw peeled *tomatoes* until they are almost in a purée. Stir in a few dice of *cucumber*, 2 chopped cloves of *garlic*, a finely sliced *spring onion*, a dozen stoned *black olives*, a few strips of *green pepper*, 3 tablespoons of *olive oil*, a tablespoon of *wine vinegar*, *salt*, *pepper* and a pinch of *cayenne pepper*, a little chopped fresh *marjoram*, *mint*, or *parsley*. Keep very cold until it is time to serve the soup, then thin with 300ml/½ pint of iced water, add a few cubes of coarse *brown bread*, and serve with broken-up ice floating in the bowl.

Sometimes gazpacho is presented in large deep cups, sometimes in shallow soup plates.

Enough for four people.

FRESH GREEN PEA SOUP

30g/1oz butter, half a small onion, 30g/1oz ham, 1 teacup shelled green peas, salt, pepper, sugar, mint, 50ml/2 fl oz cream, 2 eggs, the juice of a lemon, 900ml/1½ pints veal or chicken stock.

Melt the butter; put in the finely chopped onion. Do not let it brown, only soften. Add the ham cut into strips, then the peas. Let them get thoroughly impregnated with the butter. Season with salt, pepper, sugar, and add a little sprig of mint. Pour over hot water just to cover and simmer until the peas are tender. Stir in boiling cream. Remove from the fire and stir in the eggs beaten up with the lemon juice. Pour the boiling stock over this mixture, stirring all the time, or the soup will curdle. Serve at once. A lovely soup.

Enough for four people.

TOMATO SOUP

Minestra di pomidoro

In the summer this soup can be eaten iced, accompanied by hot crostini.

Melt 750g/1½lb chopped and skinned *tomatoes* in *olive oil*; add a clove of *garlic* and some fresh *parsley* or *basil* or *marjoram*. Cook for 5 minutes, then add 600ml/1 pint meat or chicken *stock*, *salt* and *pepper*, and a pinch of *sugar*. Cook for 5 minutes more only. By this method the flavour of the tomatoes is retained, and the soup tastes very fresh.

Enough for four people.

VEGETABLE *and* HERB SOUP

Purée léontine

Léontine was the young cook of the French family in Paris with whom I lived when I was sixteen. Her food was beautiful.

1kg/2lb leeks, ½ a tumbler olive oil, salt and pepper, 1 lemon, 1 cup each of spinach, green peas and shredded lettuce, 1 tablespoon each of chopped parsley, mint and celery.

Clean and cut the leeks into chunks. Into a thick-bottomed saucepan put the olive oil and when it is warm put in the leeks, seasoned with salt, pepper and the juice of ½ the lemon. Simmer slowly for about 20 minutes. Now add the spinach, the peas and the lettuce, stir a minute or two, and add 1.25 litres/2 pints of water. Cook until all the vegetables are soft – about 10 minutes – then press the whole mixture through a sieve. If the purée is too thick add a little milk, and before serving taste and add more lemon juice if necessary. Stir in the chopped parsley, mint and celery.

This soup turns out an appetizing pale green.

Enough for six people.

MUSHROOM SOUP

Potage aux champignons à la bressane

This is an old-fashioned way of making mushroom soup in which bread rather than flour is used for the slight amount of thickening needed. It is a soup with a very fine flavour, but it does need some sort of mild chicken, veal or beef stock.

A thick slice of crustless white bread, 1 litre/1¾ pints stock, 375g/¾lb mushrooms, 60g/2oz butter, 1 clove of garlic, parsley, 100–125ml/3–4 fl oz double cream, salt and pepper, nutmeg or mace.

Soak the bread in a little of the stock. Rinse the mushrooms in cold water and wipe them dry and free of grit with a soft damp cloth. Do not peel them or remove the stalks. Cut them in small pieces. Melt the butter in a heavy saucepan, put in the mushrooms and let them soften; when the moisture starts to run add a very small piece of chopped garlic, a tablespoon of chopped parsley, a little salt, freshly ground pepper, grated nutmeg or mace, and let the mushrooms continue to stew in the butter for several minutes.

Now squeeze the moisture out of the bread and add the bread to the mushrooms. Stir until it amalgamates with the mushrooms. Add the stock, and cook for about 15 minutes until the mushrooms are quite soft. Put the soup through the coarse mesh of the mouli, then through the next finest one. Or blend the soup in a liquidizer. You will not get the thick or smooth purée usually associated with mushroom soup, but rather a mixture of the consistency of thin cream broken by all the minuscule particles of the mushrooms. Return it to the rinsed-out saucepan and when it is reheated boil the cream and add to the soup with another tablespoon of parsley, this time chopped very fine indeed.

Enough for four people.

- les crênes
- direct du

JERUSALEM ARTICHOKE SOUP

Potage de topinambours à la provençale

Chop up 1kg/2lb of *Jerusalem artichokes* and cook in 1.8 litres/3 pints of salted water. Sieve, and heat up, adding gradually 300ml/½ pint of *milk*.

In a small frying pan heat 2 tablespoons of *olive oil* and in this fry 2 chopped *tomatoes*, a clove of *garlic*, a small piece of chopped *celery*, a little *parsley* and 2 tablespoons of chopped *ham or bacon*. Let this mixture cook only a minute or two, then pour it, with the oil, into the soup. Heat, and serve quickly.

Enough for four people.

COURGETTE *and* TOMATO SOUP

Soupe menerboise

250g/½lb courgettes, salt, olive oil, 2 onions, 500g/1lb tomatoes, 2 small potatoes, a handful of shelled and peeled broad beans, 45g/1½oz small pasta, pepper, several cloves of garlic, fresh basil, 2 egg yolks, Parmesan cheese.

Cut the courgettes into squares, salt them lightly, and leave them in a colander for an hour so that some of the water drains from them. In an earthenware casserole warm 5 tablespoons of olive oil. Into this put the sliced onions and let them melt but not fry. Add the courgettes and let them melt in the oil slowly for 10 minutes before adding all but 2 of the tomatoes, roughly chopped. When these have softened put in the potatoes cut into small squares and pour about 1.25 litres/2 pints of hot water over the whole mixture. Simmer gently for 10 minutes until the potatoes are nearly cooked; then add the broad beans, the pasta and seasoning of salt and pepper.

In the meantime grill the remaining tomatoes, remove their skins; in a mortar pound the garlic, then the tomatoes, and a small bunch of basil. Add the egg yolks, so that you have a sauce somewhat resembling a thin mayonnaise. The pasta in the soup being cooked, stir a ladleful of the soup into the sauce, then another. Return the mixture to the pan, and let it heat gently, stirring all the time to prevent the egg curdling. At the last minute stir in 2 large spoonfuls of grated Parmesan cheese.

A substantial soup for four to six people.

SPICED LENTIL SOUP

An interesting soup, oriental in flavour, very easy to make, cheap and a comforting standby on which many variations can be made.

Basic ingredients are 125g/4oz ordinary red lentils and 2 celery stalks. Others, which can be varied, are 1 small onion, 2 large or 4 small cloves of garlic, 2 teaspoons of cumin seeds (either whole or ground), 1 teaspoon of ground cinnamon, olive oil or butter, water or stock, lemon juice, parsley or dried mint, salt.

In a soup pot, saucepan or casserole of not less than 3-litre/5-pint capacity, warm about 6 tablespoons of clarified butter, ghee, or light olive oil or 45g/1½oz of butter. In this melt the chopped onion. Stir in the spices. Let them warm thoroughly before adding the crushed garlic cloves and then the lentils – it is not necessary to soak them – and the celery, cleaned and cut into 5-cm/2-inch chunks.

Let the lentils soak up the oil or butter before pouring over them 1.5 litres/2½ pints of water or stock, which could be made from lamb, veal, pork, beef, chicken, turkey or duck. No salt at this stage. Cover the pot and let the lentils cook steadily, but not at a gallop, for 30 minutes. Now throw in 2 teaspoons of salt or to taste and cook for another 15 minutes.

By this time the lentils should be completely soft. It will be a matter of moments to sieve them through the mouli or purée them in the blender. I prefer the former method.

Return the soup to a clean saucepan, and when it is reheated, taste for seasoning – it may need a little extra ground cumin and perhaps a sprinkling of cayenne pepper – stir in a tablespoon or two of chopped parsley, or a little dried mint. Lastly, a good squeeze of lemon juice.

Enough for four to six people.

SPICED LENTIL SOUP (2)

As above, but instead of cinnamon and cumin use 1 teaspoon of garam masala, and 1 teaspoon of whole cumin seeds. (The cardamom in the garam masala mixture makes the whole difference to the flavour.) For those who do not mind a rough soup, it is not even necessary to sieve the lentils or whizz them in a blender. Just beat them to a purée with a wooden spoon or a whisk. In this case, it is best to cook the lentils with 900ml/1½ pints water only and to add broth when they are cooked and reduced to a purée.

Enough for four to six people.

MUSSEL SOUP

Zuppa di cozze

This is only one of the many ways of making a mussel soup. Other shellfish can be added, such as large prawns, allowing 2 or 3 for each person, but they should be bought uncooked, and the tails slit down the centre before adding them to the soup.

Olive oil, 1 onion, celery, garlic, fresh marjoram, thyme or basil, ground pepper, 1kg/2lb tomatoes, white wine, 3 litres/5 pints mussels, parsley, lemon peel, bread.

Cover the bottom of a large and fairly deep pan with olive oil. When it is warm put in the onion, sliced very thinly. As soon as it begins to brown add a tablespoon of chopped celery, 3 cloves of garlic, sliced, some fresh marjoram, thyme or basil, and ground black pepper (no salt). When this has cooked a minute or two put in the skinned and sliced tomatoes and let them stew 3 or 4 minutes before adding a glass of white wine (about 125ml/4fl oz). Let all bubble 2 minutes before covering the pan and turning down the flame.

Cook until the tomatoes are almost reduced to pulp, then pour in a tumbler of hot water, enough to make the mixture about the consistency of a thick soup, and leave to simmer a few more minutes. The basis of the soup is now ready. (It can be prepared beforehand.)

The final operations must be carried out only immediately before serving. Heat the prepared soup and add the carefully cleaned and bearded mussels. Let them cook fairly fast until all are opened, which will take 10–12 minutes. Before serving sprinkle some cut parsley and a scrap of grated lemon peel over the mussels; have ready 3 or 4 slices of toasted French bread for each person, and a large bowl on the table to receive the empty shells as the mussels are eaten.

Enough for four people.

CONFORT ANGLAIS, FRENCH FARE

How gloriously different a matter is French food when you can buy and cook it yourself from that offered at the restaurant meals imposed when you stay in hotels, was brought home to me most forcibly in the early months of 1984. With a friend I was lent, by another and mutual friend, a charming town house in the little south-western city of Uzès. With high ceilings, tall windows, comfortable bedrooms, a bathroom for each, blessedly hot water, central heating, simple and appropriate furniture, good lighting, a large kitchen, electric kettles wherever needed, shelves filled with weeks and weeks of reading, plus all the necessary maps and guide books, the whole place was the most engaging possible blend of traditional French building with unaggressive modern English comforts.

Two minutes' walk from the house was one of those small-town casinos, emporiums of modest size and indeed modest content, but efficiently run, open long hours of every day and providing many of the necessities of life, from butter to electric light bulbs, mineral water to toilet paper, a selection of wines, spirits and liqueurs, adequate cheeses, vegetables, fruit and salad stuffs. Across the road were the food shops, a butcher, a charcuterie, a greengrocery, the market place, the Crédit Lyonnais. Three doors down from the house a fine small bakery provided fresh bread six days a week. As well as everyday baguettes and other white loaves, we had a choice of four or five different varieties of brown bread, including rye and *pain biologique*, France's version of the loaf made from organically grown whole wheat, in this case a very great improvement on the equivalent product of the English health-food shop. As well as good bread the little bakery offered takeaway temptations such as flaky pastry turnovers filled with *brandade de morue*, the creamed salt cod of the region, and an old-fashioned Provençal pissaladière baked in rectangular iron trays and sold by the slice. They call it pizza now. People have forgotten the old name, and will tell you it comes from Italy. I can tell them it comes from no nearer Italy than Marseille where I used to buy it when I lived on a boat tied up in the Vieux Port. That was 1939, before the war started. I used to go ashore every morning and walk up a narrow street to a bakery to buy my pissaladière fresh out of the oven. It was a treat to find my anchovy-and-tomato-spread pissaladière once again in Uzès, and even handier to the house than the Marseille bakery had been to my boat.

L'ECONOME

Market day at Uzès is Saturday morning. It was February when I was there, not the most propitious time of year for fresh produce, and on the first Saturday of my stay the mistral was blowing so ferociously that it was difficult to stand up. Even the hardy stallholders were shivering and anxious to pack up and climb into the shelter of their vans. Nevertheless, even on a day like that we could buy quite a good variety of vegetables and salads. Among the greatest pleasures, as always in France, were the good creamy-fleshed firm potatoes. Then, even in February, there were little round, crisp, bronze-flecked, frilly lettuces, baskets of mesclun or mixed salad greens, great floppy bunches of chard, leaf artichokes, trombone-shaped pumpkins which make admirable soup, fat fleshy red peppers, new-laid eggs, eight or nine varieties of olives in basins and barrels, thick honey and clear honey, in a variety of colours, in jars and in the comb, and honey soap in golden chunks, bouquets of mixed fresh flowers, tulips, dark purple anemones, marigolds. And then cheeses, cheeses. There are the locally made goats' milk cheeses called *pélardons*, small round and flattish and to be bought in various stages of maturity. Is it for immediate consumption, do you wish to keep it a few days, is it for toasting, roasting, grilling? Try the *magnane à la sarriette*, another goat cheese, strewn with the savory leaves they call *poivre d'âne* across the Rhône in Provence. Or how about the St Marcellin? Or the fresh ewes' milk cheeses? 'They are my own,' says the lady on the stall. We buy two. They are delicious, but they are horribly expensive, as anyone who has a taste for Roquefort well knows.

Given the very small yield of milk, about ½ litre/17 fl oz per milking, all ewes' milk cheese is a luxury. Here we are not all that far from the place where that great and glorious Roquefort is produced and matured, and in Uzès market, from another cheese stall, we have our pick of three or four grades. Within two or three minutes we have spent £7.00 and have not yet bought our Parmesan or Gruyère for grating on to the delicate little ravioles we have bought from the goat cheese lady. They are tiny, these ravioles, filled with a mixture of parsley and comté, the Gruyère-like cheese of Franche Comté. They take one minute to cook, warns the lady. She imports them from the other side of the Rhône, from Royans near Romans in the Drôme where ravioles have long been a local speciality.

By now we have nearly finished our shopping. We have bought as much as we can carry. But we spend another pound's worth of francs on one of the goat cheese lady's specialities, one of her own. It is something she calls a *tourte à la crème*, or *tourteau*. It is a light, puffy, yeast-leavened tourte, round, like an outsize bun, with a layer of subtly flavoured sweet, creamy cream cheese in the centre, and with a characteristically blackened top. It is deliberate, this charred top, and traditional, says the lady.

Lunch is going to be a feast. Our red peppers are to be impaled on the electric spit and roasted until their skins are charred as black as the top of the *tourteau*. Then we shall peel them, cut them in strips, dress them with the good olive oil we have bought direct from the little oil mill at Bédarrides on the Tarascon road out of Fontvieille. Over them we strew chopped parsley and garlic and leave them to mature in their dressing. We shall eat them after we have had our bowls of hot ravioles, cooked one minute, according to instructions, in a good chicken broth made from the carcass of a spit-roasted, maize-fed chicken we had a couple of days ago. With fresh brown bread – it always has a good crackly crust – our *sarriette*-strewn *magnane* and a nice creamy little St Marcellin, plus a hunk of that excellent *tourteau* with our coffee, we marvel for the twentieth time in a week that we have such a remarkable choice of provisions here. Pâtés and terrines, large jars of freshly made fish stock, saddle of rabbit rolled and stuffed, ready for roasting or baking, good sausages and *cayettes*, green with the chard so much loved in Rhône Valley cooking, skilfully cut and enticingly trimmed lamb and beef, all the good things from the bakery, the fresh eggs which really are fresh (one stallholder was apologetic because his were three days old), all play their part in making every meal a treat as well as extraordinarily simple to prepare. And in how many towns of no more than 7,500 inhabitants can one choose, on market day, from about seventy different kinds of cheese, at least sixty-five of them French, the rest Italian, Swiss and Dutch?

I must add that Lawrence Durrell, who lives not far away, and who I hadn't seen for a long while, reminded me that many years ago, about 1950, he and I happened to meet in Nîmes and that I complained angrily about the local food, swearing that I would never go back to the region. The area was indeed then very poor. Now the tourists, foreign residents, enterprising wine-growers, motorways, have made it prosperous. Well, there are worse things than words to eat.

from An Omelette and a Glass of Wine, *1984, revised February 1986*

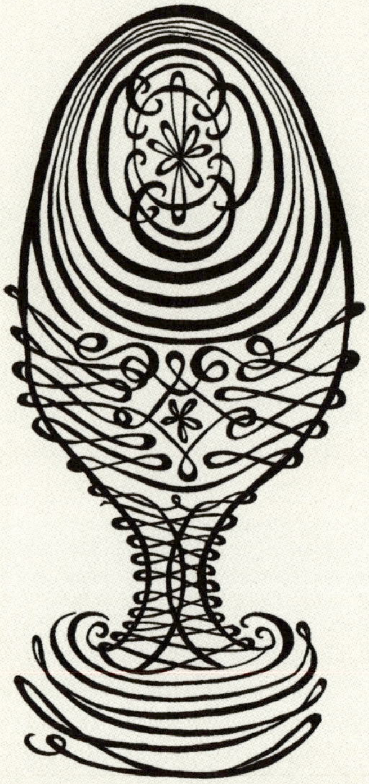

EGGS

'They reckon 685 ways of dressing eggs in the French kitchen; we hope our half-dozen recipes give sufficient variety for the English kitchen.' Doctor William Kitchiner, who wrote these words in *The Cook's Oracle*, round about 1821, therewith betrays himself as a pretty smug fellow. For the life of me I cannot see why, if our neighbours twenty-one miles across the Channel have 685 ways of cooking eggs, we should have to make do with six. Six recipes would no more than cover the basic ways of egg cookery common to all countries, but Dr Kitchiner was certainly right in so far as it is important to understand these methods thoroughly before embarking on the 679 remaining variations.

'Have ready 12 freshly poached eggs,' says the cookery book, and with a shudder you turn over the page, knowing that, allowing for disasters, those twelve eggs will probably turn into twenty and that your kitchen will be a charnel house of eggshells and a shambles of running egg yolks. Or 'shell 8 *œufs mollets*', they say, 'lay each in a puff pastry case and mask with a hollandaise sauce. Pour a cordon of melted meat glaze round each egg and brown with a salamander.' And one begins to agree with old Dr Kitchiner. For elaborate dishes of this sort are not really to be recommended for household cookery.

There are still plenty of lovely egg dishes of a much simpler kind to be made at home; with constant practice and given the time, it is perfectly possible to poach a few eggs successfully; an omelette is very easy to make in spite of all the talk about light hands and heavy frying pans.

Eggs in their own right, as well as all those allied dishes such as the onion tarts of Alsace, the cream and bacon quiches of Lorraine and all the various cheese and egg, potato and cream, and hot pastry confections of different provinces of France make the best possible dishes to serve for a first course or for a simple meal. But it cannot be claimed that these are particularly light dishes. Eggs, and especially eggs with cheese or cream, are very filling. So if you are starting with an onion tart, or a *pipérade*, it is best to make the second course something not too rich, and certainly not one requiring an egg or cream sauce. Egg dishes have a kind of elegance, a freshness, an allure, which sets them quite apart from any other kind of food, so that it becomes a great pleasure to be able to cook them properly and to serve them in just the right condition.

TIAN *with* SPINACH *and* POTATOES

This is one version – entirely my own and a much simplified one – of a Provençal country dish called a *tian*. The *tian* takes its name from the round earthenware gratin dish used for its cooking; and the ingredients which go into it are variable and very much dependent upon individual taste as well as upon family and local tradition.

Green vegetables and eggs are the constants. Tomatoes are almost inevitable, rice or potatoes are quite frequently included. And the *tian* is, like the Spanish omelette or tortilla and the Italian frittata, very often eaten cold as a picnic dish, or as a first – or only – course for the summer midday meal.

When mixing the *tian* ingredients, it's preferable that the vegetables be hot when they are mixed with the beaten eggs, and it is important that as soon as the mixture is ready it be poured into the cooking dish and transferred immediately to the oven. If it is kept waiting in the dish, the eggs tend to rise to the top, so you get a dish in two layers, instead of one integrated and nicely marbled cake.

250–350g/8–11½oz potatoes boiled in their skins, olive oil, salt and pepper, 500g/1lb fresh spinach, garlic, anchovy fillets, 5–6 eggs, 2–3 tablespoons grated cheese.

First peel the cooked potatoes. Cut them in cubes, put them in an earthenware dish (20.5cm/8½ inches) with 2 tablespoons of olive oil and seasonings of salt and pepper. Let them warm in the uncovered dish in a low oven at 150°C/gas 2 while you wash the spinach and cook it very briefly in just the water clinging to the leaves. Season with a little salt. Drain and squeeze dry. Chop it roughly, adding a little garlic if you like, and half a dozen anchovy fillets torn into short lengths. Stir this mixture into the beaten eggs and cheese, then add the cubed potatoes.

Tip the whole mixture into the dish, sprinkle the top with a little oil, return it, uncovered, to the oven, now heated to 190°C/gas 5. Leave the tian to bake for 25–30 minutes until it is well and evenly risen.

A few pine nuts make a delicious and characteristic addition to this *tian*. An alternative to the potatoes is cooked rice. Allow about 100g/3½oz uncooked weight, for this size of *tian*.

Enough for four people.

TIAN *of* COURGETTES

Please do not be daunted by the length of the recipe which follows. Once this dish has been mastered – and it is not at all difficult – you find that you have learned at least three dishes as well as a new way of preparing and cooking courgettes.

The quantities given should be enough for four people but the proportions are deliberately somewhat vague because the *tian* is essentially a dish to be made from the ingredients you have available. If, for instance, you have 250g/½lb only of courgettes, make up the bulk with 4 tablespoons of cooked rice, or the same bulk in diced cooked potatoes.

500g/1lb courgettes, salt, 750g/1½lb tomatoes (or use 500g/1lb fresh tomatoes and make up the quantity with Italian tinned whole peeled tomatoes and their juice), 1 small onion, 2 cloves of garlic, fresh basil when in season, and in the winter dried French marjoram or tarragon, 4 large eggs, a handful (i.e. about 3 tablespoons) of grated Parmesan or Gruyère cheese, a handful of coarsely chopped parsley, freshly ground pepper, nutmeg. For cooking the courgettes and tomatoes, a mixture of butter and olive oil.

To prepare the courgettes, wash them and pare off any parts of the skins which are blemished, leaving them otherwise unpeeled. Slice them lengthways into four, then cut them into 1-cm/½-inch chunks. Put them at once into a heavy frying pan or enamelled cast-iron skillet or gratin dish, sprinkle them with salt, and set them without fat of any kind over a very low flame. Watch them carefully, and when the juices, brought out by the salt, start to seep out, turn the courgettes with a spatula, and drop into the pan 30g/1oz or so of butter, then a tablespoon or two of olive oil. Cover the pan, and leave the courgettes over a low heat to soften.

While the courgettes are cooking prepare the tomatoes. Pour boiling water over them, skin them, chop them roughly. Peel and chop the onion. Heat a very little butter or olive oil in a pan. First melt the chopped onion without letting it brown. Then put in the tomatoes, season them, add the peeled and crushed garlic. Cook, uncovered, over low heat until a good deal of the moisture is evaporated. Now add the tinned tomatoes. These, and their juices, give colour, body and the necessary sweetness to the sauce. Sprinkle in the herb of your choice, let the tomato mixture cook until it is beginning to reduce and thicken.

Now amalgamate the courgettes and the tomato mixture. Turn them into a buttered or oiled earthenware gratin dish. For the quantities given, use one of approximately 18-cm/7-inch diameter and 5-cm/2-inch depth.

Put the gratin dish, covered with a plate if it has no lid of its own, in a moderate oven, 170°C/gas 3, for about half an hour, until the courgettes are quite tender.

To finish the *tian*, beat the eggs very well with the cheese, add plenty of seasonings (don't forget the nutmeg) and the coarsely chopped parsley.

Amalgamate the eggs and the vegetable mixture, increase the heat of the oven to 180–190°C/gas 4 or 5, and leave the *tian* to cook until the eggs are set, risen in the dish, and beginning to turn golden on the top. The time varies between 15 and 25 minutes depending on various factors such as the depth of the dish, the comparative density of the vegetable mixture, the freshness of the eggs, and so on.

When the *tian* is to be eaten cold, leave it to cool in its dish before inverting it on to a serving dish or plate. It should turn out into a very beautiful-looking cake, well-risen and moist. For serving cut it in wedges. Inside, there will be a mosaic of pale green and creamy yellow, flecked with the darker green of the parsley and the red-gold of the tomatoes.

To transport a *tian* on a picnic, it can be left in its cooking dish, or turned out on to a serving plate. Whichever way you choose, cover the tian with greaseproof paper and another plate, then tie the whole arrangement in a clean white cloth, knotted Dick Whittington fashion.

Enough for four people.

OMELETTES

As everybody knows, there is only one infallible recipe for the perfect omelette: your own. Reasonably enough; a successful dish is often achieved by quite different methods from those advocated in the cookery books or by the professional chefs, but over this question of omelette-making, professional and amateur cooks alike are particularly unyielding. Argument has never been known to convert anybody to a different method, so if you have your own, stick to it and let others go their cranky ways, mistaken, stubborn and ignorant to the end.

It is therefore to anyone still in the experimental stage that I submit the few following points which I fancy are often responsible for failure when that ancient iron omelette pan, for twenty years untouched by water, is brought out of the cupboard.

First, the eggs are very often beaten too savagely. In fact, they should not really be beaten at all, but stirred, and a few firm turns with two forks do the trick. Secondly, the simplicity and freshness evoked by the delicious word 'omelette' will be achieved only if it is remembered that it is the eggs which are the essential part of the dish; the filling, being of secondary importance, should be in very small proportion to the eggs. Lying lightly in the centre of the finished omelette, rather than bursting exuberantly out of the seams, it should supply the second of two different tastes and textures; the pure egg and cooked butter taste of the outside and ends of the omelette, then the soft, slightly runny interior, with its second flavouring of cheese or ham, mushrooms or fresh herbs.

As far as the pan is concerned, a 25-cm/10-inch omelette pan will make an omelette of 3 or 4 eggs. Beat them only immediately before you make the omelette, lightly as described above, with two forks, adding a light mild seasoning of salt and pepper. Allow about 15g/½oz of butter. Warm your pan, don't make it red hot. Then turn the burner as high as it will go. Put in the butter and when it has melted and is on the point of turning colour, pour in the eggs. Add the filling, and see that it is well embedded in the eggs. Tip the pan towards you and with a fork or spatula gather up a little of the mixture from the far side. Now tip the pan away from you so that the unset eggs run into the space you have made for them.

When a little of the unset part remains on the surface the omelette is done. Fold it in three with your fork or palette knife, hold the pan at an angle and slip the omelette out on to the waiting dish. This should be warmed, but only a little, or the omelette will go on cooking.

An omelette is nothing to make a fuss about. The chief mistakes are putting in too much of the filling and making this too elaborate. Such rich things as foie gras or lobster in cream sauce are inappropriate. In fact, moderation in every aspect is the best advice where omelettes are concerned. Sauces and other trimmings are superfluous, a little extra butter melted in the warm omelette dish or placed on top of the omelette as you serve it being the only addition which is not out of place.

OMELETTE *with* HERBS

Omelette fines herbes

Prepare 1 tablespoon of mixed finely chopped *parsley*, *tarragon*, *chives* and, if possible, *chervil*. Mix half of this, with *salt* and *pepper*, in the bowl with the *eggs*, and the other half when the eggs are in the pan. If you like, put a little knob of *butter* on top of the omelette as it is brought to the table.

TOMATO OMELETTE

Omelette à la tomate

One *tomato*, skinned and chopped small, cooked hardly more than a minute in *butter*, with *salt* and *pepper*, is added to the eggs already in the pan.

BACON OMELETTE

Omelette au lard

Add a tablespoon of finely chopped *bacon* softened a minute or so in its own fat, to the *eggs* already in the pan; take care not to salt the eggs too much.

Enough for one person.

SPANISH OMELETTE
Tortilla

A Spanish tortilla is a thick, unfolded omelette, consisting only of eggs, potatoes and seasonings. It is cooked in olive oil, should be compact and have almost the appearance of a cake, can be eaten hot or cold, and makes a splendid picnic dish, especially for a car journey. A big tortilla will keep moist for three days.

The following recipe, in note form, is exactly as I wrote it down while watching Juanita, the village girl who once cooked for the photographer Anthony Denney in his house in the province of Alicante. The notes seem to me to convey the essential points about making a tortilla more vividly than would a conventional recipe, and I have used them often without in any way altering the method, except to cook the potatoes rather more gently than Juanita did – she was never a patient girl.

About 500g/1lb potatoes for 4 eggs. Use a 22-cm/8½-inch or 24-cm/9½-inch pan.

Potatoes all cut up small. Soaked in plenty of water (like for gratin Dauphinois).

Cooked in olive oil (she lets it smoke) in shallow earthenware dish directly on butagaz. Tiny piece of garlic. Stirred fairly often, and pressed with flat, iron spatula-spoon. Salt. In the end the potatoes are almost in a cohered mass. If any pieces too big she cuts them as they cook with her iron implement.

She beats the eggs in a bowl, tips in the potatoes (slightly cooled; they have been transferred to a bowl) and mixes them well. The tortilla is cooked in an iron omelette pan with smoking oil. It puffs up. She holds a deep plate in her left hand and turns the tortilla into it. Then back into the pan. And process repeated (sometimes twice, it depends if she is satisfied with its appearance).

Enough for four to six people.

Notes:

1. For the initial cooking of the potatoes I still use a Spanish earthenware dish over direct heat, as did Juanita, although an ordinary frying pan serves perfectly well.
2. About that spatula-spoon: this is a characteristic Spanish kitchen implement, a round flat pusher, as it were, with a long handle, used mainly when the paella is cooking, and just right for moving the rice and other ingredients around in the pan. I use a thin wooden spatula or palette knife instead.
3. Really fresh eggs are necessary for a tortilla. Stale ones don't puff up, and so produce a flat omelette.

BAKED EGGS
Œufs en cocotte

Have your little fireproof china dishes ready with a good lump of *butter* in each, and an *egg* for each person ready broken into separate saucers. Put the little dishes into the oven at 190°C/gas 5 and take them out as soon as the butter has melted, slide an egg into each, pour a large tablespoon of *cream* on to the egg, avoiding the yolk, return them to the oven. They will take 4–5 minutes to cook, allowing perhaps ½ a minute less for those on the top shelf.

If you leave them too long, the yolks get hard and the dish is ruined, so be on the alert to see that they are taken out of the oven at the exact moment.

Experience and knowledge of the idiosyncrasies of one's own oven are the mediums of success here. No pepper or salt should be added, except at table, but a very little cut fresh tarragon when they come out of the oven is an acceptable addition.

Françoise Sagan
Les violons parfois

POACHED EGGS

This is what Dr Kitchiner, author of *The Cook's Oracle* (1829) has to say about poached eggs:

> The cook who wishes to display her skill in Poaching, must endeavour to procure Eggs that have been laid a couple of days, those that are quite newlaid are so milky that, take all the care you can, your cooking of them will seldom procure you the praise of being a Prime Poacher: You must have fresh Eggs, or it is equally impossible.
>
> The beauty of a Poached Egg is for the yolk to be seen blushing through the white – which should only be just sufficiently hardened, to form a transparent Veil for the Egg.
>
> My own method for poaching eggs I learnt from a cookery book published by the Buckinghamshire Women's Institute, and it has proved infallible.

First boil a saucepan of water, and into this dip each egg whole, in its shell, while you count about thirty, then take it out. When it comes to actually poaching the eggs, have a pan of fresh water boiling, add a dessertspoon of vinegar, stir the water fast until a whirlpool has formed, and into this break the eggs, one at a time. 1–1½ minutes cooks them. Take them very carefully out with a draining spoon. They will be rounded and the yolks covered with a 'transparent Veil' instead of the ragged-looking affair which a poached egg too often turns out to be, and the alternative of the egg-poaching pan, which produces an over-cooked sort of egg-bun, is equally avoided.

It is interesting to note that Dr Kitchiner instructs his readers to place poached eggs on bread 'toasted on one side only'. How right he is; I have never been able to understand the point of that sodden toast . . .

Try serving poached eggs on a piece of fresh, buttered bread; alternatively on a purée of some kind – split peas, sweet-corn or mushrooms, with pieces of fried bread around, but not under, the egg.

PIPÉRADE

Pipérade is the best known of all Basque dishes, and various recipes for it have appeared in English cookery books. It is a mixture of sweet peppers, tomatoes and onions, with eggs added at the end; the final result is a creamy scrambled-egg effect deliciously blended with the vegetables in which the sweet pepper flavour slightly dominates. Sometimes one meets it with the purée of onions, tomatoes and peppers topped with fried eggs, sometimes in the form of an omelette; the scrambled-egg version is the most characteristically Basque.

Pork fat or olive oil, 500g/1lb onions, 3 fairly large sweet red peppers or about 6 small green ones, in season in the Basque country long before the red ones, 500g/1lb tomatoes, salt and pepper, marjoram, 6 eggs.

In a heavy frying or sauté pan melt some pork fat (sometimes olive oil is used for this dish, but pork, or even bacon fat, suits it better). Put in the sliced onions, and let them cook slowly, turning golden but not brown: then put in the peppers, cut into strips; let this cook until it is soft, then add the chopped tomatoes, with a seasoning of salt, ground black pepper and a little marjoram. Cook with the cover on the pan.

When the whole mixture has become almost the consistency of a purée, pour in the beaten eggs, and stir gently, exactly as for ordinary scrambled eggs. Take care not to let them get over-cooked.

With the pipérade are served slices of the famous Jambon de Bayonne, most of which is in fact made at Orthez, in the Béarn.

The Jambon de Bayonne is something like the Italian Prosciutto and imparts its particular flavour to many Basque and Béarnais *garbures* and daubes. Brochettes of calf's liver are sometimes served with the pipérade and a very good combination it is.

Enough for four people.

CHATCHOUKA

This dish of eggs and vegetables is of Tunisian origin. It is made with a variety of vegetables – artichokes, broad beans, carrots, peas – according to the season. Chatchouka with tomatoes and peppers is a popular summer dish. Sometimes a little chopped or minced chicken or meat is cooked with the peppers, sometimes onions, and sometimes the chatchouka is cooked in individual earthenware egg dishes.

6 small green peppers, butter or olive oil, 8 tomatoes, salt and pepper, 4 eggs.

Remove the cores and seeds from the peppers, and cut them in strips. Heat a little oil or butter in a shallow earthenware dish. In this stew the peppers, and add the tomatoes, whole, when the peppers are half cooked. Season with salt and pepper. When the tomatoes are soft, break in the eggs, whole, and cover the pan until they are cooked. Serve in the dish in which they have cooked.

Enough for four people.

QUICHE LORRAINE

As in all regional dishes of ancient origin which have eventually become national as well as purely local property, there have been various evolutions in the composition of a quiche. Also called, in different parts of the province, *galette*, *fiouse*, *tourte*, *flon* and *flan*, a quiche is a flat open tart, and originally it was made of bread dough just like the Provençal pissaladière and the Neapolitan pizza. Gradually the bread dough came to be replaced with pastry while the fillings, of course, vary enormously, from sweet purple quetsch plums or golden mirabelles to savoury mixtures of onion, of chopped pork and veal, of cream flavoured with poppy seeds, of cream and eggs and bacon, of cream and cream cheese. According to its filling the tart will be called a *quiche aux pruneaux*, *quiche à l'oignon*, and so on. The one universally known as the quiche Lorraine contains smoked bacon, cream and eggs. Parisian, and English, cooks often add Gruyère cheese, but Lorrainers will tell you that this is not the true quiche Lorraine, whose history goes back at least as far as the sixteenth century.

For the pastry: *60g/2oz butter, 125g/4oz plain flour, sieved, salt, 1 egg, a little water.*

For the filling: *6 thin rashers of streaky bacon, 300ml/½ pint double cream, 3 egg yolks, 1 whole egg, pepper, salt.*

Cut the butter into little pieces and crumble it thoroughly with the sieved flour, adding a good pinch of salt. Break in the egg and mix the dough with your hands. Add enough water (2 to 4 tablespoons) to make the dough soft, but it should still be firm enough to come away clean from the bowl or board. Simply knead it into a ball, wrap it in greaseproof paper and leave it for a minimum of 2 hours. When the time comes to use it, roll it out very thin and line a 20-cm/8-inch flan tin with it, and with a fork prick the surface.

Preheat the oven to 200°C/gas 6. For the filling cut the rashers of streaky bacon into 2-cm/1-inch-wide strips. Cook them in a frying pan for a minute so that some of the fat runs. Arrange them in circles on the pastry. Have ready the double cream mixed with the very well-beaten yolks of 3 eggs plus 1 whole egg, and well seasoned with freshly ground pepper and a little salt (taking into account the saltiness of the bacon). Pour this mixture over the bacon and transfer immediately to the preheated oven. Leave it for 20 minutes, then cook for another 10 minutes at a lowered temperature, 180°C/gas 4. By this time the filling should be puffed up almost like a soufflé, and golden brown. Let it rest a minute or two after you take it from the oven, to make it easier to cut, but don't wait until it has fallen before serving it.

Enough for four people.

ONION TART
Tarte à l'oignon

This is the famous Alsatian speciality. It makes a truly lovely first course.

For the pastry: *125g/4oz plain flour, sieved, 60g/2oz butter, 1 egg, salt, water.*

For the filling: *750g/1½ lb onions, butter and oil for cooking the onions, salt, nutmeg and plenty of freshly ground pepper, 3 egg yolks, 150ml/¼ pint thick cream.*

Make a well in the sieved flour, put the butter cut in small pieces, the egg and a good pinch of salt in the middle. Blend quickly and lightly but thoroughly, with the fingertips. Add a very little water, just enough to make the dough moist, but it should come cleanly away from the bowl or board. Place the ball of dough on a floured board and with the heel of your palm gradually stretch the paste out, bit by bit, until it is a flat but rather ragged-looking sheet. Gather it up again, and repeat the process. It should all be done lightly and expeditiously, and is extremely simple although it sounds complicated written down. Roll it into a ball, wrap it in greaseproof paper and leave it to rest in a cold larder or refrigerator for a minimum of 2 hours, so that it loses all elasticity and will not shrink or lose its shape during the baking. This is one version of the *pâte brisée* or *pâte à foncer* used for most open tarts in French cookery. Without being as rich or as complicated as puff pastry, it is light and crisp. But those who already have a satisfactory method for tart and flan pastries may prefer to stick to their own. In spite of all the cookery rules, the making of pastry remains a very personal matter.

For the filling, peel and slice the onions as finely as possible, taking care to discard the fibrous parts at the root of the onions. Melt 60g/2oz of butter and a little oil in a heavy frying pan. In this cook the onions, covered, until they are quite soft and pale golden. They must not fry, and they should be stirred from time to time to make sure they are not sticking. They will take about ½ an hour. Season with salt, nutmeg and pepper. Stir in the very well-beaten yolks and the cream, and leave until the time comes to cook the tart.

Oil a 20-cm/8-inch tart or flan tin. Roll out your pastry as thinly as possible (the great thing about this dish, as also the quiches of Lorraine, is that there should be a lot of creamy filling on very little pastry). Line the tin with the pastry, pressing it gently into position with your knuckle. Pour in the filling, cook in the centre of a fairly hot oven, with the tin standing on a baking sheet, at 200°C/gas 6, for 30 minutes. Serve very hot.

Enough for four people.

LEEK *and* CREAM PIE

Flan de poireaux à la berrichonne

Under the name of *flamiche* or *flamique* a very similar dish is made in Picardy and other parts of northern France, but does not usually include the ham, more leeks (1.5kg/3lb) and less cream (150ml/¼ pint) being used for the filling. Sometimes a bread dough or yeast pastry is used (in this case, reduce the amount of filling by one third, to allow for the rising of the pastry) and sometimes the *flamiche* is covered over with a lid of pastry so that it becomes more like a pasty.

Line a 20-cm/8-inch pie tin with *pastry*, as for the onion tart on page 90 or the quiche Lorraine, page 89. Chop the white part of 1kg/2lb of *leeks* and let them melt in *butter*. Add 60g/2oz of lean *ham* cut into dice. Spread this mixture on the pastry.

Beat together 3 *egg yolks* and 300ml/½ pint of *cream*; season with *salt* and *pepper*. Pour this mixture over the leeks, put a few small pieces of butter on the top, and cook in a medium hot oven at 190°C/gas 5 for 30–40 minutes.

Enough for four people.

PASTA ASCIUTTA

On the 15th of November 1930, at a banquet at the restaurant Penna d'Oca in Milan, the famous Italian futurist poet Marinetti launched his much publicized campaign against all established forms of cooking and, in particular, against pastasciutta. 'Futurist cooking,' said Marinetti, 'will be liberated from the ancient obsession of weight and volume, and one of its principal aims will be the abolition of pastasciutta. Pastasciutta, however grateful to the palate, is an obsolete food; it is heavy, brutalizing, and gross; its nutritive qualities are deceptive; it induces scepticism, sloth, and pessimism.'

The day after this diatribe was delivered the Italian press broke into an uproar; all classes participated in the dispute which ensued. Every time pastasciutta was served either in a restaurant or a private house interminable arguments arose. One of Marinetti's supporters declared that 'our pastasciutta, like our rhetoric, suffices merely to fill the mouth'. Doctors, asked their opinions, were characteristically cautious: 'Habitual and exaggerated consumption of pastasciutta is definitely fattening.' 'Heavy consumers of pastasciutta have slow and placid characters; meat eaters are quick and aggressive.' 'A question of taste and of the cost of living. In any case, diet should be varied, and should never consist exclusively of one single element.' The Duke of Bovino, Mayor of Naples, plunged into the fight with happy abandon. 'The angels in Paradise,' he affirmed to a reporter, 'eat nothing but *vermicelli al pomodoro*.' To which Marinetti replied that this confirmed his suspicions with regard to the monotony of Paradise and of the life led by the angels.

Marinetti and his friends proceeded to divert themselves and outrage the public with the invention and publication of preposterous new dishes. Most of these were founded on the shock principle of combining unsuitable and exotic ingredients (mortadella with nougat, pineapple with sardines, cooked salame immersed in a bath of hot black coffee flavoured with eau-de-Cologne, an aphrodisiac drink composed of pineapple juice, eggs, cocoa, caviar, almond paste, red pepper, nutmeg, cloves and Strega). Meals were to be eaten to the accompaniment of perfumes (warmed, so that the bald-headed should not suffer from the cold), to be sprayed over the diners, who, fork in the right hand, would stroke meanwhile with the left some suitable substance – velvet, silk or emery paper.

Marinetti's bombshell contained a good deal of common sense; diet and methods of cookery must necessarily evolve at the same time as other habits and customs. But behind this amiable fooling lurked a sinister note: the fascist obsession with nationalism and patriotism, the war to come. 'Spaghetti is no food for fighters.' In the 'conflict to come the victory will be to the swift', 'Pastasciutta is anti-virile . . . A weighty and encumbered stomach cannot be favourable to physical enthusiasm towards women.' The costly import of foreign flour for pastasciutta should be stopped, to boost the national cultivation of rice. The snobbery of the Italian aristocracy and *haute bourgeoisie*, who had lost their heads over American customs, cocktail parties, foreign films, German music, and French food, was damned by Marinetti as *esterofil* (pro-foreign) and anti-Italian.

Marinetti's effort was not the first that had been made to reform the Italian diet. In the sixteenth century a Genoese doctor had denounced the abuse of pasta. Towards the end of the eighteenth century a campaign was instituted against the consumption of excessive quantities of macaroni. Innumerable volumes from the hands of eminent scientists and men of letters proved unavailing. Not only was the passion for pastasciutta too deeply rooted in the tastes of the people, but there was also a widely diffused superstition that macaroni was the antidote to all ills, the universal panacea.

Another effort was made in the first half of the nineteenth century by the scientist Michele Scropetta; he, again, achieved nothing concrete. Had it not been for the war Marinetti's campaign might have achieved a certain success; but however aware enlightened Italians may be of the unsuitability of pasta as a daily food, the fact remains that the majority of southern Italians (in the north it is replaced by rice or polenta) continue to eat pastasciutta at midday and probably some kind of *pasta in brodo* at night. Considering the cost of living, this is not surprising; freshly made pasta such as tagliatelle and fettuccine is cheap and versatile. According to circumstances it may be eaten economically with tomato sauce and cheese, with fresh tomatoes when they are cheap, with butter and cheese, with oil and garlic without cheese. The whole dish will cost rather less than two eggs, is immediately satisfying, and possesses the further advantage that every Italian could prepare a dish of spaghetti blindfold, standing on his head in his sleep.

from Italian Food, *1954*

PASTA

The different varieties of pasta are countless, and to add to the confusion each province has different names for almost identical kinds. There are two main distinctions to be made with regard to genuine Italian pasta. There is *pasta fatta in casa* (home-made pasta), and the kind which is mass-produced and dried in the factory and which will keep almost indefinitely.

When you see the words *pasta di pura semola di grano duro* printed on the label of a packet of spaghetti or other pasta, it means that the product is made from fine flour obtained from the cleaned endosperm or heart of the durum (hard) wheat grain; the cream of the wheat, in fact. What we know as semolina is produced in a similar way, but is more coarsely milled.

Some kinds of factory-produced pasta are made with eggs, some without. Pasta coloured green with spinach is also sold in packets. The Italians have brought the manufacture of pasta to a fine art, and the difference between home-made and dried pasta is chiefly one of texture. Dried must, of course, be cooked for about 15 minutes, whereas freshly made pasta takes only about 5 minutes.

In Italy the amount of pasta allowed for each person is 90–125g/3–4oz, whether home-made or dried. The latter is usually cooked in a large quantity of boiling salted water. It should be cooked *al dente*, that is, very slightly resistant, and it should be strained without delay. A warmed serving dish should be ready, and the pasta should be eaten as soon as it has been prepared.

An alternative, but little known, way of cooking manufactured pasta is to calculate 1 litre or 1¾ pints of water to every 125g or ¼lb of dried pasta. Bring the water to the boil; add *a* tablespoon of salt for every 2 litres or 3½ pints of water and add the pasta. After it comes back to the boil let it continue boiling for 3 minutes. Turn off the heat, cover the saucepan with a towel and the lid, leave it for 5–8 minutes according to the thickness of the pasta, e.g. 5 minutes for spaghettini, 8 for *maccheroni rigati,* which are short tubes, ridged and thick. At the end of this time the pasta should be just *al dente*.

I learned this excellent method from the directions given on a packet of Agnesi pasta bought in the early 1970s. I find it infinitely preferable to the old-fashioned way.

The addition of a generous lump of butter left to melt on the top of the pasta as it is served, or of a little olive oil put into the heated dish before the cooked pasta is turned into it, are both valuable improvements. Whether the sauce is served separately or stirred into the pasta is a matter of taste.

TAGLIATELLE *with* BOLOGNESE SAUCE

Tagliatelle alla bolognese

Ragù is the true name of the Bolognese sauce which, in one form or another, has travelled round the world. In Bologna it is served mainly with *lasagne verdi*, but it can go with many other kinds of pasta. Fresh butter must be served as well, and plenty of grated Parmesan. This dish of pasta, known by name all over the world, is served in such a vast number of astounding ways, all of them incorrect (which would not matter if those ways happened to be successful), that it is a revelation to eat it cooked in the true Bolognese fashion. This is the recipe given me by Zia Nerina, a splendid woman, titanic of proportion but angelic of face and manner, who in the 1950s owned and ran the Trattoria Nerina in Bologna. Zia Nerina's cooking was renowned far beyond the confines of her native city.

90g/3oz bacon or uncooked ham ('both fat and lean'), butter, 1 onion, 1 carrot, 1 small piece of celery, 250g/8oz lean minced beef, 125g/4oz chicken livers, 3 tablespoons concentrated tomato purée, 1 wine glass white wine, salt and pepper, nutmeg, 2 wine glasses stock or water.

Cut the bacon or ham into very small pieces and brown them gently in a small saucepan in about 15g/½oz of butter. Add the onion, the carrot and the celery, all finely chopped. When they have browned, put in the raw minced beef, and then turn it over and over so that it all browns evenly. Now add the chopped chicken livers, and after 2 or 3 minutes the tomato purée, and then the white wine. Season with salt (having regard to the relative saltiness of the ham or bacon), pepper, and a scraping of nutmeg, and add the meat stock or water. Cover the pan and simmer the sauce very gently for 30–40 minutes. Some Bolognese cooks add at the last 1 cup of cream or milk to the sauce, which makes it smoother. When the *ragù* is to be served with spaghetti or tagliatelle, mix it with the hot pasta in a heated dish so that the pasta is thoroughly impregnated with the sauce, and add a good piece of butter before serving. Hand the grated cheese separately.

Enough sauce for six generous helpings of pasta.

PENNE *with* MASCARPONE

Mascarpone is a pure, double cream cheese made in northern Italy and sometimes eaten with sugar and strawberries in the same way as the French Crémets and Cœur à la Crème. We have several varieties of double cream cheese here. It makes a most delicious sauce for pasta. The ordinary milk curd cheese can also be used for a pasta sauce, but the double cream variety produces a dish altogether more subtle.

One or other variety of small pasta such as little shells, pennine (small quills) and so on can equally be used for this dish; as can tagliatelle, the narrow ribbon noodles, usually called fettuccine in Rome. The green ones are particularly attractive for this dish because of the contrast of the green pasta with the cream sauce.

The sauce is prepared as follows: in your serving dish melt a lump of *butter* and 125–180g/4–6oz double *cream cheese*. It must just gently heat, not boil. Into this mixture put your cooked and drained *pasta*. Turn it round and round, adding 2 or 3 tablespoons of grated *Parmesan*. Add a dozen or so shelled and roughly chopped *walnuts*. Serve more grated cheese separately.

This is an exquisite dish when well prepared, but it is filling and rich, so a little goes a long way.

Enough sauce for three or four people.

FETTUCCINE *with* FRESH TOMATO SAUCE

Fettuccine alla marinara

Fettuccine are home-made ribbon noodles. The ready-made kind will, however, do just as well for this dish, which is Neapolitan.

Cook the *fettucine* as usual; 5 minutes before they are ready make the sauce. Into a frying pan put a good covering of *olive oil*; into this when it is hot but not smoking throw at least 3 cloves of sliced *garlic*; let them cook half a minute. Add 6 or 7 ripe *tomatoes*, each cut in about 6 pieces; they are to cook for about 3 minutes only, the point of the sauce being that the tomatoes retain their natural flavour and are scarcely cooked, while the juice that comes out of them (they must, of course, be ripe tomatoes) amalgamates with the oil and will moisten the pasta. At the last moment stir in several leaves of fresh *basil*, simply torn into 2 or 3 pieces each, and season the sauce with *salt* and *pepper*. Pour the sauce on top of the fettuccine in the serving dish, and serve the grated *cheese* separately.

This sauce is also thoroughly to be recommended for all kinds of pasta, rice and dried vegetables such as haricot beans and chick peas.

Enough sauce for four people.

MACARONI CARBONARA

A Roman dish, and a welcome change from the customary pasta with tomato sauce. It can be made with any shaped macaroni, spaghetti or noodles. Sometimes rigatoni (short, thick, ribbed macaroni) are used for this dish; and streaky salt pork rather than ham or bacon.

Cook the *pasta* in the usual way, in plenty of boiling salted water. Strain it and put it into a heated dish. Have ready 125g/4oz *ham*, or *coppa* (Italian cured pork shoulder) cut into short matchstick lengths, and fried gently in *butter*. When the macaroni is ready in its dish add to the ham or coppa 2 beaten *eggs* and stir as you would for scrambled eggs, pouring the whole mixture on to the macaroni at the precise moment when the eggs are beginning to thicken, so that they present a slightly granulated appearance without being as thick as scrambled eggs. Give the whole a good stir with a wooden spoon so that the egg and ham mixture is evenly distributed, add some grated *Parmesan*, and serve more Parmesan separately.

Enough sauce for four people.

SPAGHETTI *with* CLAMS

Spaghetti alle vongole

One of the regular dishes of Roman restaurants as well as of Naples and the southern coast. Vongole are very small clams. If you can't get hold of them, use mussels, other small clams or fresh cockles instead. If ready-cooked cockles are bought from a fishmonger, keep them in a colander under running water for as long as possible, for they are sure to be gritty and probably salty.

2.5 litres/4 pints clams or cockles if they are in their shells, 250g/½lb if they are already cooked and shelled. If using mussels allow 3 litres/5 pints. Olive oil, an onion, 2 or 3 cloves of garlic, tomatoes, parsley.

Clean the shellfish carefully, scrubbing them first and leaving them under running water until all the grit and sand have disappeared. Put them into a pan over a fairly fast flame and let the shells open. Strain them. Remove the shells. In a little warmed olive oil, sauté a chopped onion and 2 or 3 cloves of garlic (more if you like). Add 750g/1½lb of chopped and skinned ripe tomatoes (or the contents of 450g/14oz tin of Italian peeled tomatoes), and when this has been reduced somewhat, add the clams, cockles or mussels and a handful of chopped parsley. As soon as the shellfish are hot the sauce is ready. Pour it over the cooked spaghetti in the dish.

Cheese is never served with *spaghetti alle vongole*.

Enough sauce for four people.

SPAGHETTI *with* OIL *and* GARLIC

Spaghetti all'olio e aglio

Pasta is often eaten in Italy with no embellishment but oil and garlic. Those who are particularly addicted to spaghetti and to garlic will find this dish excellent, others will probably abominate it. It is essential that the oil be olive oil and of good quality.

When your *spaghetti* is cooked, barely warm a cup of *oil* in a small pan, and into it stir whatever quantity of finely chopped *garlic* you fancy. Let it soak in the oil a bare minute, without frying, then stir the whole mixture into the spaghetti. You can add chopped *parsley* or any other herb, and of course grated *cheese* if you wish, although the Neapolitans do not serve cheese with spaghetti cooked in this way. If you like the taste of garlic without wishing actually to eat the bulb itself, pour the oil on to the spaghetti through a strainer, leaving the chopped garlic behind.

SPAGHETTI *with* OIL, GARLIC *and* CHILLI

Spaghetti all'olio, aglio e saetini

Cook the *spaghetti* in the usual way, put it into a hot dish, and pour over it a generous amount of very hot *olive oil* in which have been fried several coarsely chopped cloves of *garlic* and some *red pepper flakes*.

TRENETTE *with* PESTO

This is perhaps the best pasta dish in the whole of Italy. Trenette are the Genoese version of fine pasta, about the thickness of a match, and the same shape, but in long pieces. The pasta is cooked as usual, and when it is ready in the serving dish, about 2 tablespoonfuls of pesto (which is neither cooked nor heated) are heaped up on the top, and on top of the pesto a large piece of butter. The butter and the sauce are mixed into the pasta at the table. Grated Parmesan or Pecorino is served separately. Spaghetti, lasagne, tagliatelle, in fact any pasta you fancy, can be served with pesto.

This sauce is eaten by the Genoese with all kinds of pasta, with gnocchi and as a flavouring for soups. The Genoese claim that their basil has a far superior flavour to that grown in any other part of Italy, and assert that a good pesto can only be made with Genoese basil. As made in Genoa it is certainly one of the best sauces yet invented for pasta and 1 tablespoon of pesto stirred in at the last minute gives a most delicious flavour to a minestrone. Try it also with baked potatoes instead of butter.

1 large bunch of fresh basil, garlic, salt, 30g/1oz each of pine nuts and grated Sardo or Parmesan cheese, 45–60ml/1½–2fl oz olive oil.

Pound the basil leaves (there should be about 60g/2oz when the stalks have been removed) in a mortar with 1 or 2 cloves of garlic, a little salt and the pine nuts. Add the cheese. (Sardo cheese is the pungent Sardinian ewe's milk cheese which is exported in large quantities to Genoa to make pesto. Parmesan and Sardo are sometimes used in equal quantities, or all Parmesan, which gives the pesto a milder flavour.)

When the pesto is a thick purée start adding the olive oil, a little at a time. Stir it steadily and see that it is amalgamating with the other ingredients, as the finished sauce should have the consistency of a creamed butter. If made in larger quantities pesto may be stored in jars, covered with a layer of olive oil.

Enough sauce for four people.

GREEN GNOCCHI

Gnocchi verdi

This quantity is sufficient for four people for a first course. If they are to be the mainstay of a meal make the quantities half as much again; but as the cooking of these gnocchi is an unfamiliar process to most people, it is advisable to try out the dish with not more than the quantities given.

375g/12oz cooked and chopped spinach (i.e. 500g/1lb to start with), salt, pepper, nutmeg, a little butter, 250g/8oz ricotta, 2 eggs, 3 tablespoons of flour, 45g/1½oz grated Parmesan cheese, and for the sauce plenty of melted butter and grated Parmesan cheese.

Cook the cleaned spinach with a little salt but no water. Drain it, press it absolutely dry, then chop it finely. Put it into a pan with salt, pepper, nutmeg, a nut of butter and the mashed ricotta. Stir all the ingredients together over a low flame for 5 minutes. Remove the pan from the fire and beat in the eggs, the flour and the grated Parmesan. Leave the mixture in the refrigerator for several hours, or, better, overnight.

Spread a pastry board with flour, form little croquettes about the size of a cork with the spinach mixture, roll them in the flour, and when they are all ready drop them carefully into a large pan of barely simmering, slightly salted water.

(Do not be alarmed if the mixture seems rather soft; the eggs and the flour hold the gnocchi together as soon as they are put into the boiling water.)

Either the gnocchi must be cooked in a very large saucepan or else the operation must be carried out in two or three relays, as there must be plenty of room for them in the pan. When they rise to the top, which will be in 5–8 minutes, they are ready. They will disintegrate if left too long. Take them out with a perforated draining spoon, drain them carefully in a colander or sieve, and when the first batch is ready slide them into a shallow ovenproof dish already prepared with 30g/1oz of melted butter and a thin layer of grated Parmesan cheese. Put the dish in a low oven to keep hot while the rest of the gnocchi are cooked. When all are done, put another 30g/1oz of butter and a generous amount of cheese over them and leave the dish in the oven for 5 minutes.

The MARKETS *of* FRANCE: Cavaillon

It is a Sunday evening in mid-June. The cafés of Cavaillon are crammed. There isn't an inch to park your car. The noise is tremendous. In the most possible of the hotels – it goes by the name of Toppin – all the rooms are taken by seven o'clock. But the little Auberge La Provençale in the rue Chabran is quite quiet and you can enjoy a good little dinner – nothing spectacular, but genuine and decently cooked food well served – and go to bed early. The chances are you won't sleep much though, because Monday is the big market day in Cavaillon and soon after midnight the carts and lorries and vans of the big fruit farmers' co-operatives, of the market gardeners, of the tomato and garlic and onion growers, will start rattling and roaring and rumbling into the great open market in the place du Clos.

At dawn they will be unloading their melons and asparagus, their strawberries and redcurrants and cherries, their apricots and peaches and pears and plums, their green almonds, beans, lettuces, shining new white onions, new potatoes, vast bunches of garlic. By six o'clock the ground will be covered with *cageots*, the chip vegetable and fruit baskets, making a sea of soft colours and shadowy shapes in the dawn light. The air of the Place is filled with the musky scent of those little early Cavaillon melons, and then you become aware of another powerfully conflicting smell – rich, clove-like, spicy. It is the scent of sweet basil, and it is coming from the far end of the market where a solitary wrinkled old man sits on an upturned basket, scores and scores of basil plants ringed all around him like a protective hedge. With a beady eye he watches the drama of the market place. The dealers, exporters and wholesalers walking round inspecting the produce, discussing prices, negotiating; the hangers-on standing about in groups smoking, chatting; the market police and official inspectors strolling round seeing that all is in order.

On the whole the scene is quiet, quieter at least than you would expect, considering that this is one of the most important wholesale fruit and vegetable markets in France, the great distributing centre for the primeurs of the astonishingly fertile and productive areas of the Vaucluse and the

EXTRA
PROVENCE
ail frais
6,90 €
le kg

Comtat Venaissin – areas which less than a hundred years ago were desperately poor, inadequately irrigated, isolated for lack of roads and transport, earthquake-stricken, devastated by blights which destroyed the cereal crops and the vines.

It was with the building of the railways connecting Provence with Paris and the north, with Marseille and the ports of the Mediterranean to the south, that the possibilities of the Rhône and Durance valleys for intensive fruit and vegetable cultivation first began to be understood. New methods of irrigation, the planting of fruit trees in large areas where the vines had been stricken, the division of the land into small fields broken with tall cypress hedges as windbreaks against the scourging mistral, the ever-increasing demand in Paris and the big towns of the north for early vegetables, and the tremendous industry of these Provençal cultivators have done the rest. And to such effect that last year eighty thousand kilos of asparagus came into Cavaillon market alone between 15 April and 15 May; in the peak month of July three hundred tons of melons daily; five hundred tons of tomatoes every day in July and August. Altogether some hundred and sixty thousand tons of vegetables and fruit leave Cavaillon every year, about fifty per cent by rail, the rest by road. And Cavaillon, although the most important, is by no means the only big market centre in the neighbourhood. Avignon, Châteaurenard, Bolléne, Pertuis, all dispatch their produce by special trains to the north; vast quantities of fruit are absorbed locally by the jam and fruit-preserving industries of Apt and Carpentras; and every little town and village has its own retail vegetable and fruit market, every day in the bigger towns, once or twice a week in less populated places.

But now seven o'clock strikes in the market at Cavaillon. The lull is over. This is the moment when the goods change hands. Pandemonium breaks loose. The dealers snatch the baskets of produce they have bought and rush them to waiting lorries. A cartload of garlic vanishes from under your nose. A mountain of melons evaporates in a wink. If you try to speak to anybody you will be ignored, if you get in the way you'll be knocked down in the wild scramble to get goods away to Paris, London, Brussels and all the great centres of northern and eastern France. Suddenly, the market place is deserted.

At eight o'clock you emerge from the café where you have had your breakfast coffee and croissant. The market place is, to put it mildly, astir once more. It is surrounded by vans and lorries disgorging cheap dresses and overalls, plastic kitchenware, shoes and scarves and bales of cotton, piles of plates and jugs, nails and screws and knives, farm implements and packets of seeds, cartons of dried-up-looking biscuits and trays of chemically coloured sweets.

You dive down a side street where you have spied a festoon of pretty cotton squares, and there, under gaudy painted colonnades, lilac and orange, cinnamon and lemon and rose, in patterns more typical of Marseille or the Levant than of Cavaillon, the retail market stalls are already doing business. The displays seem rather tame after the wholesale market and there is not a melon to be seen. It is too early in the season, they are still too expensive for the housewives of Cavaillon. Five thousand francs a kilo they were fetching today, and a week later in London shops 12s. 6d. each for little tiny ones. But the street opposite the painted colonnades leads into the square where more and more food stalls are opening and the housewives are already busy marketing. Here you can buy everything for a picnic lunch. Beautiful sprawling ripe tomatoes, a Banon cheese wrapped in chestnut leaves, Arles sausages, pâté, black olives, butter cut from a towering monolith, apricots, cherries.

It is still early and you can drive out towards Apt and branch off across the Lubéron. The roads are sinuous but almost empty, and they will take you through some of the most beautiful country in Provence. Perched on the hillsides are typical old Provençal villages, some, like Oppède-le-Vieux, crumbling, haunted, half-deserted, others like Bonnieux with a flourishing modern village built below the old one, and up beyond Apt, through the dramatic stretch of ochre-mining country, the strange red-gold village of Roussillon appears to be toppling precariously on the edge of a craggy cliff. Round about here, the network of caves under the ochreous rocks has been turned into vast *champignonnières*, and at the modest little Restaurant David (no relation) you can eat the local cultivated mushrooms cooked *à la crème* or *à la provençale* with, naturally, olive oil, parsley and garlic. And the Rose d'Or, a little hotel opened only a few weeks ago, promises a welcome alternative to the establishments of Apt, Aix and Cavaillon.

from Vogue, 1960

VEGETABLES

What, I am sometimes asked, is the difference between fresh and frozen vegetables; surely they are exactly the same? Astonishing though such a question may seem to anyone who knows what is really meant by fresh vegetables, I think the explanation is that to a great many English people vegetables mean simply an accompaniment to meat. Gravy and horseradish, mustard and mint, to say nothing of the meat itself, distract attention from second-rate or inadequately cooked vegetables. Eaten for themselves alone, as a separate dish, vegetables take on a very different significance. Both their charms and their defects become more apparent. Apart from cauliflower cheese, we haven't much tradition in the way of vegetable dishes which stand on their own. But we have plenty of vegetables, and often it is the commonplace ones like onions and beetroot, carrots and spinach and leeks which make the most delicious dishes.

It is in the matter of vegetables and fruit that a country's eating habits evolve most rapidly. There was a time, after all, when there were no potatoes in England, when the tomato was new to Italy, when petits pois were first brought to France (and caused a furore at the court of Louis XIV), when bananas, grapefruit and the cultivated mushrooms we now take for granted were exciting novelties. Not so long ago, French beans meant only coarse scarlet runners, but now we can buy several varieties of string beans and dwarf beans. Aubergines, sweet peppers and avocado pears have become commonplace in our shops. Enterprising English growers are supplying us with little courgettes as an alternative to gigantic vegetable marrows.

So, I wonder if, eventually, we shall not come round to the habit, taken for granted in French cookery, of regarding vegetable dishes as an important part of the meal rather than simply as an adjunct to the roast. If we do, we shall surely find that we enjoy the meat course more as well as the vegetables, for both must, when required to stand on their own, be more carefully bought and more meticulously cooked.

VENETIAN ARTICHOKES

Carciofi alla veneziana

Globe artichokes are almost one of the staple vegetables of Italy. There are several different varieties and they are cooked in a good many different ways. The large green ones, which are so tender that the whole vegetable can be eaten, are at their best in the famous Roman dish *carciofi alla Giudea* (fried whole in oil), or *alla Romana*, stewed in oil and garlic. They can be cut into slices and fried, sometimes in batter, and served as part of a *fritto misto*. Very tiny artichokes are preserved in oil. The medium-sized ones with violet-coloured leaves are perfectly delicious stewed in oil and white wine, and equally good cut in papery slices and either cooked in butter as an accompaniment to veal or served raw with a seasoning of oil and lemon. Hearts of artichokes are often combined with eggs in a frittata, also in a kind of omelette cooked in the oven, and are an important ingredient of the excellent *torta pasqualina*, Genoese Easter pie.

In some parts of Italy artichoke hearts are sold ready prepared for cooking. You take off the outside leaves and with a sharp knife cut off two thirds of the top of the artichoke. Take out the choke and trim round the outside so that only the heart and a few of the inside leaves are left. As each one is ready throw it into cold water in which you have squeezed lemon juice.

For this dish the small dark violet-leaved *artichokes* are used. Put 6 or 8 of them, with only the outer leaves cut away, into a braising pan, covered with equal parts of *olive oil*, *white wine* and water. Stew them gently, with the cover on the pan, for an hour, then take off the lid, turn up the flame, and let the liquid reduce until only the oil is left.

Enough for three to four people.

TURKISH AUBERGINES

Aubergines à la turque

Aubergines are particularly successful when mixed with tomatoes in some form or other and they also make interesting purées and salads, the kind of little dishes which are served either as an hors d'œuvre or with meat, like a chutney (see recipe on page 31). Aubergines are best cooked in olive oil rather than in butter or dripping; they always have a warm southern look about them, especially when they are cooked with their purple skins on. Most aubergine dishes are as good cold as they are hot, and they can also be heated up without deteriorating in any way, so they are a most versatile vegetable.

2 large aubergines (the round variety are best for this dish), salt, olive oil, 3 large onions, 250g/½lb tomatoes, garlic, ground allspice, sugar.

Cut the unpeeled aubergines into thick, round slices. Salt them and leave them to drain in a colander for an hour or two. Fry them in oil so that they are browned on both sides. Take them out of the pan and fry the thinly sliced onions, not crisply, but just golden yellow, then add the skinned and chopped tomatoes, and a clove or two of crushed garlic. Season with salt, a teaspoon of the allspice, and a little sugar. Cook until you have a thick sauce. Arrange the aubergine slices in an oiled baking tin, put a tablespoonful of the sauce on each slice of aubergine, and bake in a moderate oven for 40–50 minutes. Can be served hot but best cold.

Enough for four people.

PROVENÇAL AUBERGINE MOUSSE

Papeton d'aubergines

The story goes that one of the Avignon Popes complained that Provençal cooking was not as good as that of Rome, and his cook invented this recipe in order to prove that he was wrong. It is also recounted that the first *papeton* was presented to the Pope in the form of a mitre.

6 aubergines, salt, olive oil, ground pepper, a clove of garlic, milk, 3 eggs.

Peel the aubergines, cut them in thick slices, salt them and leave them to drain. Stew them in olive oil in a covered pan, so that they remain moist; drain them and chop or sieve them. Season and add a chopped clove of garlic, a teacup of milk and 3 eggs. Turn into a lightly oiled mould. Cook for 25 minutes in a bain-marie. Turn out and serve covered with a thick fresh tomato sauce flavoured with fresh basil (page 305).

Instead of being turned out, the *papeton* can be served in the dish in which it has cooked, with the sauce poured on the top, or offered separately. A much easier system.

Enough for four people.

BROAD BEANS *with* BACON

Melt 60g/2oz of diced *bacon* (or ham, or cold pork) in a little *butter*. Add 1kg/2lb of cooked *broad beans*, 2 or 3 tablespoons of light *béchamel sauce* (see page 298), a little *cream*, a very little chopped *parsley*. Simmer together for 5 minutes.

Enough for four to five people.

BROAD BEANS *with* YOGHURT

A Middle Eastern dish, called *fistuqia*.

750g/1½lb broad beans, 2 tablespoons rice, a clove of garlic, salt and pepper, a small pot of yoghurt, 1 egg.

Boil the broad beans and the rice separately, strain them and mix them together while hot. Stir the pounded garlic into the yoghurt, season with salt and pepper and add the mixture to the beans and rice. Heat gently, then stir in the beaten egg. As soon as the sauce has thickened slightly, it is ready. Can be eaten hot or cold.

Enough for four people.

BROAD BEANS *with* EGG *and* LEMON

Cook 1kg/2lb *beans* in boiling salted water. When they are ready drain them, reserving a teacup of the water in which they have cooked. Add this to 2 *egg yolks* and the juice of a *lemon*. Heat over a very gentle flame, whisking all the time until the sauce is frothy and slightly thickened. Pour over the beans. Serve hot or cold.

Cooked artichoke hearts mixed with the beans are a good combination, and for an hors d'œuvre add a few large prawns or langoustines.

Enough for four to five people.

SLOW-COOKED BEANS

Fasœil al fùrn

A Piedmontese country dish which is made with dried red haricot (borlotti) beans, cooked all night in a slow oven and eaten the following day at lunch time. The Piedmontese custom is to put the dish to cook on Saturday night so that it is ready to take out of the oven when the family return from Mass on Sunday at midday.

Put 500g/1lb of *haricot beans* (white ones when red are unobtainable) to soak for 12 hours. Chop a good quantity of *parsley* with several cloves of *garlic*, and add *pepper*, *cinnamon*, ground *cloves* and *mace*. Spread this mixture on to wide strips of *pork rind or pancetta*, roll them up, put them at the bottom of a deep earthenware bean pot, cover them with the beans, and add enough water to cover the beans by about 5cm/2 inches. Put the cover on the pot, and cook in a very slow oven, regulating the heat according to the time at which the beans are to be eaten. The slower they cook, the better the dish. Serve in soup plates as a very substantial midday meal. A splendid dish when you are busy, hard up, and have hungry people to feed.

Enough for four people.

HARICOT BEANS

Fasoūlia

The Greek name for haricot beans. People who appreciate the taste of genuine olive oil in their food will like this dish.

Soak 250g/½lb of *beans* for 12 hours. Heat half a tumbler of *olive oil* in a deep pan; put in the strained beans; lower the heat; stir the beans and let them simmer gently for 10 minutes, adding 2 cloves of *garlic*, a *bay leaf*, a branch of *thyme*, and a dessertspoon of *tomato paste*. Add boiling water to cover the beans by about 2.5cm/1 inch. Cook them over a moderate heat for 3 hours. The liquid should have reduced sufficiently to form a thickish sauce. Squeeze in the juice of a *lemon*, add some *raw onion* cut into rings, some *salt* and *black pepper*, and leave them to cool.

Enough for four people.

Haricot Plat - Maroc
4 euro

CAROTTES VICHY

This is one of the best-known vegetable dishes of French cookery. It is exceedingly simple, and makes a particularly welcome dish in the spring before the new peas and beans have arrived.

The water of the Vichy region is non-chalky and is therefore said to be particularly satisfactory for the cooking of vegetables, and it is this circumstance which no doubt gives the dish its name. A pinch of bicarbonate of soda in the water helps to produce the same effect. *Carottes Vichy* can be served as a garnish to meat or as a separate dish.

New *carrots* are scraped, and sliced into bias-cut rounds about 5mm/¼ inch thick. Put them into a heavy pan with 30g/1oz of *butter*, a pinch of *salt*, 2 lumps of *sugar*, and 450ml/¾ pint of water per 500g/1lb of carrots. Cook uncovered for 20 to 25 minutes until nearly all the water has evaporated and the carrots are tender. Add another lump of butter and shake the pan so that the carrots do not stick. Add a little finely chopped *parsley* before serving.

Older carrots cut in quarters or chunks can be cooked in the same way but need a larger proportion of water. Add a teaspoon of *sugar* with the final lump of butter, and let this mixture cook until it has formed a thick syrup which coats the carrots, but don't let it turn to toffee.

Enough for four people.

PROVENÇAL LEEKS

Poireaux à la provençale

1.5kg/3lb leeks, 2 tablespoons olive oil, salt and pepper, 250g/½lb tomatoes, 12 black olives, juice of 1 lemon, 1 dessertspoon finely chopped lemon peel.

Chop the cleaned leeks into 1-cm/½-inch lengths. Into a shallow heatproof dish put the oil and when it is warm, but not smoking, put in the leeks, add a little salt and pepper, cover the pan and simmer for 10 minutes. Add the tomatoes cut in halves, the stoned olives, the lemon juice and the chopped lemon peel and cook slowly for another 10 minutes. Serve in the dish in which it has been cooked. This is excellent cold as a salad.

Enough for four people.

CHICORY BRAISED *in* BUTTER

Endives au beurre

Allow 1½ to 2 *chicory* per person. Peel off any brown outside leaves; wipe the chicory with a cloth. With a stainless knife cut each into 1-cm/½-inch lengths. Melt a good lump of *butter* in a frying pan. Put in the vegetables; let them cook a few seconds, turning them about with a wooden spoon, before adding *salt*, turning down the heat and covering the pan. By this method they will be sufficiently cooked in about 10 minutes (as opposed to over an hour when they are cooked whole) but uncover them and shake the pan from time to time to make sure the chicory are not sticking. Before serving add a squeeze of *lemon juice*.

A variation is to add a few little cubes of *bacon or ham*. Leeks are excellent prepared and cooked in the same way.

TOMATOES BAKED *with* GRUYÈRE

Tomates fromagées

Choose *medium-sized tomatoes*, cut off the tops, scoop out the flesh, sprinkle them with *salt*, turn them upside down and leave them to drain.

In a double saucepan melt some *Gruyère cheese* with black *pepper*, *cayenne*, a little *French mustard*, a drop of *white wine* and a pounded clove of *garlic*.

Fill the tomatoes with the mixture, which should be about the consistency of a Welsh rarebit. Bake for 10 minutes in the oven (180°C/gas 4) and finish under the grill.

ARMENIAN MUSHROOMS

Mushrooms à l'arménienne

Mushrooms cooked in this way can be served as a separate course, as a garnish for scrambled eggs or omelettes, or eaten cold as a starter.

250g/½lb mushrooms, olive oil, garlic, 2 rashers of bacon, a glass of wine (red or white), parsley.

Slice the mushrooms, sauté them in 2 tablespoons of olive oil; add a few very fine slivers of garlic, and the bacon cut in squares.

Let this cook a few minutes before pouring in a glass of wine, then cook fiercely for just 1 minute (to reduce the wine), turn the heat down, add the chopped parsley and simmer for 5 more minutes.

Enough for four people.

HOSTELLERIE AUBERGE
des SEIGNEURS
et du LION D'OR

SWEET PEPPER *and* TOMATO STEW

Peperonata

A large onion, olive oil, butter, 8 red peppers, salt, 10 good ripe tomatoes.

Brown the sliced onion very lightly in a mixture of olive oil and butter. Add the peppers, cleaned, the seeds removed, and cut into strips; season them with salt. Simmer them for about 15 minutes, with the cover on the pan. Now add the tomatoes, peeled and quartered, and cook another 30 minutes. There should not be too much oil, as the tomatoes provide enough liquid to cook the peppers, and the resulting mixture should be fairly dry. Garlic can be added if you like.

To store for a few days in the refrigerator, pack the *peperonata* in a jar, and float enough olive oil on the top to seal the contents. Enough for six or seven people, but *peperonata* is so good when reheated that it is worth making a large amount at one time.

GREEN PEAS *and* HAM

Piselli al prosciutto

The green peas which grow round about Rome are the most delicious I have ever tasted anywhere. Small, sweet, tender, and very green, they are really best simply stewed in butter. Cooked in this way they make a most delicate sauce for finely cut home-made pasta, or for *riso in bianco*. The Romans adore these green peas cooked with ham. Try this method with young English green peas before they become wrinkled and floury.

A small onion, lard or butter, 1kg/2lb peas, 90g/3oz very good cooked ham, cut into strips.

Melt the chopped onion in the lard or butter, and let it cook very gently, so that it softens without browning. Put in the shelled peas and a very little water. After 5 minutes add the ham. In another 5–10 minutes the peas should be ready.

Enough for four people.

PÉRIGORD POTATOES

Pommes de terre à l'échirlète

This is a way of cooking potatoes from the Périgord district, first class with grilled steak or roast game or by themselves.

Cook whole fairly small *potatoes*, in just enough water or, better still, *stock*, to cover them, adding 2 cloves of *garlic*; cover the pan. By the time the liquid is absorbed they should be cooked. Now put them in a pan with a tablespoon of *goose or pork fat* and the garlic and cook them slowly until they are brown all over. Turn them over two or three times.

Large potatoes cut in halves or quarters can also be successfully cooked by this excellent method.

500g/1lb potatoes are enough for four to five people.

POTATOES COOKED *in* MILK

This recipe demonstrates a method which turns old potatoes into something special, and makes new ones, as the French say, *extra*. For each 500g/1lb of peeled and thickly sliced old *potatoes* or of small whole new ones, allow 600ml/1 pint of *milk*. Pour the cold uncooked milk over the potatoes in a saucepan, add a very little *salt*, simmer (if you let them gallop, the milk will boil over and the potatoes will stick, so look out), until the potatoes are just tender but not breaking up. Strain off the milk – it makes good vegetable soup stock – transfer the potatoes to a shallow ovenproof dish, sprinkle them very lightly with grated *nutmeg* and a little *thyme or basil*, add 3 or 4 tablespoons of the milk, and leave them uncovered in a low or moderate oven for about 15 minutes.

Delicious with a plain roast, with steak, chicken, or just by themselves.

500g/1lb potatoes are enough for four to five people.

GRATIN DAUPHINOIS

Gratin dauphinois is a rich and filling regional dish from the Dauphiné. Some recipes include cheese and eggs, making it very similar to a *gratin savoyard*: but other regional authorities declare that the authentic *gratin dauphinois* is made only with potatoes and thick fresh cream. I give the second version, which is, I think, the better one; it is also the easier. And if it seems to the thrifty-minded outrageously extravagant to use half a pint of cream to one pound (300ml to 500g) of potatoes, I can only say that to me it seems a more satisfactory way of enjoying cream than pouring it over tinned peaches or chocolate mousse.

It is not easy to say how many people this will serve; two, or three, or four, according to their capacity, and what there is to follow. Much depends also upon the quality of the potatoes used. Firm waxy varieties such as the kipfler and the pink fir-apple make a gratin lighter and also more authentic than that made with routine commercial King Edwards or Majestics which are in every respect second best.

Two more points concerning the proportions of a *gratin dauphinois*: as the quantity of potatoes is increased the proportion of cream may be slightly diminished. Thus, for 1.5kg/3lb of potatoes, 750ml/1¼ pints of cream will be amply sufficient; and the choice of cooking dish is also important, for the potatoes and cream should, always, fill the dish to within approximately 1.5cm/¾ inch of the top.

Peel 500g/1lb of yellow *potatoes*, and slice them in even rounds no thicker than a penny; this operation is very easy with the aid of a mandoline. Rinse them thoroughly in cold water – this is most important – then shake them dry in a cloth. Put them in layers in a shallow earthenware dish which has been rubbed with *garlic* and well buttered. Season with *pepper* and *salt*. Pour 300ml/½ pint of thick *cream* over them; strew with little pieces of butter; cook them for 1½ hours in a low oven, 150°C/gas 2, During the last 10 minutes turn the oven up fairly high to get a fine golden crust on the potatoes. Serve in the dish in which they have cooked.

The best way, in my view, of appreciating the charm of a *gratin dauphinois* is to present the dish entirely on its own, as a first course to precede grilled or plain roast meat or poultry, or a cold joint to be eaten with a simple green salad.

POTATOES *in a* PAPER BAG

Potatoes en papillote

Nicolas Soyer, grandson of the famous Alexis, spent years perfecting the system of paper-bag cookery and in 1911 published a book extolling its advantages. Indeed they are many. I can vouch for the excellence of this method for new potatoes.

Preheat the oven to 190°C/gas 5. Scrape 24 very small *new potatoes*. Put them on a fair-sized piece of greaseproof paper, with 2 leaves of *mint*, a little *salt* and 60g/2oz of *butter*. Fold the paper over and then fold down the two edges so that the bag is completely sealed. Put it into the preheated oven, on to the grid, and cook for about 35 minutes. They will come out perfectly cooked, buttery and full of flavour. Larger potatoes can be cut in half.

Enough for four people.

POTATO PIE

Torta di patate

1kg/2lb potatoes, 4 tablespoons milk, 90g/3oz butter, salt, pepper, nutmeg, 3 tablespoons breadcrumbs, 90g/3oz cheese (Gruyère or Bel Paese), 90g/3oz cooked ham, ham sausage or mortadella, 2 eggs.

Sieve the boiled potatoes, add milk and 60g/2oz butter; season with salt, pepper and nutmeg. Line a 20-cm/8-inch pie plate with butter and half the breadcrumbs. Spread a layer of potatoes smoothly into the tin. On top arrange the cheese and the ham cut into squares, and the 2 eggs, boiled for 6 minutes, shelled and cut into quarters. Cover the ham, cheese and eggs with the rest of the mashed potatoes. Spread the remaining breadcrumbs on the top, pour over a little melted butter, and cook the pie for about 40 minutes in a fairly hot oven (190°C/gas 5).

Enough for five to six people.

SPINACH PIE

Spanakopittá

This is a Greek (and also Turkish) dish made with filo pastry.

1kg/2lb spinach, 90g/3oz butter, 90g/3oz filo pastry leaves, 125g/¼lb Gruyère cheese.

Clean and cook the spinach in the usual way, and squeeze it very dry. Chop it not too finely, and heat it in a pan with 30g/1oz of butter. Season well. Butter a square cake tin, not too deep. In the bottom put 6 leaves of filo pastry cut to the shape of the tin and a fraction larger, brushing the top of each leaf with melted butter before covering it with the next leaf.

Over the 6 layers of pastry spread the prepared spinach, then a layer of the grated Gruyère. Cover with 6 more layers of pastry, again buttering between each layer, and buttering also the top. See that the edges of the pastry are also well buttered, and cook in a moderate oven, 180°C/gas 4 for 30–40 minutes. Leave to cool for a few minutes, turn upside down on to a baking dish, and return to the oven for 10 minutes or so for the underside to get crisp and golden.

Enough for four people.

SPINACH *with* SULTANAS
Spinaci con uvetta

1kg/2lb spinach, salt, 30g/1oz butter, olive oil, a clove of garlic, pepper, 30g/1oz sultanas, 30g/1oz pine nuts.

Clean the spinach and put it into a large saucepan with a little salt but no water. Plenty of moisture comes out as it cooks. When it is cooked drain it, pressing it hard so that as much of the moisture as possible is removed. In a wide saucepan or frying pan warm the butter and 2 tablespoons of olive oil. Add the spinach, the chopped garlic and a little pepper. Turn the spinach over and over; it should not fry, and neither should the garlic. When it is thoroughly hot put in the sultanas, which should have soaked for 15 minutes in a cup of warm water, and the pine nuts. Cover the pan, and continue to cook very gently for another 15 minutes.

Enough for two to three people.

MY DREAM KITCHEN

So frequently do dream kitchens figure in the popular newspaper competitions, in the pages of shiny magazines and in department store advertising that one almost begins to believe women really do spend half their days dreaming about laminated work-tops, louvered cupboard doors and sheaves of gladioli standing on top of the dishwasher. Why of all rooms in the house does the kitchen have to be a dream? Is it because in the past kitchens have mostly been so underprivileged, so dingy and inconvenient? We don't, for example, hear much of dream drawing-rooms, dream bedrooms, dream garages, dream boxrooms (I could do with a couple of those). No. It's a dream kitchen or nothing. My own kitchen is rather more of a nightmare than a dream, but I'm stuck with it. However, I'll stretch a point and make it a good dream for a change. Here goes.

This fantasy kitchen will be large, very light, very airy, calm and warm. There will be the minimum of paraphernalia in sight. It will start off and will remain rigorously orderly. That takes care of just a few desirable attributes my present kitchen doesn't have. Naturally there'll be, as now, a few of those implements in constant use – ladles, a sieve or two, whisks, tasting spoons – hanging by the cooker, essential knives accessible in a rack, and wooden spoons in a jar. But half a dozen would be enough, not thirty-five as there are now. Cookery writers are particularly vulnerable to the acquisition of unnecessary clutter. I'd love to rid myself of it.

The sink will be a double one, with a solid wooden draining-board on each side. It will be (in fact, is) set 760mm/30 inches from the ground, about 152mm/6 inches higher than usual. I'm tall, and I didn't want to be prematurely bent double as a result of leaning over a knee-high sink. Along the wall above the sink I envisage a continuous wooden plate rack designed to hold serving dishes as well as plates, cups and other crockery in normal use. This saves a great deal of space, and much time spent getting out and putting away. Talking of space, suspended from the ceiling would be a wooden rack or slatted shelves – such as farmhouses and even quite small cottages in parts of Wales and the Midland counties used to have for storing bread or drying out oatcakes. Here would be the parking place for papers, notebooks, magazines – all the things that usually get piled on chairs when the table has to be cleared. The table itself is, of course, crucial. It's for writing at and for meals, as well as for kitchen tasks, so it has to have comfortable leg room. This time round I'd like it to be oval, one massive piece of scrubbable wood, on a central pedestal. Like the sink, it has to be a little higher than the average.

Outside the kitchen is my refrigerator and there it will stay. I keep it at the lowest temperature, about 4°C/40°F. I'm still amazed at the way so-called model kitchens have refrigerators next to the cooking stove. This seems to me almost as mad as having a wine rack above it. Then, failing a separate larder – in a crammed London house that's carrying optimism a bit too far – there would be a second and fairly large refrigerator to be used for the cool storage of a variety of commodities such as coffee beans, spices, butter, cheese and eggs, which benefit from a constant temperature of say 10°C/50°F.

All the colours in the dream kitchen would be much as they are now, but fresher and cleaner – cool silver, grey-blue, aluminium, with the various browns of earthenware pots and a lot of white provided by the perfectly plain china. I recoil from coloured tiles and beflowered surfaces and I don't want a lot of things coloured avocado and tangerine. I'll just settle for the avocados and tangerines in a bowl on the dresser. In other words, if the food and the cooking pots don't provide enough visual interest and create their own changing patterns in a kitchen, then there's something wrong. And too much equipment is if anything worse than too little. I don't a bit covet the exotic gear dangling from hooks, the riot of clanking ironmongery, the armouries of knives, or the serried rank of sauté pans and all other carefully chosen symbols of culinary activity I see in so many photographs of chic kitchens. Pseuds corners, I'm afraid, many of them.

When it comes to the cooker I don't think I need anything very fancy. My cooking is mostly on a small scale and of the kind for intimate friends, so I'm happy enough with an ordinary four-burner gas stove. Its oven has to be a good size, though, and it has to have a drop-down door. Given the space I'd have a second, quite separate oven just for bread, and perhaps some sort of temperature-controlled cupboard for proving the dough. On the whole though it's probably best for cookery writers to use the same kind of domestic equipment as the majority of their readers. It doesn't do to get too far away from the problems of everyday household cooking or take the easy way out with expensive gadgetry.

What it all amounts to is that for me – and I stress this is purely personal, because my requirements as a writing cook are rather different from those of one who cooks mainly for a succession of guests or for the daily meals of a big family – the perfect kitchen would really be more like a painter's studio furnished with cooking equipment than anything conventionally accepted as a kitchen.

Article from Terence Conran's The Kitchen Book, *1977*

RICE

Every amateur cook, however gifted and diligent, has some weak spot, some gap in her knowledge or experience which to anyone critical of her own achievements can be annoying and humiliating. To some it may be a question of not being able to get a roast precisely right; to others, a cream sauce which only spasmodically comes off; and even to those who admit to having little talent for pastry or cakes, it is irritating to be defeated by a process which to others appears so effortless. Some regard the confection of a mayonnaise as the easiest thing in the world, some with terror and despair. There are those who have a talent for perfect rice dishes, while for others the stuff invariably turns to a mush. And it is no coincidence that when dishes go wrong, it nearly always happens when they are cooked for guests, and consequently in larger quantities than those with which one is accustomed to dealing.

Sometimes this is due to something so obvious as cooking for eight in the same utensils as those normally used for four, or to the cook having overlooked the fact that even a good-tempered dish like a meat and wine stew may disloyally change its character and appearance, losing all its professional-looking finish, if kept waiting too long in the oven. Or perhaps the joint, twice as large as usual, has been cooked twice as long, whereas what should really have been taken into consideration was not the weight but the shape and thickness of the joint.

Sometimes, of course, the trouble is more psychological than technical. Take rice, for example. Because a rice dish has gone wrong once, no doubt because the cook had no experience of cooking the particular rice she was using, she will ever after be scared stiff of making it. There is something rather specifically dismal about a failed rice dish. And I would never recommend anybody to cook a risotto for a dinner party which had to be managed single-handed, because it is a bad dish to keep waiting. But there are so many other ways of cooking rice and some of them appear to be specially designed for the kind of meals we all cook these days – meals consisting of dishes which simply must not be of the kind requiring split-second timing. Good-quality rice is essential, though. The two kinds to look for are the long-grained Patna type, of which basmati is the best, and the round-grained Piedmontese rice called avorio or arborio, which has a hard core in the centre of the grain so that it is almost impossible to ruin by overcooking. The flavour of this Piedmontese rice is also much more pronounced than that of the Patna type, which makes it a good one to use when the rice itself, rather than any flavouring or sauce, is the main point of the dish.

A good point to remember about the boiling of rice is that ten times the volume of water to that of rice is an ample quantity to calculate. So measure the rice in a cup or glass, and then reckon the amount of water accordingly.

MILANESE RISOTTO

Risotto alla milanese

Rice is to the northern provinces of Italy (Lombardy, Piedmont and the Veneto) what pasta is to the south. I wish I knew who was the genius who first grasped the fact that Piedmontese rice was ideally suited to slow cooking and that its particular qualities would be best appreciated in what has become the famous Milanese risotto. The fact that this rice can be cooked contrary to all rules, slowly, in a small amount of liquid, and emerge in a perfect state of creaminess with a very slightly resistant core in each grain gives the risotto its particular character.

The classic *risotto alla milanese* is made simply with chicken stock and flavoured with saffron; butter and grated Parmesan cheese are stirred in at the end of the cooking, and more cheese and butter served with it. The second version is made with beef marrow and white wine; a third with Marsala. In each case saffron is used as a flavouring.

Into a heavy pan put 30g/1oz *butter*. In the butter fry a *small onion* cut very fine; let it turn pale gold but not brown; then add 30g/1oz of *beef marrow* extracted from marrow bones; this gives a richer quality to the risotto, but can perfectly well be left out. Now add *Italian rice*, allowing about 90g/3oz per person (in Italy they would allow a good deal more; the amount rather depends upon whether the risotto is to constitute a first course only or a main dish). Stir the rice until it is well impregnated with the butter. It must remain white.

Now pour in two thirds of a tumbler of *dry white wine* and let it cook on a moderate flame until the wine has almost evaporated. At this moment start adding the *stock*, which should be a light chicken consommé and which is kept barely simmering in another pan; add about a ladle at a time, and keep your eye on the risotto, although at this stage it is not essential to stir continuously. As the stock becomes absorbed add more; in all you will need about 1.2 litres/2 pints of stock for 300–400g/10–14oz of rice, and if this is not quite enough, dilute it with hot water. Towards the end of the cooking, which will take 20–30 minutes, stir continuously using a wooden fork rather than a spoon, which tends to crush the grains. When you see that the rice is tender, the mixture creamy but not sticky, add the *saffron*.

The proper way to do this is to pound the strands to a powder (three or four strands will be enough for 400g/14oz of rice), steep the powder in a coffee cup of the stock for 5 minutes, and strain the liquid obtained into the rice. Having stirred in the saffron, add 30g/1oz each of butter and grated *Parmesan* cheese, and serve the risotto as soon as the cheese has melted. More butter and grated cheese must be served separately.

Enough for four people.

RISOTTO *with* GREEN PEAS

Risi e bisi, a Venetian dish

A small onion, 45g/1½oz butter, 60g/2oz ham, 1kg/2lb green peas in the pod (or 375g/12oz shelled peas), 1.85 litres/3 pints chicken or meat stock, 2 teacups of risotto rice, Parmesan cheese.

Put the chopped onion to melt in 15g/½oz of butter. Add the chopped ham, which should be fat and lean in equal quantities. Let it melt slightly, add the shelled peas. When they are impregnated with the butter pour in a large cup of hot stock, and when it is bubbling, add the rice. Now pour over more hot stock, about 600ml/1 pint, and cook gently without stirring; before it is all absorbed, add more. *Risi e bisi* is not cooked in quite the same way as the ordinary risotto, for it should emerge rather more liquid; it should not be stirred too much or the peas will break. It is to be eaten, however, with a fork, not a spoon, so it must not be too soupy. When the rice is cooked stir in 20g/1oz each of butter and grated Parmesan, and serve more cheese separately.

To make a less rich dish cook the rice with water instead of stock, which will produce soothing food for tired stomachs.

Enough for four to five people.

CHICKEN RISOTTO

Risotto alla sbirraglia

Most recipes for chicken risotto require a chicken stock made from the bones of the bird, but in this case the liquid from the previously stewed pieces of chicken supplies sufficient richness, so that it is really preferable to use water and reserve the carcass and bones of the chicken for a soup.

Half a chicken, 2 small onions, butter or oil, a slice of ham or Bologna sausage, 3 or 4 tomatoes, a piece of celery, sliced, a clove of garlic, sliced, a green or red pepper, cleaned and cut into strips, a few dried mushrooms, a glass of white wine, seasoning and herbs, risotto rice, Parmesan cheese.

For four people use half a chicken weighing about 1.8kg/3½lb (the other half can be used for another meal).

Remove the skin, take all the flesh off the bones, and cut into fairly large, long slices. In a thick pan sauté a sliced onion in butter or oil, and when it is golden add the pieces of chicken, the ham, and the other vegetables. Let them fry for a few minutes, then pour in the wine, leaving it to bubble for 3 or 4 minutes. Add seasoning and fresh herbs (marjoram, thyme or basil). Add hot water barely to cover the contents of the pan, put on the lid, and cook very slowly for about ¾ of an hour, preferably in the oven. (This preparation can be made beforehand and heated when the time comes to make the risotto.)

For the risotto allow 2 good teacups of rice for four people. In a large, shallow and heavy pan heat 30g/1oz of butter or olive oil, and in it melt the second onion, sliced very finely; add the rice and stir, allowing it to soak up the butter. Now add boiling water to cover the rice, stir again, and when the water is absorbed add more, cooking all the time over a moderate flame, and stirring frequently so that the rice does not stick. Season with a little salt. When you see that the rice is all but cooked pour in the chicken mixture, sauce and all, and continue stirring until the liquid is absorbed and the rice tender. At this moment stir in 2 tablespoons of grated Parmesan and 30g/1oz of butter. The risotto can be served in the pan in which it has cooked, or it can be turned out on to a hot dish.

Enough for four people.

PILAFF RICE

There are Egyptian, Turkish, Persian, Indian, Chinese and goodness knows how many other systems of cooking and flavouring pilaff rice. This is one of my own recipes, evolved by combining an Indian method with flavourings which are predominantly Levantine.

Measurements for pilaff rice cookery are nearly always based on volume rather than weight. The use of a cup or glass for measuring the rice simplifies the recipes because the cooking liquid is measured in the same vessel, the success of the process depending largely upon the correct proportions of liquid to rice. The cooking pot is also important, especially to those unfamiliar with the routine. Choose a saucepan or a two-handled casserole not too deep in proportion to its width. Whether of aluminium, iron, cast iron, copper or earthenware is not important provided the base is thick and even.

Those unfamiliar with rice cookery are advised to start by making a small quantity of pilaff, enough for say two or three people. The recipe once mastered, it is easy to increase the quantities, in proportion, and to experiment with different flavourings.

Using thin-grain basmati rice the initial ingredients and preparations are as follows: 1 tumbler of rice, 2 tumblers of water. (The tumbler I use for measuring holds 175g/6oz basmati rice and 175ml/6fl oz water).

For the flavouring: *30g/1oz clarified butter (or ghee bought from an Indian provision store), 1 small onion, 4 cardamom pods, 2 teaspoons of cumin seeds, or ground cumin, 1 teaspoon of turmeric powder, 2 teaspoons of salt, a bayleaf or two, 2 tumblers of water.*

Put the rice in a bowl and cover it with water. Leave it to soak for an hour or so.

Melt the butter in your rice-cooking pot or saucepan (for this quantity a 1.5–1.8-litre/2½–3-pint one is large enough) and in it cook the sliced onion for a few seconds, until it is translucent. It must not brown. This done, stir in the cardamom seeds extracted from their pods and the cumin seeds, both pounded in a mortar, and the turmeric. The latter is for colouring the rice a beautiful yellow, as well as for its flavour, and the object of cooking the spices in the fat is to develop their aromas before the rice is added. This is an important point.

Drain the rice, and put it into the butter and spice mixture. Stir it around until it glistens with the fat. Add the salt. Pour in the 2 tumblers of water and let it come to the boil fairly fast. Put in the bayleaf.

Let the rice cook steadily, uncovered, over a medium heat until almost all the water is absorbed and holes begin to appear in the mass. This will take almost 10 minutes.

Now turn the heat as low as possible. Over the rice put a thickly folded absorbent tea cloth, and on top of the cloth (use an old one; the turmeric stains) the lid of the pan. Leave undisturbed, still over the lowest possible heat, for 20–25 minutes. At the end of this time the rice should be quite tender and each grain will be separated. Fork it round, turn into a warmed serving bowl. The rice should be a fine yellow colour and mildly spiced.

The pilaff can be eaten as an accompaniment to spiced lamb or beef kebabs, but to my mind is even nicer on its own, with the addition of a few sultanas or raisins, soaked for an hour in water, heated up in a little saucepan and mixed into the rice just before it is turned out of the saucepan for serving. Oven-toasted almonds or pine kernels make another attractive addition.

Enough for four people.

QUICK KEDGEREE

For a party I make a kedgeree with rice boiled in advance, then kept hot, with all its extra ingredients, in a big bowl standing in a saucepan of simmering water.

For an impromptu dish for two or three people I use a quick and easy method which, once you've understood the principle, has infinite possibilities. You can apply the same system to prawns, mussels, vegetables, chicken, meat – with one proviso. Good-quality rice, either long-grained basmati or the hard round-grained Italian variety is essential. Soft pudding rice will turn to just that – pudding.

3 smoked haddock fillets, 2 tablespoons olive oil, 1 medium onion, a scant teaspoon curry powder, 4 heaped tablespoons rice, 2 tablespoons sultanas or currants, seasonings, 2 hard-boiled eggs, parsley, water, a lemon, mango chutney.

First pour boiling water over the haddock fillets. Leave them 2 or 3 minutes, drain them, peel off the skin and divide the fish into manageable pieces.

Heat the oil in a heavy 25-cm/10-inch frying or sauté pan. In this fry the sliced onion until pale yellow. Stir in the curry powder. Add the rice (don't wash it). Stir all round together. Add the washed sultanas or currants. Pour in 600ml/1 pint of water. Cook steadily, not at a gallop, and uncovered, for 10 minutes. Put in the haddock. Continue cooking until the liquid is all absorbed and the rice tender – approximately 10 minutes. But keep an eye on it to see it doesn't stick, and stir with a fork, not a spoon, which breaks the rice. Taste for seasoning. Salt may or may not be required. Turn on to a hot serving dish. On the top strew the chopped eggs and parsley – and, if you like, a nice big lump of butter. Surround with lemon quarters and serve with mango chutney.

Enough for four people.

KHICHRI

The dish from which the English evolved kedgeree. The original contains no fish, and is simply a mixture of lentils and rice cooked with spices. It is very cheap and filling.

Khichri can be eaten on its own or as an accompaniment to a meat or chicken curry. In either case a little dish of chutney and another of fresh cucumber with a yoghurt and mint dressing or some other such refreshing little preparation should be offered at the same time. The spices can be altered to suit individual taste. Those who do not like ginger (a little fresh ginger root is far better than the powdered variety) or cloves could substitute cumin and turmeric, and if you have no cardamom seeds – well, perhaps you will invent some new and perfect spice mixture. If English kedgeree can evolve from *khichri*, then in cookery anything at all can happen.

6 allspice berries, 6 white peppercorns, the seeds from 6 cardamom pods, ¼ teaspoon each of ground ginger and cloves, 30g/1oz clarified butter or ghee, 1 small onion, ¾ of a glass (approximately 125g/4oz) each of ordinary red lentils and Patna or basmati rice, salt, a tablespoon or two of the liquid part of rather sharp mango chutney or, more correctly, of tamarind pulp, 3 glasses of water, lemon juice.

Pound the allspice, peppercorns and cardamoms. Mix them with the ground spices.

In the clarified butter or ghee melt the thinly sliced onion. Do not let it brown. Stir in the spices, let them fry for a minute or so. Add the lentils, then the rice. Stir both round in the fat. Season with salt – about 1 heaped dessertspoon. Add the chutney or tamarind pulp. Pour in 3 glasses of cold water.

Cook, uncovered, over medium heat. Stir from time to time with a fork, for about 15 minutes, until all the water is absorbed. By this time the lentils are nearly cooked but the rice is not. Turn the heat as low as possible, put the saucepan on a heat-diffuser mat, cover the rice and lentils with a folded tea cloth and the lid of the saucepan. Leave for 20 minutes. Turn into a heated dish, squeeze lemon juice over and serve at once, very hot.

There should be enough for three or four, depending upon what other dishes are to be given.

ITALIAN FISH MARKETS

Of all the spectacular food markets in Italy, the one near the Rialto in Venice must be the most remarkable. The light of a Venetian dawn in early summer – you must be about at four o'clock in the morning to see the market coming to life – is so limpid and so still that it makes every separate vegetable and fruit and fish luminous with a life of its own, with unnaturally heightened colours and clear stencilled outlines. Here the cabbages are cobalt blue, the beetroots deep rose, the lettuces clear pure green, sharp as glass. Bunches of gaudy gold marrow-flowers show off the elegance of pink and white marbled bean pods, primrose potatoes, green plums, green peas. The colours of the peaches, cherries and apricots, packed in boxes lined with sugar-bag blue paper matching the blue canvas trousers worn by the men unloading the gondolas, are reflected in the rose-red mullet and the orange *vongole* and *canuestrelle* which have been prised out of their shells and heaped into baskets. In other markets, on other shores, the unfamiliar fishes may be vivid, mysterious, repellent, fascinating, and bright with splendid colour; only in Venice do they look good enough to eat. In Venice even ordinary sole and ugly great skate are striped with delicate lilac lights, the sardines shine like newly minted silver coins, pink Venetian scampi are fat and fresh, infinitely enticing in the early dawn.

The gentle swaying of the laden gondolas, the movements of the market men as they unload, swinging the boxes and baskets ashore, the robust life and rattling noise contrasted with the fragile taffeta colours and the opal sky of Venice – the whole scene is out of some marvellous unheard-of ballet.

A very different kettle of fish, indeed, is the market of Genoa. Nothing will shake my conviction that *Genova la superba* is the noisiest city on earth. (This is nothing new; travellers have constantly remarked upon the fact.) The market place will therefore be quite a rest; here one is oblivious of the uproar, spellbound by the spectacle of the odd fish which come up from these waters. Their names are descriptive enough: the angler or frogfish, the praying-fish, the sea hen, the scorpion, the sea cat, the sea date, the sea truffle, sea snails, sea strawberries, and a mussel with a hair-covered shell called *cozze pelose*. No wonder that anybody with a spark of imagination is prepared to put up with the ear-splitting din of Genoa, the crashing of trams and trains, the screeching of brakes, and even the agonized wailing of itinerant musicians in the taverns, in order to taste some of these sea beasts when they have been converted into *burrida*, the Genoese fish stew, or into the immense edifice of crustaceans, molluscs, fish, vegetables and green sauce, which is known as *cappon magro*.

TORREFAZIONE - ALIMENTARI

€5
EURO

Along the coast at Santa Margherita the fish market is famous; here the fish are less forbidding and savage of aspect, but their brilliance of colour is phenomenal. Huge baskets are filled with what from a distance one takes to be strawberries but which turn out to be huge prawns (they are scarlet by nature, before they are cooked); dark green and grey *tonnetto*, gleaming silver with phosphorescence, are thrust head downwards, like so many French loaves, in a high basket; *moscardini*, brown and pale green, are arranged in rows, like newly washed pebbles; the tiny *calamaretti*, *fragoline di mare*, are black and grey (cooked in a wine sauce they turn a deep pink); the rose-coloured slippery little fish called *signorini* are for the *frittura*; the scampi are pallid compared to the brilliant prawns; an orange langouste is a tamed beast beside a black lobster, lashing furiously.

Another market with its own very characteristic flavour is that of Cagliari, in the island of Sardinia. Spread out in flat baskets large as cartwheels are all the varieties of fish which go into *ziminù*, the Sardinian version of fish soup; fat, scaly little silver fish streaked with lime green; enormous octopus, blue, sepia, mauve and turquoise, curled and coiled and petalled like some heavily embroidered marine flower; the *pescatrice* again, that ugly hooked angler fish; cold stony little clams, here called *arselle*; *tartufi di mare*; silvery slippery sardines; rose-red mullets in every possible size, some small as sprats, like doll's-house fish; the fine lobsters for which Sardinia is famous. To eat the plainly grilled or fried fish in this island is an experience from which any town dweller, accustomed to fish which must have been in the ice at least a day or two, will derive great pleasure. The mullet, the thin slices of fresh tuna, the little clams, seem to have been washed straight from the sea into the frying pan, so fresh and tender is their flesh. In such conditions there is no necessity to create complicated sauces and garnishes; and, indeed, for the cooking of fish Italian cooks are mainly content to concentrate their skill on the arts of frying, grilling and roasting.

from Italian Food, *1954*

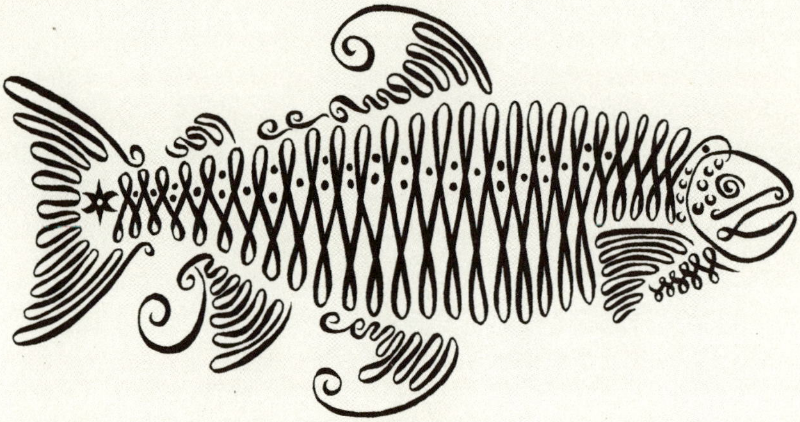

FISH, SHELLFISH *and* CRUSTACEA

Boiled salmon with cucumber and mayonnaise is an admirable dish, but anyone visiting this country for the first time and dining out frequently might well be excused for supposing that salmon is the only fish procurable in England during the whole of the summer. In fact, salmon is at its best in the very early spring; later, it scarcely justifies its high price. Salmon trout, in season all summer until the end of August, is an exquisite fish. If it is a cold dish that is needed and there is money to spend, fillets of sole make a very welcome change from the eternal salmon. Then there are some excellent lesser-known fish, such as John Dory, sea bream, Cornish bass and grey mullet which are comparatively cheap; so it is well worth knowing how to deal with them.

Rock salmon and mackerel make good cheap cold dishes, and red mullet, although more expensive, makes one of the best and most beautiful of summer fish dishes when grilled on a bed of dried fennel stalks. Fresh brown trout fried or grilled and served with plenty of melted butter are a rare treat, but the little rainbow trout are often rather disappointing. An interesting sauce, however, does a great deal for them. A grilled herring has always seemed to me one of those cheap luxuries of which there are all too few; herrings are out of season in May and June, but later in the summer they can be enjoyed with fresh herbs and butter and perhaps French mustard. Remember soft herring roes too; with a little ingenuity they make most excellent little dishes, at a very small cost.

Crabs are useful for all sorts of soups, salads and soufflés, but a little, unlike other crustaceans of which one needs a lot, goes a long way. Unless you know your fishmonger pretty well, it is not advisable to buy 'dressed' crab from him; it is often mixed with bread, and sometimes not of the first freshness.

For those who like fish plain grilled, fried, baked or poached, there are the delicious classic French sauces, hollandaise, maltaise, Bercy, remoulade, and a few lesser-known sauces made with herbs, almonds, walnuts, avocado pears, which will often liven up a rather dull fish. Of all vegetables, I think perhaps sorrel is the one which goes best with coarse fish. Spinach not being a good substitute, the next best vegetables are tomatoes, and, for more delicate fish, mushrooms, lettuce, courgettes, and watercress cooked a few seconds in butter, then chopped.

GRILLED RED MULLET *with* AÏOLI *and* SAUCE ROUILLE

Rougets à la provençale

For the *aïoli*: *2 large cloves of garlic pounded in a mortar, 2 egg yolks, a little salt, 200ml/⅓ pint of olive oil, mixed exactly as for a mayonnaise (see page 299).*

For the red part of the sauce: *pound 250g/8oz grilled and skinned red peppers with a teaspoon of paprika; add a teacup of fresh breadcrumbs, softened in water, then pressed dry, to the pounded peppers.*

Score large red mullets obliquely, twice, on each side, and paint them with olive oil. Grill them for about 10 minutes on each side and serve with a combination of two Provençal sauces, *aïoli* and *sauce rouille*. At the last minute amalgamate the two sauces, adding the *aïoli* gradually to the pepper mixture. Grey mullet may be served in the same way.

Allow one fish, or half if very large, per person.

BAKED BREAM

Marinate a medium to large sea bream for an hour in olive oil and lemon juice, with a bay leaf, parsley, thyme, salt and pepper.

Cook it in an open baking dish in a fairly hot oven, at 190°C/gas 5, so that the skin gets nicely golden and crackling.

Serve with the following sauce: a chopped shallot in a glass of white wine reduced to half: add ½ teaspoon of French mustard, 60g/2oz of butter, 2 pounded hard-boiled egg yolks, salt, pepper and chopped parsley.

A large grey mullet may be cooked in the same way, but make sure it is very well cleaned, and washed under running water, as these fish sometimes have a slightly muddy taste.

Enough for two to three people.

GREY MULLET *with* OLIVES *and* WHITE WINE

Mulet aux olives et au vin blanc

A very simple and effective recipe which can be applied to many sorts of fish, including red mullet, sea bream, sea bass, whiting and mackerel.

2 medium-sized fish, each weighing approximately 500g/1lb gross weight, 5 tablespoons olive oil, if possible, a little sprig of thyme or fennel or a bay leaf, salt and pepper, 2 or 5 tablespoons white wine, a dozen stoned black olives, some slices of orange or lemon.

Put the cleaned fish into a shallow oval ovenproof dish, pour the oil over them, add your herbs, a sprinkling of salt and pepper and the white wine. Bake, uncovered, for 15–20 minutes in a medium oven at 180°C/gas 4.

Now add the stoned black olives and cook another 5 minutes. The mullet can be served in the dish in which they have cooked, or be transferred to a flat serving dish, in either case with their own juice and slices of orange or lemon arranged along each fish. May be served hot or cold.

Enough for two to three people.

SEA BASS *with* MUSHROOMS *and* POTATOES

Bar à la marseillaise

Bar or *loup de mer* is one of the most delicate fish of the Mediterranean; grilled on a bed of fennel stalks it makes the famous Provençal *grillade au fenouil*. The bass which come from Cornwall are the English equivalent and are well worth buying.

A bass weighing 1.25–1.5kg/2½–3lb, a coffee-cup olive oil, a small glass dry white wine, a little bouquet of fennel leaves, 2 cloves of garlic, 250g/½lb onions, 250g/½lb mushrooms, 500g/1lb yellow waxy potatoes, salt and pepper.

Put the fish in a baking dish, pour over it the oil and wine, cover with the chopped fennel and garlic, round it arrange the sliced onions, mushrooms and thinly sliced potatoes. Season with salt and pepper, add 600ml/1 pint of water and cook in a fairly hot oven, at 190°C/gas 5 for about an hour.

Serve with an *aïoli* or *rouille* (see recipe for Grilled red mullet, page 178).

Enough for four people.

EPICERIE M. FLORIET

BAKED SALMON TROUT

Truite saumonée au four

Few of us now possess fish kettles in which a large whole fish can be poached, but the system of wrapping the fish in greaseproof paper or foil and cooking it in the oven produces, if anything, better results.

Sea bass (*loup de mer*) is excellent cooked in the same way.

Cut a piece of aluminium foil about 15cm/6 inches longer than your salmon trout. Butter it copiously, or if the fish is to be served cold, paint it with oil. Lay the fish in the middle, gather up the edges and twist them together, so that no juices can escape. Also twist the two ends very securely, taking particular care that the paper touching the tail and the head is well buttered or oiled, as these are the parts which stick easily.

Have your oven already heated for 10 minutes at a very low temperature, 140°C/gas 1. Place your wrapped fish on a baking sheet and leave it severely alone for the whole cooking time – 1 hour for a 1-kg/2-lb fish. All you have to do when it is cooked is to lay it on a warmed serving dish, unwrap the paper and slide the fish and all its juices off the paper on to the dish. A hot salmon trout does not really need any sauce other than its own juices and a little bowl of fresh melted butter. If it is to be served cold, have with it a *sauce verte* (page 300) or, best of all, I think, Escoffier's horseradish and walnut-flavoured sauce (page 304). It also makes serving easier if the skin is removed while the fish is still warm; this is not difficult so long as the fish has not been overcooked but, of course, it must be done gently and patiently.

There is one more point. A cold salmon trout eaten a couple of hours after it is cooked is infinitely superior to one cooked and kept until the following day.

FILLETS *of* SOLE *with* CREAM *and* ONION SAUCE

Fillets de sole deauvillaise

Sole cooked *à la deauvillaise* is a curious combination, perhaps, but one much liked by those who share the Norman fondness for onions.

Fillets of John Dory, sea bream, whiting or even plaice can be prepared in this way.

180g/6oz onions, butter, 2 fine soles, filleted, cider/wine, lemon, salt, 300ml/½ pint cream, nutmeg, pepper, French mustard, breadcrumbs.

Weigh the onions after they have been peeled; chop them. Melt 45g/1½oz of butter in a thick pan; in this cook the onions very gently, so that they turn transparent and yellow but not brown. In the meantime make a little fish stock by cooking the carcass of the soles for 10 minutes with 150ml/¼ pint of cider or white wine, 300ml/½ pint of water, a slice of lemon and a little salt. Strain. Sieve the onions to a purée, add about 2 tablespoons of the prepared stock and the cream; stir till smooth and fairly thick. Season with grated nutmeg, a little freshly ground pepper, salt if necessary and a scant teaspoon of French mustard. All this can be done in advance.

When the time comes to cook the fish, poach the fillets in the remainder of the stock. About 5 minutes is enough. Remove them to a heated oval gratin dish. Cover them with the sauce, gently reheated. Sprinkle breadcrumbs on the top, and add a few little pieces of butter. Put under the grill for about 3 minutes and serve at once, with little triangles of bread fried in butter arranged round the dish.

Enough for four people.

TURBOT *with* CREAM *and* HERB SAUCE

Turbot sauce messine

For those who can lay hands on tarragon and chervil, a herb and cream mixture called *sauce messine*, from Lorraine, is one of the most delicious of summer sauces to serve with fish. Buy a piece of turbot weighing a little over 1kg/2lb (the bones are very large, so this is not too much for four people).

First chop together the leaves of half a dozen sprigs of *tarragon*, the same of *parsley* and *chervil* and 2 small *shallots*. Then work together 60g/2oz of *butter* and a teaspoon of *flour*, add a teaspoon of *French mustard*, two beaten *egg yolks* and 300ml/½ pint of *thin cream*. Blend with the herb and shallot mixture, season, and put all in a small saucepan. Heat with the saucepan standing in hot water, stirring all the time until the sauce thickens. Do not let it boil. Put the *turbot* in a baking dish and cover it completely with half *water* and half *milk*. Cut turbot is much apt to dry up during cooking, and so should have plenty of moisture. Add *salt* and a sprig of fresh tarragon and parsley.

Bake, covered with buttered greaseproof paper, in a fairly slow oven, 160°C/gas 3, for about 55 minutes, until you see that the flesh comes easily away from the bones. One side of the turbot is thicker than the other, so the timing depends a little bit on whether you have a thick or thin piece. Lift out the fish on to a hot serving dish, and have the sauce ready to be served separately. Immediately before serving, squeeze in the juice of a small *lemon*.

FISHERMAN'S CLAMS

Vongole alla marinara

A rough and ready dish, often served in seaport taverns. Even in London mussels cooked in this way preserve a good deal of their flavour of the sea.

Wash and scrub 2 litres/4 pints of *little clams* (or mussels) and put them to open in a heavy pan over a fairly hot flame. They are to cook in their own liquid only. Cover the pan to start with, and take the lid off when the shells start to open. At this moment add *chopped parsley* and *garlic*.

Serve as soon as all the clams are opened, with their own juice.

Enough for three to four people.

SCALLOPS *with* WHITE WINE *and* BACON

Here is an excellent little scallop dish; the mixture of pork or bacon with the fish sounds odd, but it is an old-fashioned and good one.

15g/½oz butter, a shallot or two, 60g/2oz streaky salt pork or unsmoked bacon, 4 large scallops, pepper, 1 teaspoon flour, 1 small glass dry white wine, parsley.

Melt the butter in a frying pan, put in the finely chopped shallots and the pork or bacon cut into tiny cubes. Cut the cleaned scallops into larger cubes, season them with pepper but no salt, sprinkle them with flour and put them in the pan when the shallots have turned pale yellow and the pork is beginning to frizzle. Cook very gently for 2–3 minutes, then lift the scallops out with a slotted spoon and put them in a serving dish. Add the wine to the pan, boil to reduce a little while stirring; pour the sauce over the scallops and serve, garnished with parsley.

Enough for two people.

MUSSELS *with* SPICED RICE

Moules au riz à la basquaise

In small quantities this dish is excellent hot or cold, as a starter. In larger quantities it makes a nice party dish. The quantity of liquid is always twice that of the volume of rice – i.e. 4 cups of stock, including the olive oil, to 2 cups of rice.

1½ teacups long-grain basmati rice, 2¾ teacups veal or fish stock and ¼ teacup olive oil, 90–125g/3–4oz chorizo sausage (or other coarsely cut pork sausage) half a red or green pepper, paprika, 1 litre/2 pints mussels, a few prawns.

Boil the rice for 7 minutes in plenty of water, without salt. Drain it, and hold the colander under the running cold tap until all starch is washed away.

Put it in an earthenware or other oven dish with the stock, the olive oil, the sausage cut into little cubes, the pepper, freed of all seeds and core, sliced into thin rounds, and a teaspoon of paprika. Bring to simmering point on top of the stove. Cover with a folded cloth, a lid, and put in a moderate oven, at 180°C/gas 4. In 20–25 minutes the rice will have absorbed all the liquid and be beautifully cooked and well spiced. Open the mussels in a pan over a hot flame, with just a little water, and leave them in their shells. Gently fry the prawns in a little oil. Turn the rice into a hot shallow dish, add the mussels and the prawns. Garnish with quarters of lemon.

Enough for four people.

MOULES MARINIÈRE

There are several versions of *moules marinière*. Here are three of them.

1 small onion, 1 clove of garlic, a small piece of celery, 1 small glass white wine, pepper, 3 litres/6 pints mussels, 30g/1oz butter, 15g/½oz flour, parsley.

Put the chopped onion, garlic and celery into a large pan with the white wine and about 600ml/1 pint of water. Add pepper but not salt. Put in the well-cleaned mussels, cover the pan and cook until the shells open. Take out the mussels, keep them hot, and thicken the liquid in which they have cooked with 30g/1oz of butter and 15g/½oz of flour. Pour the sauce over the mussels in a large tureen and sprinkle with parsley. Serve very hot.

To be eaten out of soup plates, with a fork and a soup spoon.

Another way is to prepare the sauce first; make a little white roux in the pan with butter, flour, chopped onion, celery and the white wine. Add the water and put the mussels in when the liquid has the consistency of a thin soup. The mussels can then be served directly they are opened, a great advantage, as they then do not lose their freshness and savour, which they are apt to do if they are reheated. On no account must the sauce be over-thickened, or you will simply have mussels in a white sauce.

Perhaps the most usual way of cooking *moules marinière* is simply to put the mussels into the pan with the white wine but no water, throw chopped parsley and onion or garlic over them as they are opening and serve as soon as they are all open.

Always serve plenty of French bread with *moules marinière*.

Enough for four to six people.

RAGOÛT *of* SHELLFISH

12 cooked scampi or Dublin Bay prawns, 2 litres/4 pints mussels, 1 onion, 15g/1oz butter, 1 tablespoon concentrated tomato purée, 4 cloves of garlic, seasoning, 1 dessertspoon sugar, tarragon, 1 tablespoon flour, 300ml/½ pint white wine, 125g/¼lb mushrooms, 6 scallops, lemon juice, parsley.

First of all split the scampi tails in half, retaining 6 halves in their shells for the garnish. From the remaining shells remove the flesh and cut it into fairly large pieces. Clean the mussels carefully.

In a deep pan sauté a sliced onion in butter. When golden add the tomato purée, the chopped garlic, salt, pepper and the sugar and tarragon. Simmer for 5 minutes. Stir in the flour. When thick, pour over the heated wine, and cook this sauce for 15–20 minutes. Add the flesh of the scampi, the sliced mushrooms, the scallops cut into 2 rounds each, and the mussels. Turn up the heat and cook until the mussels have opened. At the last minute add the reserved scampi in their shells. Turn into a deep dish, squeeze over a little lemon, sprinkle with chopped parsley and serve very hot, in soup plates.

The black shells of the mussels and the pink of the prawns make a very decorative dish. The tails of large crawfish (langouste) can be used instead of the Dublin Bay prawns or scampi, but of course fewer will be needed, and they can be cut into four or six pieces each.

Enough for four to six people as a first course.

LOBSTER COURCHAMPS

This is not a classic regional or other recognized traditional dish, so you can call it what you please. It has no name of its own. I have named it after the Comte de Courchamps, author of the first of the three books in which I found the recipe. The others were by Dumas the Elder and the Baron Brisse. Highly imaginative as they were, all three gentlemen called it Sauce for Boiled Lobster.

1 freshly boiled, medium large (about 750g/1½lb) hen lobster or langouste, 2 small shallots, 1 heaped teaspoon tarragon leaves, 2 tablespoons chopped parsley, salt, pepper, a scant teaspoon of strong yellow French mustard, 24–30 drops of soy sauce, approximately 6 tablespoons mildly fruity Provence olive oil, the juice of half a rather small lemon, 1 teaspoon anisette de Bordeaux.

From the split lobster extract all the red and creamy parts. Pound them in a mortar. Mix with the finely chopped shallots, tarragon and parsley. Add the seasonings and the soy sauce, then gradually stir in the olive oil; add lemon juice. Finally, the anisette. Divide the sauce into two portions, and serve it in little bowls or squat glasses placed on each person's plate, so that the lobster can be dipped into it. The lobster meat can be cut into scallops and piled neatly back into the shells.

Apart from its sheer deliciousness (most cold lobster sauces, including mayonnaise, are on the heavy side for what is already rich and solid food) this sauce has other points to recommend it. Anisette is not a liqueur which, speaking at least for myself, one has a great compulsion to swig down in quantity; in my cupboard a bottle lasts for years. A small bottle of soy sauce keeps almost indefinitely, and fresh tarragon can now be bought all year. The makings of your sauce, then, are always with you. All you need is the freshly boiled hen lobster.

Enough for two people.

LANGOUSTE *in* TOMATO *and* BRANDY SAUCE

Langouste comme chez Nénette

This dish comes from the port of Sète in the Languedoc and is a variation of the better-known *homard à l'américaine*. I have quoted the recipe given to me by Madame Nénette from her restaurant.

'Cut a live crawfish into not too large pieces; put them at once into a wide and shallow pan containing a little smoking olive oil, add salt and pepper and cook until the shell turns red. Add some finely chopped shallots and a clove or two of garlic, crushed and first cooked separately in a little oil.

'Pour in a small glass of good *cognac* and set light to it; when the flames have gone out, add a half bottle of still *champagne or Chablis*, and a spoonful of *tomato purée*. Cover the pan and cook over a steady fire for about 20 minutes. Remove the pieces of crawfish, which are now cooked, and keep them hot.

'Press the sauce through a very fine sieve, let it boil up again, season with a scrap of *cayenne* and, at the last minute, add 3 good spoonfuls of *aïoli*. (See page 302.)

'Pour the sauce over the crawfish and sprinkle a little finely chopped *parsley* over the dish.'

Enough for two people.

SLOW-COOKED SQUID

Calamari in umido

500g/1lb squid, salt, lemon juice, 2 large onions, oil, 2 or 3 tomatoes, 1 dessert teaspoon tomato purée, marjoram and thyme, 3 cloves of garlic, 1 small glass of red wine.

To clean the squid, remove the insides from the pocket-like part of the fish, and pull out the thin transparent spine bone. Remove also the purplish outside skin, which comes off very easily in warm water.

From each side of the head remove the little ink bag (the whole operation is carried out in a bowl of water and is very quickly done) and take out the eyes and the hard beak-like object in the centre of the tentacles of which Dumas remarks that it is '*non pas un nez, mais l'anus (au milieu du visage!)*'. Rinse the squid in running water until it is quite free of grit. When clean they are milky white.

Cut the body of the squid into rings, about 5mm/¼ inch wide, and the tentacles into strips. Season them with salt and lemon juice. Now put the onions, cut into rings, into a pan in which you have warmed enough olive oil to cover the bottom. Let them turn golden and add the squid. After 2 minutes put in the chopped tomatoes, some marjoram and thyme, and the garlic, and after 2 more minutes pour in a small glassful of red wine; let this reduce a little and add a dessertspoon, not more, of tomato purée. Add enough hot water to reach the level of the ingredients in the pan, put on the lid, and cook very slowly for 1½ hours. Serve with rice or with toasted French bread.

Enough for two to three people.

DISHES *for* COLLECTORS

A dish of pork and prunes seems a strange one to chase two hundred miles across France, and indeed it was its very oddity that sent me in search of it. The combination of meat with fruit is not only an uncommon one in France, it is one which the French are fond of citing as an example of the barbaric eating habits of other nations, the Germans and the Americans in particular. So to find such a dish in Tours, the very heart of sane and sober French cookery, is surprising, even given the fact that the local prunes are so renowned.

I knew where we would go to look for the dish because I had seen it on the menu of the Rôtisserie Tourangelle on a previous occasion, when there were so many other interesting specialities that it just hadn't been possible to get round to the *quasi de porc aux pruneaux*. But this time I hoped perhaps to find out how the dish was cooked as well as in what manner such a combination had become acceptable to conservative French palates.

Driving out of Orléans towards Tours I observed for the first time the ominous entry in the new *Guide Michelin* concerning the Rôtisserie Tourangelle: '*Déménagement prévu,*' it said. Very well, we would get to Tours early, we would enquire upon entering the town whether by some ill-chance the restaurant was at this moment in the throes of house-moving. If so, we would not stay in Tours, but console ourselves by driving on to Langeais, where there was a hotel whose cooking was said to be worth the journey. The evening was to be our last before driving north towards Boulogne, so we specially didn't want to make a hash of it. But we had plenty of time, the afternoon was fine, the Loire countryside lay before us in all its shining early summer beauty. We dawdled along, making a detour to Chenonceaux on the way.

So in the end it was after seven o'clock by the time we had battled into the main street of Tours, found the Office of the Syndicat d'Initiative, and made our enquiry. No, said the pretty and efficient young lady in charge, the house-moving of the Rôtisserie Tourangelle had not yet started. All was well. '*Déménagement prévu*, indeed,' said my companion, 'what a fuss. It'll be *prévu* for the next two years.' Fifteen minutes later the car had been manœuvred into the courtyard of the charming Hotel Central, we had booked our room, the luggage was unloaded. As we were about to get into the lift I returned to the desk and asked the lady in charge if she would be so kind as to telephone chez Charvillat and book us a table, for we were already late. As I walked away, I heard her saying into the telephone '*Comment, vous êtes fermé*?'

Yes, the *déménagement* had started that day. Closed for a fortnight. Well it was hardly the fault of the charming girl at the Syndicat, but . . . anyway, it was now too late to move on to Langeais. We must eat at Tours and make the best of it. By the time I had explained the magnitude of the disaster to Madame at the desk, she and I were both nearly in tears. For she perfectly grasped the situation, and did not think it at all odd that we had driven two hundred miles simply to eat chez Charvillat. But all the restaurants in Tours, she said, were good. We would eat well wherever we went. Yes, but would we find that dish of *porc aux pruneaux* which by this time had become an obsession? And in any case what restaurant could possible be as nice, charming, as comfortable, as altogether desirable as that of M. Charvillat?

Madame spent the next twenty minutes telephoning round Tours on our behalf, and eventually sent us, somewhat consoled, to a well-known restaurant only two minutes' walk from the hotel. I wish I could end this story by saying that the place was a find, a dazzling revelation, a dozen times better than the one we had missed. But it was not as dramatic as that. It was indeed a very nice restaurant, the head waiter was friendly, and we settled down to some entirely entrancing white Vouvray while they cooked our *alose á l'oseille* – shad grilled and served with a sauce in the form of a runny sorrel purée. In this respect at least we had timed things properly, for the shad makes only a short seasonal appearance in the Loire. It was extremely good and nothing like as bony as shad is advertised to be. Then came this restaurant's version of the famous pork dish, which turned out to be made with little noisettes of meat in a very remarkable sauce and of course we immediately felt reproved for doubting for one moment that an intelligent French cook could make something splendid out of even such lumpish sounding ingredients as pork and prunes.

It was worth all the fuss, even for the sauce alone. But, almost inevitably, it was something of an anticlimax. The combination of a long day's drive, the sampling during the day of the lovely, poetical wines of Pouilly and of Sancerre *sur place* (and whatever anyone may say, they do taste different on the spot), a hideously ill-advised cream cake at an Orléans patisserie, the alternating emotions of triumph and despair following so rapidly one upon the other, not to mention a very large helping of the shad and sorrel, had wrecked our appetites. By this time it was known throughout the restaurant that some English had arrived especially to eat the *porc aux pruneaux*. The helpings, consequently, were very large. By the time we had eaten through it and learned how it was cooked, we were near collapse, but the *maître-d'hôtel* and the *patronne* were just warming up. If we were interested in local recipes, what about their *brochet au beurre blanc* and their *poulet á l'estragon*, and their *dodine de canard*? To be sure, we should have had that duck as an hors d'œuvre, but just a slice or two now, to taste, and then at least we would have some local cheeses and a sweet?

Curiosity overcame prudence. We did indeed try their *dodine de canard,* which was not the daube of duck in red wine usually associated with this name, but a very rich cold duck galantine, which would have been delicious as an hors d'œuvre, but after all that pork . . . Cravenly, we ordered coffee. No salad? No cheese? No dessert?

As we paid our bill, expressed our thanks, and left with the best grace we could muster, I was miserably aware that we had failed these kindly hospitable people and left them with the feeling that we did not appreciate their food.

It was a long time before I had the courage to set to work on that recipe. When I did, and saw once more the row of little pork noisettes, the bronze and copper lights of the shining sauce, the orderly row of black, rich, wine-soaked prunes on the long white dish, I thought that indeed it had been worth the journey to learn how to make something as beautiful as that. One day, with a better appetite and more stamina, I will go back to that restaurant in Tours and make amends for the evening when justice to their cookery was not done.

(See pages 250–51 for the pork and prunes recipe.)

from Vogue, *November 1958*

MEAT

French cooks, it is sometimes alleged, have perfected their particular brand of magic with second-class materials because they have no first-class ones. This, of course, is nonsensical. French cooks hold good-quality materials in the highest esteem, and certainly have plenty to work with. But the attitude of a French cook or housewife is extremely realistic. Appreciating the fact that not every fish that comes out of the sea is a sole, and that not even carefully nurtured animals are entirely constructed of prime steaks and cutlets, they have made it their business to know how to present coarser fish, elderly birds and second- or third-grade cuts of meat with the identical skill and ceremony accorded to luxury roasts and showpieces.

A good French butcher takes as much trouble over the cutting, trimming and presentation of his cheap cuts as with the prime joints. Such things as shoulder and breast of lamb, shoulder cuts, skirt and briskets of beef, shins of veal and belly of pork are so neatly prepared that when the housewife buys them she knows exactly what she is getting; there will be no trimming or boning for her to do at home and so no waste, of either time or materials. Beef for braising or for *bœuf mode*, *bœuf bourguignon* or the *pot-au-feu* will be on display at the butcher's without her having to order it specially, to have it larded or to explain what is to be done. And this is where we come up against a difficulty when we want to cook French meat dishes in England, for it is not only the meticulous cutting and seaming, trimming and larding and tying which is differently approached in France, but the separation of the carcasses into their various cuts is done on a different system, particularly in regard to beef and veal, so that it is not easy to get, in England, the precise equivalent of a French shoulder cut of beef for a *pot-au-feu*, of a leg cut for a daube, of a noix of veal for roasting, or escalopes for frying.

In the meat recipes, therefore, I have tried wherever possible to indicate English equivalents or alternatives to the French cuts.

PROVENÇAL BEEF *and* WINE STEW

La daube de bœuf provençale

There must be scores of different recipes for daubes in Provence alone, as well as all those which have been borrowed from Provence by other regions, for a daube of beef is essentially a country housewife's dish. In some daubes the meat is cut up, in others it is cooked in the piece; what goes in apart from the meat is largely a matter of what is available, and the way it is served is again a question of local taste.

This daube is a useful dish for those who have to get a dinner ready when they get home from the office. It can be cooked for 1½ hours the previous evening and finished on the night itself. Provided they have not been overcooked to start with, these beef and wine stews are all the better for a second or even third heating up. The amounts I have given are the smallest quantities in which it is worth cooking such a stew, and will serve four or five people, but of course they can be doubled or even trebled for a large party; if the meat is piled up in layers in a deep pan it will naturally need longer cooking than if it is spread out in a shallow one.

This is an easy recipe, but it has all the rich savour of these slowly cooked wine-flavoured stews. The pot to cook it in may be earthenware, cast iron, or a copper oven pot of about 1 litre/2 pints capacity, wide rather than deep.

1kg/2lb top rump of beef, about 175g/6oz unsmoked streaky bacon or salt pork, 2 carrots, 2 onions, about 90g/3oz fresh pork rinds, 2 tomatoes, 2 tablespoons olive oil, 2 cloves of garlic, a bouquet of thyme, bay leaf, parsley and a little strip of orange peel, seasoning, a glass of red wine.

Have the meat cut into squares about the size of half a postcard and about 8mm/⅓ inch thick. Buy the bacon or salt pork in the piece and cut it into small cubes.

Scrape and slice the carrots; peel and slice the onions. Cut the rinds, which should have scarcely any fat adhering to them and are there to give body as well as savour to the stew, into little squares. Skin and slice the tomatoes.

In the bottom of the pot put the olive oil, then the bacon, then the vegetables and half the pork rinds. Arrange the meat carefully on top, the slices overlapping each other. Bury the garlic cloves, flattened with a knife, and the bouquet, in the centre. Season and cover with the rest of the pork rinds. With the pan uncovered, start the cooking on a moderate heat on top of the stove.

After about 10 minutes, put the wine into another saucepan; bring it to a fast boil; set light to it; rotate the pan so that the flames spread. When they have died down pour the bubbling wine over the meat. Cover the pot with greaseproof paper or foil, and a well-fitting lid. Transfer to a very slow oven, at 140°C/gas 1, and leave for 2½ hours.

To serve, arrange the meat with the bacon and the little pieces of rind on a hot dish; pour off some of the fat from the sauce, extract the bouquet, and pour the sauce round the meat. At the serving stage, a *persillade* of finely chopped garlic and parsley, with perhaps an anchovy and a few capers, can be sprinkled over the top. Or stoned black olives can be added to the stew half an hour before the end of the cooking time.

Although in Italy pasta is never served with a meat dish, in Provence it quite often is. The cooked and drained noodles, or whatever pasta you have chosen, are mixed with some of the gravy from the stew, and in this case the fat is not removed from the gravy, because it lubricates the pasta. Sometimes this *macaronade*, as it is called, is served first, to be followed by the meat. Nowadays, since rice has been successfully cultivated in the reclaimed areas of the Camargue, it is also quite usual to find a dish of rice, often flavoured with saffron, served with a meat stew.

Enough for four to six people.

SUSSEX STEWED STEAK

This is one of the excellent old English dishes in which mushroom ketchup and ale or stout make a rich-looking and interesting gravy. Creamy mashed potatoes and perhaps a few fried or grilled mushrooms – if you can get large flat ones – go well with this casserole of steak. The whole dish takes scarcely five minutes to prepare for cooking.

1.25kg/2½lb of a cheap cut such as chuck steak, top rump or thick flank cut in one piece, salt and pepper, a tablespoon or two of flour, an onion, 5 to 6 tablespoons each of port and stout, 2 tablespoons mushroom ketchup or wine vinegar.

Season the meat, rub flour on both sides. Put it flat in a shallow baking dish in which it just fits. Over it slice a large onion. Pour in the port, stout, and ketchup or vinegar. Cover with a double sheet of greaseproof paper and the lid of the dish. Put it in a very low oven, at 140°C/gas 1, and leave it for about 3 hours – a little less or longer won't matter. The toughest piece of meat emerges beautifully tender, and the gravy rich, bright brown, excellently flavoured.

Enough for four people.

BEEF *with* RED WINE, ONIONS *and* MUSHROOMS

Bœuf à la bourguignonne

This is a favourite among those carefully composed, slowly cooked dishes which are the domain of French housewives and owner-cooks of modest restaurants rather than of professional chefs. Generally supposed to be of Burgundian origin, *bœuf à la bourguignonne* has long been a nationally popular French dish, and is often referred to, or written down on menus, simply as '*bourguignon*'. Such dishes do not, of course, have a rigid formula, each cook interpreting it according to her taste, and the following recipe is just one version. Incidentally, when I helped in a soup kitchen in France many years ago, this was the dish for feast days and holidays.

If more convenient, the first 2 hours' cooking can be done in advance, the stew left to cool and the fat removed; it can then be reheated gently with the bacon, mushrooms and onions added. There are those who maintain that the dish is improved by being heated up a second time; the meat has time to mature, as it were, in the sauce.

To make a cheaper dish, chuck (shoulder) beef may be used instead of topside, and an extra 45 minutes' cooking time allowed. And when really small onions are not available it is best simply to cook a chopped onion or two with the stew, and to leave onions out of the garnish, because large ones are not suitable for the purpose.

For formal occasions a boned joint of beef may be cooked whole and served with a similar sauce and garnish, and then becomes *pièce de bœuf à la bourguignonne*.

1kg/2lb topside of beef, salt and pepper, a large onion, thyme, parsley and bay leaves, 2 tablespoons olive oil, 150ml/¼ pint red wine, meat dripping or butter, 125g/4oz salt pork or streaky bacon (unsmoked for preference), a dozen or so small whole onions, 1 tablespoon flour, 300ml/½ pint meat stock, preferably veal, a clove of garlic, 250g/½lb small mushrooms.

Cut the meat into slices about 6cm/2½ inches square and 5mm/¼ inch thick. Put them into a china or earthenware dish, seasoned with salt and pepper, covered with the large sliced onion, herbs, olive oil and red wine. Leave to marinate for 5–6 hours.

Put a good tablespoon of beef dripping or butter into a heavy stewing-pan of about 2.5 litres/4 pints capacity. In this melt the salt pork or bacon, cut into 5-mm/¼-inch-thick match-length strips. Add the whole peeled small onions, and let them brown, turning them over frequently and keeping the heat low. Take out the bacon when its fat becomes transparent, and remove the onions when they are nicely coloured. Set them aside with the bacon. Now put into the fat the drained and dried pieces of meat and brown them quickly on each side. Sprinkle them with the flour, shaking the pan so that the flour amalgamates with the fat and absorbs it. Pour over the strained marinade. Let it bubble half a minute; add the stock. Put in a clove of garlic and a bouquet of thyme, parsley and bay leaf tied with a thread. Cover the pan with a close-fitting lid and let it barely simmer on top of the stove for about 2 hours.

Now add the bacon and onions, and the whole mushrooms washed but not peeled and already cooked in butter or dripping for a minute or so to rid them of some of their moisture. Cook the stew another half-hour. Remove the bouquet and garlic before serving.

There should be enough for four to six people.

BEEF *and* WINE STEW *with* BLACK OLIVES

Bœuf à la gardiane

A dish from western Provence and the Camargue demonstrating the stewing of a tough piece of meat in red wine without the addition of any stock or thickening for the sauce.

The old Nîmoise cook who showed me how to make this particular version of the dish used Châteauneuf du Pape to cook it in (we were in the district, so it wasn't so extravagant as it sounds, and it most definitely pays to use a decent and full-bodied wine for these beef stews) and she garnished the dish with heart-shaped croûtons of fried bread instead of rice.

1kg/2lb top rump of beef, butter and olive oil, 4 tablespoons brandy, 1 large glass red wine, salt and pepper, a bouquet of thyme, parsley and bay leaf, plus a little strip of orange peel and a crushed clove of garlic, about 175g/6oz stoned black olives.

The meat should be cut into small neat cubes, not more than 2.5cm/1 inch square. Brown them in a mixture of butter and olive oil. Warm the brandy in a soup ladle, pour it over the meat, set light to it, shake the pan until the flames go out. The flaming with brandy, although not absolutely essential, burns up the excess fat and makes quite a difference to the flavour of the finished sauce, which will be a short one, most of the liquid having been absorbed by the meat. Add the red wine; let it bubble fast for about half a minute. Season with only very little salt and pepper, put in the bouquet tied with thread, turn the flame as low as possible, cover the pan with at least two layers of greaseproof paper or foil and the lid.

Cook as gently as possible, on top of the stove for about 3½ hours. Ten minutes before serving remove the bouquet and put in the stoned black olives. Taste for seasoning before serving. A dish of plain boiled rice can be served separately.

Enough for four or five people.

PAUPIETTES *of* BEEF

For the stuffing: *2 onions, finely chopped, 60g/2oz each of bacon and mushrooms, dripping or oil, 1 dessertspoon finely chopped lemon peel, 1 tablespoon breadcrumbs, a handful of parsley, salt and pepper, 1 egg.*

8 thin slices of beef cut from the round, without fat and each weighing approximately 30g/1oz, salt and pepper, thyme, flour, dripping or oil, 1 clove of garlic, 1 tablespoon French mustard.

Fry the onions, bacon and mushrooms in a little dripping or oil, then mix in the lemon peel, breadcrumbs, chopped parsley and seasoning, and a beaten egg.

Flatten out each slice of beef; season with salt, pepper and thyme. On each slice lay a little heap of stuffing, roll up the meat and secure with a tooth-pick, or tie with string. Roll them in flour and brown them in dripping or oil, in a small sauté pan. Add water just to cover, and simmer very slowly for 30 minutes. Now with the point of a knife crush a small piece of garlic and add this to the sauce, together with the French mustard, and cook for another 30 minutes. The sauce should be creamy and piquant. The dish can be made beforehand and heated up.

Serve with either boiled rice or a purée of potatoes.

Enough for four people.

SPICED BEEF LOAF

1.75kg/3½lb fairly finely minced beef bought from a reliable butcher, 125g/4oz fat bacon, 1 teaspoon each of dried basil and ground allspice, 2 heaped teaspoons salt, 1 dozen peppercorns, 1 very small clove of garlic, 4 tablespoons port, sherry or red wine, 1 tablespoon wine vinegar.

Put the beef into a big china bowl, add the roughly chopped bacon, all the seasonings and garlic crushed together, the wine and the vinegar. Mix very thoroughly, and if possible leave for a couple of hours so that all the flavours have a chance to penetrate the meat.

Turn the whole mixture into a 1.5–2-litre/2½–3-pint loaf tin, or two smaller tins. The mixture will shrink during the cooking, so that, initially, the containers should be packed full to the brim. Stand the tins in a shallow baking tin filled with water and cook uncovered in the centre of a slow oven, at 160°C/gas 3, for 1½ hours.

If the top of the loaf looks like it's getting too brown, cover with buttered foil or greaseproof paper.

Leave to cool, then store in the refrigerator or a cool larder. To turn the loaf out of its tin simply run a knife round the edges and ease the loaf out on to a dish. Carve it in rather thin slices, and serve with a salad and/or sweet-sour pickled fruits, mild fruit chutney, or a mustardy sauce.

Enough for eight to ten people.

OXTAIL STEWED *with* WHITE GRAPES

La queue de bœuf des vignerons

Oxtail 'as cooked by the wine growers' is a lovely dish made out of what should be inexpensive ingredients, but as in England grapes are not to be had just for the picking, one should perhaps only attempt it when imported grapes are plentiful and cheap. To make the lengthy cooking worthwhile buy at least 2 oxtails, cut into the usual 5-cm/2-inch lengths by the butcher. A dish of potatoes boiled in their skins, or a potato purée, should accompany the dish.

2 oxtails cut into 5-cm/2-inch lengths, 100–125g/3–4oz salt pork or a cheap cut of fat unsmoked bacon bought in one piece, 2 large onions, 4 large carrots, a bouquet of 2 bay leaves, parsley, thyme and 2 crushed cloves of garlic tied in a little bunch, seasonings of salt and freshly ground pepper and a little mace or allspice, 1kg/2lb white grapes.

Steep the oxtail in cold water for a minimum of 2 hours, so that the blood soaks out.

Cut the pork or bacon, without the rind, into little cubes. Chop the onions and dice the carrots. At the bottom of a heavy cooking pot put the bacon with the vegetables on top. Start off on a low flame and cook for 10 minutes until the fat from the bacon is running. Now put in the pieces of oxtail, and put the bouquet in the centre. Season the meat. Cover the pot and cook gently for 20 minutes. Pick the grapes off their stalks and crush slightly in a bowl. Add them to the pot and cover the pot with two sheets of greaseproof paper and the lid. Transfer to a very slow oven, at 140°C/gas 1, and cook for a minimum of 3½ hours. Oxtail varies very much in quality, and sometimes takes a good deal longer, and unless the meat is so soft and tender it is almost falling from the bones it will not be good. Once cooked, quickly transfer the pieces of oxtail and a few of the little bits of bacon to another terrine or to a serving dish, and keep them hot while you sieve all the rest of the ingredients through a fine mesh. Pour the resulting sauce over the oxtail.

An alternative method is to cook the dish for half an hour less, take out the oxtail, and leave the sieved sauce separately so that excess fat can be removed from the top when it is cold. Having done this, pour the sauce, warmed, over the meat and heat on top of the stove rather than in the oven, because all-round heat tends to make the sauce oily, whereas with direct heat it will retain its consistency. The dish can, as a matter of fact, be reheated two or three times without damage.

Two oxtails should make six to eight ample helpings.

BRAISED SHIN *of* VEAL

Ossi buchi milanese

To make the dish as it should be, very tender veal from an animal not more than three months old should be used. A dish of *risotto alla milanese* (see page 160) always accompanies *ossi buchi*. Incidentally, I have seen it asserted that *ossi buchi* means drunken bones. It doesn't. It means bones with holes, or hollow bones.

1kg/2lb shin of veal (if from a full-grown calf allow 2kg/4lb) sawn into pieces 5cm/2inches thick, 60g/2oz butter, 150ml/¼ pint each of white wine and stock, 375g/¾lb tomatoes, salt and pepper, parsley, a clove of garlic, a lemon.

In a wide shallow pan, brown the slices of veal shin in the butter. Once browned, arrange them in the pan so that they remain upright, in order that the marrow in the bone may not fall out as the meat cooks. Pour the white wine over them, let it cook for 10 minutes, then add the skinned and chopped tomatoes; let them reduce; add the stock. Season. Cook for 1½–2 hours keeping the pan covered for the first hour.

Prepare a handful of chopped parsley, a clove of chopped garlic and the grated peel of half a lemon. The Milanese call this mixture *gremolata*, and it is an essential part of the traditional *ossi buchi Milanese*. It is to be sprinkled on the top of the *ossi buchi* before serving.

Enough for four people.

BRAISED MEAT ROLL

Polpettone

1kg/2lb raw minced veal, beef or pork, 4 eggs, garlic, an onion, a handful of parsley, salt and pepper, butter.
For the stuffing: *2 hard-boiled eggs, 60g/2oz cooked ham, 60g/2oz provolone or Gruyère cheese, seasoning.*

Mix the meat, the eggs, the chopped garlic, onion and parsley together, and season them. Flatten the mixture out on a floured board. In the centre put the stuffing of hard-boiled eggs, ham and cheese, all coarsely chopped and seasoned. Roll the meat up into a large sausage. Enclose it in a piece of buttered greaseproof paper. Melt some butter in an ovenproof dish and cook the *polpettone* in a very slow oven or on top of the stove for 1½ hours. If the fat dries up, add a little water or stock, and keep the pan covered. Serve hot but also very good cold.

Nowadays I cook this dish in rather the same way as a meat loaf, in a rectangular tin or terrine.

Enough for eight people.

ESCALOPES *of* VEAL *with* VERMOUTH *and* CREAM SAUCE

Escalopes à la savoyarde

It is always difficult to decide what vegetables, if any, should go with this creamy veal dish. On the whole it is best simply to serve a few little croûtons fried in butter, or some small plain boiled potatoes as a garnish, and to keep green vegetables for a separate course.

2 escalopes cut from the topside or thick flank of veal, each weighing approximately 120g/3½oz, salt and pepper, lemon juice, 30g/1oz butter, 4 or 5 tablespoons dry white vermouth, 150ml/¼ pint thick cream.

Season your escalopes with salt, pepper and lemon juice. Cook them rapidly on each side in foaming butter; pour in the vermouth; let it bubble. Moderate the heat. Add the cream. Shake the pan so that the cream and wine amalgamate; now lower the heat again and simmer for another 3 or 4 minutes, until the cream has thickened.

Enough for two people.

TEL - RESTA

URANT DE L

MUTTON STEWED *with* BRANDY *and* GARLIC

Tranches de mouton à la poitevine

Have two thick slices cut from a leg of *mutton*, with the bone, weighing about 375g/¾lb each. Brown them in *butter* in a heavy shallow pan with a well-fitting lid. *Salt and pepper* them; pour over about 125ml/4floz *brandy* and the same amount of water. Add a dozen peeled cloves of *garlic*. Cover with paper and the lid, lower the flame, and cook as slowly as possible for about 2½ hours. There will only be a little concentrated juice when the dish is ready, but the mutton will be very tender with a highly aromatic flavour. You can, of course, use less garlic if you like, but some there must be. Almost any root or dried vegetables go well with this dish, either braised or plain boiled, or in a purée.

Slices of shoulder of lamb can be stewed in the same way, allowing 1¾–2 hours' cooking time.

There should be enough for four people.

SHOULDER *of* LAMB BAKED *with* POTATOES

Épaule d'agneau boulangère

The boning and rolling of a shoulder of lamb or mutton is not really a mystery; any decent butcher will do it for you, and the system certainly does make the joint very simple to carve. This particular way of cooking a boned shoulder owes its name to the fact that it was a dish which would be prepared at home and carried to the bakery to be cooked in the oven after the bread was baked. It makes an excellent and quite economical dish for a large household.

The boned shoulder will weigh about 2kg/4lb. Press *salt*, *pepper*, chopped fresh *thyme* or *marjoram*, and for those who like it, *garlic*, into the inside of the rolled meat. People who like the flavour of garlic without wishing to find it in the meat might try putting a clove or two under the joint in the pan while it is cooking. In this way it will flavour the gravy and the potatoes, but will scarcely be perceptible in the meat itself. Personally, I find a little garlic with lamb as indispensable as others find mint sauce.

Melt 30g/1oz of *butter* and a tablespoon of *oil* in a large pan; brown the seasoned meat in it. Transfer it to an oven dish; put in the garlic and 1kg/2lb of whole *new potatoes*. In the same fat fry a sliced *onion* until it turns golden; pour over 2 teacups of *meat stock*, which can have been made from the bones of the joint, cook a minute or so and pour over the meat and potatoes. Cover with a piece of buttered greaseproof paper and the lid of the dish. Cook in a slow oven at 160°C/gas 3, for 2 hours or a little under if you like the meat faintly pink. Before serving, salt the potatoes and sprinkle with more *fresh herbs*. The stock, reduced a little by fast boiling, will serve as a sauce.

Enough for six to eight people.

LAMB *and* AUBERGINE STEW

In countries where aubergines flourish and are cheap, and where meat is scarce and expensive, a dish such as this one would be made with more aubergines and less meat, and the rice would be the really filling element of the meal. It can be cooked in a frying pan or sauté pan, or any wide and shallow utensil of rather large capacity.

Should you have a little mutton or lamb stock available – about 300ml/½ pint – omit the tomatoes and use the stock instead, adding it at the same stage of the cooking. This system makes a dish which has more distinction than the tomato-enriched version.

2 small aubergines, salt, 4 tablespoons of oil, 1 large onion, 750g–1kg/1½–2lb shoulder or middle neck of lamb boned and cut into 2.5-cm/1-inch cubes, fresh or dried mint or basil, pepper, 250g/½lb tomatoes, a clove of garlic and 2 heaped teaspoons of cumin seeds or ground cumin if you prefer.

Slice the unpeeled aubergines into quarters and then into 1-cm/½-inch cubes, put them in a colander, sprinkle them with a tablespoon of salt, put a plate and a weight on the top and leave them for at least an hour so that the excess moisture drains out. Before cooking them press them as dry as you can.

Heat the oil in a heavy 25–30cm/10–12-inch frying or sauté pan and put in the thinly sliced onion. When it has just begun to take colour put in the meat, plentifully sprinkled with the herbs, salt and pepper. Turn the meat cubes over and over until they are nicely browned. (If this operation is neglected the dish will be pallid and sad-looking.) Remove the meat and onion to a dish with a draining spoon and into the same oil put the aubergine cubes. Cover the pan and let them cook gently for 10 minutes, giving a stir from time to time.

Now return the meat and onions to the pan, add the skinned and roughly chopped tomatoes, the crushed garlic and the heated and pounded cumin seeds. Cover the pan again, let it simmer very gently for 1 hour. Or, if it is more convenient, cook it only for 45 minutes and then heat it up very slowly for half an hour the next day. Strew with more mint or basil before serving. Plain boiled rice or pilaff rice goes with this dish.

Ample for four people.

BEST END *of* NECK *of* LAMB *with* HARICOT BEANS

Carré d'agneau aux haricots à la bretonne

The *carré* is the French butcher's term for the best end of neck joint, consisting of eight cutlets. It is trimmed exactly as the cutlets would be if they were to be cut separately for grilling, with the chine bone and most of the fat removed, so that only the actual cutlets with their bones are left. Neatly tied, it makes a compact little joint, very easy to cook and carve, and suitable for a small party when a leg or saddle would be too much.

First of all, prepare a stock from the bones and trimmings, with an *onion*, *garlic*, *carrot* and *seasoning*, and water barely to cover. Simmer for an hour or so, strain, leave to cool and skim off the fat. This stock is for basting the joint, so only about a cup is needed. Red wine instead of stock can, if preferred, be used for basting. In this case, pour a large glass of *red wine* into a saucepan, add either a couple of chopped *shallots* or 3 or 4 whole cloves of *garlic*, and boil until the wine is reduced by half. Use in the same way as the stock.

Preheat the oven to 190°C/gas 5. To cook the joint, butter a roasting tin, lay the joint in it fat side up, and cover with a piece of thickly buttered greaseproof paper or foil. Put a lid on the roasting tin, and put in the centre of the preheated oven. After about 20 minutes remove the paper and baste the meat with the juices in the pan and some of the prepared stock, heated. Altogether, the joint will take about 50 minutes to cook and should be basted three or four times, being left uncovered for the last 10 minutes so that the outer coating of fat browns.

When the meat is cooked, keep it hot in a large shallow serving dish. Put the rest of your stock or wine into the roasting pan, scrape up all the juices, let it bubble a minute and add a little of it to the prepared haricot beans and serve the rest separately.

For the beans: 375g/12oz medium-sized and long, rather than round, *white haricot beans* are soaked overnight if for lunch, or for 6–8 hours (which is quite long enough provided the beans are those of the current season and not a couple of years old) if for dinner. Drain them, simmer them in water to cover by 5cm/2 inches, with a *carrot*, an *onion*, a *bouquet of herbs* and a piece of *celery*. According to the quality of the beans they may take anything from 1½ to 3 hours. So it is best, if you don't know your beans, to prepare them in advance. They have to be reheated anyhow. When they are tender, but not broken, drain them, reserving the liquid, and season them well with *salt*. Extract the carrot and the herbs and throw them away. Chop the onion and fry it in *butter*. Add 3 or 4 skinned and chopped tomatoes and cook till soft, thinning with a little of the reserved cooking liquid. The beans are gently reheated in this mixture, the juice from the roast being added when they are ready. The beans are then turned into the serving dish round the meat or, if preferred, served in a separate dish. Little paper frills are slipped on to the end of the bones, and the joint is carved straight down into cutlets.

If you like, a béarnaise sauce (page 294) can be served with the lamb: in which case you wouldn't really need the gravy as well, except a little to mix with the beans.

The ordinary English cut of best end of neck can, of course, be cooked in the same way, allowing a little longer cooking time.

It should make ample helpings for four.

PERSIAN LAMB *with* AUBERGINES

Maqlub of aubergines

Although this is rather a trouble to make it is one of the best of all aubergine dishes, and the rice, which absorbs some of the flavour of the meat, is particularly good. A good bowl of yoghurt can be served with it, and a tomato or green salad.

4–5 medium-sized aubergines, salt, 125g/¼lb rice, ½ a teaspoon ground allspice, thyme or marjoram, 2 cloves of garlic, 375g/¾lb minced lamb cooked or raw, olive oil, 1 onion, 60g/2oz almonds, 450ml/¾ pint meat stock.

Cut the unpeeled aubergines in slices about 5mm/¼ inch thick, salt them and leave them for an hour. Put the rice to soak in water for an hour. Mix the spice, a little thyme or marjoram and chopped garlic with the meat. Dry the aubergines and fry them lightly in oil, then fry the sliced onion. Put a layer of the fried aubergines in a round ovenproof dish; on top put a layer of the meat. Sprinkle with a few sliced blanched almonds and the fried onion. Repeat until all the aubergines and meat are used up, and on top put the drained rice. Pour over half the meat stock, cover the dish and cook over a low flame for about 20 minutes. Add the rest of the stock and cook for another 30–40 minutes until the rice is almost cooked.

Put an ovenproof serving dish upside down over the top, turn out the contents and put in the oven for another 10–15 minutes. The rice will finish cooking and any liquid left will be absorbed.

Enough for six people. It can be reheated quite successfully, in a covered pan in a gentle oven.

COURGETTE MOUSSAKA

The more commonly known version of this excellent and useful dish is made with layers of aubergines, minced lamb and tomatoes, all rather highly flavoured with onions and spices and herbs, the whole arranged in layers and baked in a tin to make a rich, colourful and rather filling kind of pie. Sometimes courgettes or even potatoes are substituted for the aubergines, and the courgette version is particularly good.

500g/1lb small courgettes, salt, 4 tablespoons olive oil, a large onion, 500g/1lb finely chopped or minced meat which can be lamb or beef, cooked or uncooked, pepper, a teaspoon each of freshly ground allspice and dried or fresh mint, 2 eggs, 750g/1½lb tomatoes, a clove of garlic, 2 or 3 tablespoons each of stock and breadcrumbs.

Wash the courgettes but do not peel them. Cut each one lengthways into slices about 2.5mm/1 inch thick. Salt them slightly and leave them to drain for an hour or so. Shake them dry in a tea towel, fry them gently in olive oil until they are tender. When all are done, remove the courgettes, put more oil into the pan and in this fry the finely sliced or chopped onion until it is pale yellow. Put in the meat. If it is already cooked just stir it round until it is amalgamated with the onion. If it is raw meat let it cook gently for about 10 minutes until it is nicely browned. Add seasonings and herbs and, off the heat, stir in the beaten eggs.

In a separate pan put the skinned and chopped tomatoes and the crushed garlic clove and simmer until most of the moisture has evaporated. Season with salt and pepper.

Now coat a 1.25–1.5-litre/2–2½-pint square or round, and not too deep, cake tin lightly with oil. Put in a layer of courgettes, then one of meat, then one of tomatoes, and so on until all the ingredients are used up, finishing with a rather thick layer of the tomatoes. On top sprinkle breadcrumbs and then moisten with the stock. Cover the tin with a piece of foil. Cook, with the tin standing on a baking sheet, in a low oven at 160°C/gas 3, for an hour, but at half-time remove the foil. If the moussaka looks dry add a little more stock. Serve hot.

With the layers of pale green courgettes in between the red and brown of the tomatoes and meat, this is a very beautiful-looking dish, which, provided it has not been overcooked to start with, can quite successfully be reheated.

For a moussaka with aubergines instead of courgettes the proceeding is precisely the same, and you need 2 to 4 aubergines according to size, unpeeled, cut lengthways into thinnish slices and salted before being fried in oil.

Enough for four to five people.

PORK BAKED *with* WINE *and* ORANGES

1 or 2 cloves of garlic, herbs (parsley, marjoram, rosemary), salt and pepper, a joint or loin of pork, weighing about 2kg/4lb boned, skinned and tied in a sausage shape, a little olive oil, 125ml/¼ pint clear meat or chicken stock, 3 oranges, 4 tablespoons Madeira, white wine or dry vermouth, breadcrumbs.

Chop a clove or two of garlic with a little parsley, marjoram, a scrap of rosemary, and salt and pepper. Rub this all over the meat, pressing it well in along the lean side of the joint. Pour a tablespoon of olive oil into a baking dish, put in the meat and all the bones and skin which have been removed. Let it cook for 10 to 15 minutes in a fairly hot oven at 200°C/gas 6, before adding the hot stock. Then cook uncovered in a very slow oven at 150°C/gas 2, for 2½–3 hours.

From time to time baste it with a little of its own liquid. A quarter of an hour before the end of cooking, take out the bones and skin, squeeze the juice of half an orange over the meat and add the wine. Strew the breadcrumbs on the fat side of the joint and return it to the oven.

Slice the remaining 2½ oranges into thin rounds, and blanch them for about 3 minutes in boiling water. Drain carefully, and put them in the sauce round the meat for the last 5 minutes of the cooking time.

Serve with sliced oranges all round the meat, and the sauce separately. This dish is even better cold than hot, and if this is how you intend to serve it, cook the sauce for an extra half-hour or so after the meat has been removed, strain it into a bowl, chill it and remove the fat before serving it.

Enough for six to eight people.

PORK COOKED *in* MILK

Maiale al latte

45g/1½oz butter, an onion, 45g/1½oz ham, garlic, about 750g/1½lb loin of pork, or boned leg, without the rind, rolled into a sausage shape, coriander seeds, marjoram, basil or fennel, salt and pepper, 950ml/1½ pints of milk.

Melt the butter, brown the finely chopped onion in it, then the ham, also finely chopped.

Stick a clove of garlic inside the rolled meat, together with 3 or 4 coriander seeds and a little marjoram, basil or fennel. Rub it with salt and pepper and brown it in the butter with the onion and ham. In the meantime heat the milk to boiling point in another pan. When the meat has browned pour the milk over it. Add no more salt or pepper. Keep the pan steadily simmering at a moderate pace, uncovered. Gradually a golden web of skin begins to form over the top of the meat while the milk is bubbling away underneath. Don't disturb it until it has been cooking for a good hour. At this moment break the skin and scrape the sides of the pan, stirring it all into the remaining milk, which will be beginning to get thick. In about another 30 minutes the milk should have reduced to about a small cupful, full of all the delicious little bits of bacon and onion, and the meat should be encased in a fine crust formed by the milk, while it is moist and tender inside. It is at this moment that any meat or bird cooked in milk should be carefully watched, for the remaining sauce evaporates with disconcerting rapidity, leaving the meat to stick and burn.

To serve, pour the sauce, with all its grainy little pieces, over the meat. Can be eaten hot or cold. But best cold, I think.

Whatever the weight of the piece of meat to be cooked in this fashion, allow roughly 600ml/1 pint of milk per 500g/1lb. One or two readers have told me they find this recipe very tricky. It can be made easier by transferring the dish, uncovered, to a moderate oven, after the web has formed. When the meat is cooked, return the pan to the top of the stove and reduce the sauce.

Enough for six people.

PORK CHOPS BAKED *with* AROMATIC HERBS

This dish is a good example of one in which the scent of aromatic herbs makes the whole difference; it should provide ideas for many others of the same sort. If you have time, prepare the pork chops an hour or so in advance, or in the morning for the evening, so that the herbs and seasonings have already scented the meat before cooking starts.

Buy a couple of nice thick *chops* without rind. Score the meat lightly on each side. Cut a peeled clove of *garlic* in half and rub the meat with the cut surface. Press in *salt* and a little freshly ground black *pepper*. Coat each side of both chops with *olive oil*. In a baking dish arrange half a dozen twigs of wild *thyme*, several whole *bay leaves* and a dozen *fennel* stalks. On top put the chops. Put the dish under the grill, and let the chops brown lightly on each side. Now cover the dish with oiled paper or foil and transfer it to a low oven, at 160°C/gas 3, and leave for 40–50 minutes. Finally, pour off into a bowl any excess fat which has come from the meat during cooking. Serve the chops as they are, in their cooking dish, herbs and all.

A simple enough dish, deliciously flavoured; and needing no accompaniment other than a green salad, or a few sliced tomatoes dressed with oil and sprinkled with onion and parsley.

Enough for two people.

GRILLED PORK CHOPS *with* CIDER SAUCE

Côtes de porc vallée d'auge

Chop 3 or 4 *shallots* very finely with *parsley*; season with *salt* and *pepper*; score 4 *pork chops* lightly on each side and spread with the shallot mixture. Moisten with melted *butter or olive oil*, and grill. Have ready a glass of *cider* heated in a small pan and when the chops are cooked transfer the grilling pan to the top of the stove; pour in the cider; let it bubble over a very fast flame until it has amalgamated with the juices from the meat and formed a sauce, which will take 2 or 3 minutes. If *Calvados* is available, add a small quantity after the cider has been poured into the pan. It cuts the richness of the pork. Straw potatoes, or a purée, or simply a plain green salad go with the pork chops.

Enough for four people.

PORK NOISETTES *with a* PRUNE *and* CREAM SAUCE

Noisettes de porc aux pruneaux

This dish, a speciality of Tours, is a sumptuous one, rich and handsome in appearance as well as in its flavours. But it is not one to try out for the first time on guests, unless you can be sure of ten minutes or so uninterrupted in the kitchen while you make the sauce. Neither is the dish exactly a light one, and is perhaps best eaten, as pork dishes are always supposed to be, at midday rather than in the evening.

Both the utensil for cooking the pork and the dish to serve it in are important. The first should be a shallow and heavy pan to go on top of the stove, either a sauté pan or the kind of dish in which a whole flat fish is poached; failing this the meat will first have to be browned in a frying pan and then transferred to an oven dish. The serving dish should be a big oval one, preferably one which can go for a few minutes into the oven without risk.

300g/10oz very fine large juicy prunes (there should be approximately 2 dozen, and the best Californian prunes are perfect for the dish), a half-bottle of wine, which should, by rights, be white Vouvray, 6 to 8 noisettes cut from the boned and skinned chump end of the loin of pork, each one weighing about 90g/3oz, seasonings, a little flour, 60g/2oz butter, a tablespoon redcurrant jelly, approximately 300ml/½ pint thick cream (you may not use it all but it is as well to have this quantity, as I will explain presently).

First, put the prunes to steep in a bowl covered with 300ml/½ pint of the wine; this is supposed to be done overnight, but with good prunes a half-day will be sufficient. After which, cover them and put them in a very low oven to cook. They can stay there an hour or so. They should be quite tender but not mushy, and the wine must not evaporate.

Season the pork very well with freshly ground pepper and salt and sprinkle each noisette with flour. Melt the butter in the pan; put in the meat; let it gently take colour on one side and turn it. Keep the heat low, because the butter must not brown. After 10 minutes pour in the remaining 2 tablespoons or so of the white wine. Cover the pan. Cook very gently, covered, on top of the stove, or in the oven if necessary, for approximately 10–15 minutes, but the timing must depend upon the quality of the meat. Test it with a skewer to see if it is tender.

When it is nearly ready (but it will not, being pork, come to harm if left a bit longer even after it is tender), pour the juice from the prunes over the meat – this, of course, must be done over direct heat on top of the stove – and keep the prunes themselves hot in the oven. When the juice has bubbled and reduced a little, transfer the meat to the serving dish and keep it hot.

To the sauce in the pan add the redcurrant jelly and stir until it has dissolved. Now pour in some of the cream; if the pan is wide enough it will almost instantly start bubbling and thickening; stir it, shake the pan and add a little more cream, and when the sauce is just beginning to get shiny and really thick, pour it over the meat, arrange the prunes all round and serve it quickly. The amount of cream you use depends both on how much juice there was from the prunes and how quickly the sauce has thickened; sometimes it gets too thick too quickly, and a little more cream must be added. In any case there should be enough sauce to cover the meat, but not, of course, the prunes. These are served as they are, not 'boned', as the French cooks say.

On the whole, I think it is better to drink red wine than white with this dish. And, of course, you do not serve any vegetables with it. Even with light first-and last-course dishes, 8 noisettes should be enough for four people.

CAFE DU GLOBE

BARBADOS BAKED *and* GLAZED GAMMON

Serve this gammon hot with creamed spinach and jacket potatoes or a purée of red lentils, or cold with a salad of cubed honeydew melon seasoned with lemon juice and a pinch of powdered ginger.

Soak a 2–2.5-kg/4–5-lb piece of *middle leg* for 12–24 hours, and preferably for 36, in cold water to cover (and also keep a cloth or dish over the basin). Change the water two or three times. When the time comes to cook the gammon, wrap it in two sheets of aluminium cooking foil, twisting the edges together so that the joint is completely enclosed. Stand this parcel on a grid placed in a baking tin. Half fill the tin with water – the steam coming from it during cooking helps to keep the gammon moist.

Place low down in a very moderate oven, at 160°C/gas 3, and allow approximately 45 minutes per 500g/1lb. The only attention you have to give it is simply to turn the parcel over at half-time.

Remove from the oven, leave for about 40 minutes, then unwrap the foil, and peel off the rind – this is very easily done while the gammon is still hot – and score the fat in diamond shapes. Replace the gammon in the rinsed-out baking tin.

Have ready the following mixture: 2 heaped tablespoons *soft brown sugar*, 1 teaspoon *Dijon mustard* and 4 tablespoons *milk*, all stirred together. Pour this mixture over the gammon, pressing some of it well down into the fat. If you feel you must, stud the fat with whole *cloves*.

Place the tin near the top of the oven – still at the same temperature – and cook the gammon for another 20–35 minutes, basting frequently with the milk and sugar mixture, which will eventually turn into a beautiful dark golden shining glaze.

The sugar, mustard and milk-glaze mixture is by far the most effective, as well as the cheapest and most simple, of any I have ever tried. There really is no need for fanciful additions of rum, orange juice or pineapple chunks.

Whether you keep your cooked gammon or bacon in a refrigerator or a larder do keep it wrapped in clean greaseproof paper, constantly renewed. In this way it will keep sweet and moist down to the last slice.

Enough for eight to ten people.

WINE *in the* KITCHEN

Nobody has ever been able to find out why the English regard a glass of wine added to a soup or stew as a reckless foreign extravagance and at the same time spend pounds on bottled sauces, gravy powders, soup cubes, ketchups and artificial flavourings. If every kitchen contained a bottle each of red wine, white wine and inexpensive port for cooking, hundreds of store cupboards could be swept clean for ever of the cluttering debris of commercial sauce bottles and all synthetic aids to flavouring. To the basic sum of red, white and port I would add, if possible, brandy, and half a dozen miniature bottles of assorted liqueurs for flavouring sweet dishes and fruit salads, say Kirsch, Apricot Brandy, Grand Marnier, Orange Curaçao, Cointreau and Framboise. Sherry is a good addition, but should be used in cooking with the utmost discretion.

THE COOKING OF WINE

The fundamental fact to remember about the use of wine in cooking is that the wine is cooked. In the process the alcohol is volatilized and what remains is the wonderful flavour which perfumes the dish and fills the kitchen with an aroma of delicious things to come. In any dish which does not require long cooking the wine should be reduced to about half the quantity originally poured in the pan, by the process of very fast boiling. In certain soups, for instance, when the vegetables have been browned and the herbs and spices added, a glass of wine is poured in, the flame turned up, and the wine allowed to bubble fiercely for 2 or 3 minutes; when it starts to look a little syrupy on the bottom of the pan, add the water or stock; this process makes all the difference to the flavour and immediately gives the soup body and colour.

When making gravy for a roast, strain off the fat, pour a ½ glass of any wine round the roasting-pan, at the same time scraping up all the juice which has come out of the meat, let it sizzle for a minute or two, add a little water, cook gently another 2 minutes and your gravy is ready.

For a duck, add the juice of an orange and a tablespoon of redcurrant jelly; for fish which has been grilled add white wine to the butter in the pan, lemon juice and chopped parsley or capers; to the butter in which you have fried escalopes of veal add a little red wine or madeira, let it bubble and then pour in a ½ cup of cream.

TO MARINATE IN WINE

To marinate meat, fish or game is to give it a bath lasting anything between 2 hours and several days in a marinade usually composed of a mixture of wine, herbs, garlic, onions and spices, sometimes with the addition of a little vinegar, olive oil or water. A tough piece of stewing beef is improved by being left several hours in a marinade of red wine; it can then be braised or stewed in the marinade, strained of the vegetables and herbs which, by this time, have become sodden, and fresh ones added.

A leg of mutton can be given a taste approximating to venison by being marinated for several days. It is then carefully dried and roasted, the strained marinade being reduced and used for the sauce. For certain terrines I always marinate the prepared meat or game for 2 or 3 hours in white wine, but red can be used.

THE CHOICE OF THE WINE

There is no hard-and-fast rule as to the use of white or red wine, port or brandy for any particular dish. Generally speaking, of course, red wine is better for meat and game dishes, white for fish, but one can usually be substituted for the other, an exception being *moules marinière*, for which white wine is a necessity, as red turns the whole dish a rather disagreeable blue colour, and any essentially white dish, such as a delicate concoction of sole, must have white wine.

from French Country Cooking, *1951*

POULTRY *and* GAME BIRDS

The French housewife mixes chopped fresh pork or pure pork sausagemeat with eggs and herbs to stuff a big fat fowl, she poaches it with vegetables and a bouquet of herbs and the result is that *poule au pot* which good King Henry of Navarre wished that all his subjects might eat on every Sunday of the year. Or perhaps that same housewife will cook her chicken without a stuffing and serve it with a dish of rice and a cream sauce; or if it is a plump young bird, she will roast it simply in butter and serve it on the familiar long oval dish with a tuft of watercress at each end and the buttery juices in a separate sauce-boat. The farmer's wife, faced with an old hen no longer of use for laying, will (if she has inherited her grandmother's recipes and has a proper sense of the fitness of things) bone the bird, stuff it richly with pork and veal and even, perhaps, truffles if it is for a special occasion, and simmer the bird with wine and a calf's foot to make a clear and savoury jelly, so that the old hen will be turned into a fine and handsome galantine fit for celebrations and feast days.

If she is in a hurry, the French cook will cut up a roasting chicken into joints, fry them gently in butter or oil, add stock or wine, perhaps vegetables and little cubes of salt pork as well, and the result will be the *poulet sauté* which, in a restaurant, will be glorified with some classic or regional label, or named after a minister or famous writer or actress. *Parmentier* it will be if there are little bits of potato; *provençale* if there are tomatoes; *chausseur* or *forestière* if there are mushrooms.

Young game birds, pheasant, partridge and grouse (for which the nearest French equivalent is the *coq de bruyère*), are best roasted either on the spit, in the oven or in a heavy pot on top of the stove. The professional chefs, of course, like to do all sorts of elaborate and expensive dishes with them, usually involving truffles and *foie gras*. Pâtés and terrines offer an excellent solution, perhaps the best, to people who have plenty of game at their disposal, while the deep freeze is kinder to game than to vegetables, meat or fish.

CHICKEN *with* TARRAGON

Poulet à l'estragon

Tarragon is a herb which has a quite remarkable affinity with chicken, and a *poulet à l'estragon*, made with fresh tarragon, is one of the great treats of the summer. There are any amount of different ways of cooking a tarragon-flavoured chicken dish: here is a particularly successful one.

For a plump roasting *chicken* weighing about 1kg/2lb knead 30g/1oz *butter* with a tablespoon of *tarragon* leaves, half a clove of chopped *garlic*, *salt* and *pepper*. Put this inside the bird, which should be well coated with *olive oil*. Roast the bird lying on its side on a grid in a baking dish. Turn it over at half-time (45 minutes altogether in a pretty hot oven at 200°C/gas 6 or an hour in a moderate oven at 180°C/gas 4 should be sufficient; those who have a roomy grill might try grilling it, which takes about 20 minutes, and gives much more the impression of a spit-roasted bird, but it must be constantly watched and turned over very carefully, so that the legs are as well done as the breast).

When the bird is cooked, heat a small glass of *brandy* in a soup ladle, set light to it, pour it flaming over the chicken and rotate the dish so that the flames spread and continue to burn as long as possible. Return the bird to a low oven at 150°C/gas 2 for 5 minutes, during which time the brandy sauce will mature and lose its raw flavour. At this moment you can, if you like, enrich the sauce with a few spoonfuls of thick *cream* and, at la Mère Michel's Paris restaurant, from where the recipe originally came, they add *Madeira* to the sauce. Good though this is, it seems to me a needless complication.

Enough for four people.

SAUTÉD CHICKEN *with* OLIVES *and* TOMATOES

Poulet sauté aux olives de Provence

The success of all dishes in which the chicken is cut before cooking lies in having presentable portions. Nothing is more dismal than those *poulets sautés* and *fricassées de poulet*, in which all you get on your plate is an unidentifiable and bony little joint from which the dry flesh is detached only with great determination. Some skill is needed to joint a chicken into several pieces and, on the whole, it is more satisfactory to buy smaller chickens and simply split them, or have them split, in half.

One 875g–1kg/1¾–2lb chicken, 1 lemon, 1 clove of garlic, a sprig of thyme or basil, flour, olive oil.

Split the chicken in two, as for grilling. Season the halves of chicken, rub them with lemon juice and insert a very small piece of garlic and a little sprig of thyme or basil under the skin of each piece. Dust with flour. In an ordinary heavy frying pan heat 5 tablespoons of olive oil. Make it fairly hot and put in the pieces of chicken skin side down. When they are golden on one side turn them over and, when both sides are seized, turn them over again, turn the heat low and cover the pan, removing the lid only from time to time to turn the chicken. After 20 minutes, transfer the chicken and nearly all the oil to a baking dish and put in a very low oven, covered, while the sauce is made.

For this have ready: *a small glass of wine, white for preference but red if it is easier, 2 anchovy fillets roughly pounded with 2 cloves of garlic, 4 large ripe tomatoes, skinned and chopped, a sprig each of thyme, marjoram and basil, 125g/4oz stoned black olives.*

First pour in the wine, detaching any brown pieces and juices which may have adhered to the pan. Let it bubble and reduce. Add the anchovy and garlic mixture, stir well in, then add the tomatoes and the herbs. Simmer until the sauce is thick, add the olives, let them get hot and taste the sauce for seasoning.

Test the chicken by running a skewer through the thick part of the leg and, if the juices come out white, it is cooked. If still red, leave a little longer in the oven. For serving, arrange the chicken in a long dish on top of the very hot sauce.

Enough for two people.

RCUTERIE VOLAILLES
NCHE.F
VISA
VISA
CHÈQUE DE TABLE
Ticket Restaurant

CHICKEN POT-ROASTED *with* FENNEL *and* HAM

Basically, this is a dish of the old-fashioned country cooking of Tuscany. The final blaze of brandy is a modern flourish.

A half dozen each of dried fennel stalks and whole bay leaves, a 1.25kg/2½lb roasting chicken, 2 or 3 garlic cloves, a strip of lemon peel, 125–175g/4–6oz mild, cooked ham in one piece, a half dozen whole black peppercorns, 60g/2oz butter, optionally 4 tablespoons brandy.

Tie the fennel stalks and bay leaves into a bunch. Put them into an earthenware or cast-iron pot. On top put the chicken (lying on its side) stuffed with the peeled garlic cloves, the strip of lemon peel and the ham cut into finger-thick strips and liberally sprinkled with coarsely crushed black peppercorns (no salt). Add the butter in small pieces. Cover the pot, put it low down into a medium-hot oven, 190°C/gas 5. Leave for 45 minutes. Now turn the chicken, basting it with the butter, and return it to the oven. Cook for another 45–50 minutes.

Now uncover the pot, turn the chicken breast upwards and leave it to brown in the oven for 10–15 minutes.

To give the dish a spectacular finish, and to bring out to their full extent the scents and flavours of the aromatic herbs, transfer the pot to a mild heat on top of the stove. Pour the brandy into a ladle, warm it, ignite it, pour it flaming over the chicken and rotate the pan so that the flames spread. After they have died down, transfer the chicken to an ovenproof serving dish but leave the juices in the casserole to cook and mature for another 3 or 4 minutes. Pour them off into a sauce boat.

For serving, arrange the fennel stalks and bay leaves on the dish with the chicken. Make sure, when the chicken is carved, that everybody has a share of the little strips of ham from the inside of the bird.

Enough for four people.

VOLAILLES
GIBIERS

CHICKEN BAKED *with* ITALIAN SPICE *and* OLIVE OIL

A really good roasting chicken of approximately 1.8kg/3¼lb, 3–4 tablespoons good olive oil, ½ a teaspoon of the Italian spice mixture given below, and salt.

For the spice mixture: *3 teaspoons white peppercorns, approximately ½ a small nutmeg, 1 teaspoon juniper berries, ¼ teaspoon whole cloves.*

Put all the spices in a coffee mill and grind them until they are in a powder. The nutmeg takes the longest, and there are moments when the coffee grinder makes a rather angry whine. The quantity makes enough to fill a little glass jar of approximately 45g/1½oz capacity, and is sufficient to last about 6 months.

Rub the cleaned chicken with salt and paint it with about half the olive oil, then rub in the spice.

Wrap the chicken in paper or foil, put it on its side in a shallow ovenproof dish. Cook it on the centre shelf of a medium-hot oven at 180°C/gas 4, for 30 minutes before unwrapping it, painting it again with olive oil, turning it over on to the other side, re-covering it with the paper, and this time leaving it for 20 minutes. Now turn the chicken breast upwards, use the rest of the olive oil for brushing it over once more, and leave it, again covered, for the final 20 minutes.

Remove the paper or foil carefully so that the juices fall back into the baking dish. Heat them quickly, pour them into a small bowl or sauce-boat and use them as the only sauce necessary with the chicken. It will be excellent as a cold dish. Leave it to cool naturally, and serve it with a very simple salad.

The taste of the spice and the olive oil makes a delicate seasoning for the chicken which, given a properly reared bird, will be perfectly cooked, very moist, tender, and the legs still a little pink inside.

The small quantity of olive oil is all that is needed for keeping the chicken moist. All the basting considered necessary with poor-quality birds is quite redundant when you are dealing with a good one. And as for that maddening thing called a bulb baster, I never have understood what anyone could possibly need it for.

Enough for four to six people.

CHICKEN BAKED *with* GREEN PEPPER *and* CINNAMON BUTTER

This recipe also works well with pheasant. For a young bird of about 850g/1¾lb, the timing and temperature are as for the chicken. But the pheasant should be wrapped in well-buttered paper or foil.

For a 1.25–1.5-kg/2½–3-lb roasting chicken have ready 45g/1½oz of the spiced butter described below.

Lift the skin of the chicken, rub salt and then the spiced butter well over the flesh, making a few gashes with a small sharp knife in the drumsticks and thick part of the legs so that the spices will penetrate. Put a little more of the butter inside the chicken. If possible leave for an hour or two before cooking.

Put the chicken, with a few bay leaves, into a shallow baking dish into which it will just fit. Cook, uncovered, on the centre shelf of a moderate oven at 180°C/gas 4, allowing 20 minutes on each side and 20 minutes breast upwards. Baste with the juices each time the chicken is turned. At the end of the cooking time the skin should be beautifully golden and crisp.

Serve with lemon quarters and watercress, and the buttery juices poured into a little sauce boat. A simple green salad with a very light dressing is the best accompaniment.

For the green pepper and cinnamon butter, crush 2 teaspoons of *green pepper berries* with a small sliver of *garlic* and ½ a teaspoon of ground *cinnamon*. Into the mixture work 45–60g/1½–2oz of *butter*. When thoroughly amalgamated add a scant teaspoon of *salt* – less if you have used salted butter. Store in a small covered jar in the refrigerator, or make in larger quantities and store in the freezer, keeping a small jar in the refrigerator for current consumption.

Coriander, *ground cumin* and/or *ginger* can be combined with the cinnamon in this recipe, or used instead, and proportions of the spices can be increased or diminished according to taste.

Enough for four people.

MASSALÉ
SUMAC
GINGEMBRE
50 grs 4€
100 grs 7€
ANIS VERT
50 grs 4€
100 grs 7€
SAFRAN
en Pistils
d' Espagne
PIMENT DOUX
CARRY INDIAN
50 grs 4€
100 grs 7€
CARDAMOME
SPECIAL CHILI (BEANS)
50 grs 4€
100 grs 7€
Cumin
50 grs. 4€
100 grs. 7€
CARRY de BOMBAY
au goût anisé
50 grs 4€
Moutarde moulue
50 grs. 4€
100 grs. 7€
MUSCADE
Pour Quiche Lorraine
-cuisine à base de
50 Grs.
100 Grs.
PAPRIKA DOUX
POIVRE de CAYENNE
25 Grs 3€
5€
MACIS
écorce de la noix muscade
25 Grs
50 Grs. 8€

RAS EL HANOUT
GARAM MASSALA
QUATRE ÉPICES
50 grs. 4€
100 grs 7€
POIVRE de GUINÉE
POIVRE de JAMAÏQUE
CINQ PARFUMS
Mélange Chinois pour Soupe, nem.....
50 grs. 4€
100 grs 7€
SP. ROUILLE
Mélange pour Soupe de Poisson. A mélanger avec la mayonnaise....
POIVRE BLANC
100 gr. 8€
CANNELLE
50 grs. 4€
100 grs 7€
RAS EL HANOUT
Pour Tajine.
50 grs 4€
100 grs 7€
POIVRE SELIM

DUCK *with* FIGS

Put 16 fresh *figs* to marinate in a half bottle of *Sauternes* for 24 hours.

Make a stock from *veal bones*, the *giblets of the duck*, 2 sliced *onions*, 2 *carrots*, a clove of crushed *garlic*, and a branch of *thyme or marjoram*. Season the duck with *salt* and *pepper* and put a piece of *butter* and a piece of *orange peel* inside the bird. In a deep earthenware terrine with a lid put 60g/2oz of butter, and put the duck in the terrine, breast downwards, and another 30g/1oz of butter on top of the duck. Let it brown in a fairly hot oven at 200°C/gas 6 without the lid, for 15 minutes; now pour the butter off, turn the duck over, and pour in the wine from the figs; let this cook 5 minutes and add about 300ml/½ pint of the stock. Put the cover on the casserole and cook in a slow oven at 160°C/gas 3 for 1 hour, until the duck is tender.

Now take out the duck and remove the vegetables and giblets; leave the lid off the casserole, turn the oven up and let the juice bubble for 15 minutes to reduce it; put in the figs, and let them cook 5 minutes if they are the very ripe purple ones, 10 minutes if they are green figs; take them out and arrange them round the duck. Leave the stock to cool. Remove the fat and pour the liquid over the duck and figs; it should set to a light jelly.

Serve the duck with a plain green salad.

Enough for three to four people.

WELSH SALT DUCK

This method of salting and cooking a duck is adapted from a Welsh recipe dating back at least a century. (So far as I know, the first time it appeared in print was in Lady Llanover's *Good Cookery* published in 1867.) In the original, the duck was eaten hot, with an onion sauce, which would have been rather heavy, but both the preliminary salting and the slow-cooking methods are worth reviving; they produce a deliciously flavoured and tender duck; and the melon goes to perfection with cold duck. It goes without saying that, if you prefer, a salad of sliced oranges more usual with duck can be substituted. Buy and prepare your duck three days in advance.

1 large duck (about 3kg/6lb gross weight), 125g/¼lb sea or rock salt or coarse kitchen salt, 1 honeydew melon, lemon juice.

Place the duck in a deep dish. Rub it all over with the salt. Repeat this process twice a day for three days. Keep the duck covered, and in a cool place (use the giblets at once for stock, and the liver for an omelette), ideally in a larder rather than the refrigerator.

In the morning for the evening cook the duck as follows: first rinse off excess salt; then place the bird in a deep oven-dish. (I use a large oval enamelled casserole, which will stand inside a baking tin.) Cover the duck with cold water, put water also in the outer tin. Transfer the whole contraption to the centre of a very low oven, at 150°C/gas 2, and cook, uncovered, for just 2 hours.

Remove the duck from its liquid (which will probably be rather too salty to use for stock) and leave it to cool.

Serve the duck quite plain and cold, its sole accompaniment the flesh of a honeydew melon cut into small cubes and seasoned only with lemon juice. Jacket potatoes could also be served with the duck, but are hardly necessary, and do nothing to help the appreciation of this very delicately flavoured bird.

Enough for four people.

DUCK *in* SOUR-SWEET SAUCE

Anitra in agrodolce

2 large onions, 60g/2oz butter, 1 duck weighing 2–2.5kg/4–5lb, salt and pepper, flour, a pinch of ground cloves, 450ml/¾ pint chicken stock or water, a little fresh mint, 2 tablespoons sugar, 2 tablespoons wine vinegar.

Slice the onions very thin and melt them in the heated butter. Season the duck with salt and pepper, roll it in flour, and put it to brown with the onions. Add the ground cloves. When the duck is well browned pour over the heated stock or water, cover the pan, and cook gently for 2–3 hours. Turn the duck over from time to time so that it cooks evenly. When it is tender remove it from the pan and keep it warm in the oven. Pour off as much fat as possible from the sauce and stir in the chopped mint (about 2 tablespoons). Have the sugar ready caramelized – that is, heated in a pan with a little water until it turns toffee coloured. Stir this into the sauce and add the vinegar. See that the seasoning is right and serve the sauce separately as soon as it has acquired a thick syrup-like consistency. This dish is also excellent cold. Instead of pouring off the fat before adding the mint, sugar and vinegar, make the sauce as directed and remove the fat – it makes the most delicious dripping – when the sauce is cold.

Enough for four people.

TURKEY BREASTS *with* MARSALA

Filetti di tacchino al marsala

Cut the two sides of the breast of not too large a turkey into fillets. From a 4kg/8lb *turkey* you get 8–10 good-sized fillets. Flatten them out a little on a wooden board, season them with *salt* and *pepper*, and dust them very lightly with *flour*. Melt a generous amount of *butter* in a frying pan (if they are all to be done at once you will probably need to keep two pans going at the same time). Cook the fillets on both sides, gently, for the butter must not blacken or burn. When they are nearly done pour over them first a small glassful of marsala, and after it has bubbled and amalgamated with the butter the same quantity of stock. Cook in the open pan for another 2 or 3 minutes.

Enough for four to six people.

PHEASANT *with* CREAM, CALVADOS *and* APPLE

Faisan à la cauchoise

This is, I think, the best of the many versions of pheasant with apples and Calvados, usually called *faisan normand*. It goes well with a little dish of diced sweet apple, previously fried golden in butter and kept warm in the oven: 2 apples will be sufficient for one pheasant.

Cook a tender roasting *pheasant* in *butter* in a heavy iron or earthenware casserole on top of the stove, turning it over once or twice so that each side is nicely browned. It will take about 40–45 minutes to cook. Carve it, transfer it to the serving dish and keep it warm. Pour off the juices into a shallow pan; let them bubble; pour in a small glass of warmed *Calvados* (or *brandy* or *whisky*), set light to it, shake the pan and when the flames have burnt out add a good measure, 250–300ml/8–10fl oz, of *thick cream*. Shake the pan, lifting and stirring the cream until it thickens. Season with a very little salt and pepper. Pour the sauce over the pheasant.

Enough for two people.

ROAST PHEASANT *with* CHESTNUT SAUCE

A young but fully grown pheasant will weigh about 750g/1½lb and takes approximately 45 minutes to roast.

For the chestnut sauce, which can be made a day or two in advance and slowly reheated: *250g/½lb chestnuts, 45g/1½oz butter, 2 sticks of celery, one rasher of bacon, about 6 tablespoons port, a little stock or cream.*

Put a lump of butter inside the bird, wrap it in well-buttered greaseproof paper, place it on its side on a grid standing in a baking tin and cook in the centre of a preheated fairly hot oven at 190°C/gas mark 5.

Turn it over after the first 20 minutes, after another 15 minutes remove the paper and turn the bird breast upwards for the last 10 minutes.

Score the chestnuts on one side, bake them in a moderate oven at 180°C/gas 4 for 15 minutes, shell and skin them. Chop them roughly. Heat the butter, put in the chopped celery and bacon, add the chestnuts, the port, an equal quantity of water, and a very little salt. Cover the saucepan and cook very gently for about 30 minutes until the chestnuts are quite tender. When reheating, enrich the mixture with either a couple of tablespoons of rich meat or game stock or double cream.

The mixture is fairly solid, really more like a vegetable dish than a sauce proper, but whatever you like to call it, it goes to perfection with pheasant. A good creamy bread sauce or simply crisp breadcrumbs put in a baking tin with a little butter and left in the oven for about 15–20 minutes could provide an alternative, and personally I always like a few fried or baked chipolata sausages with a pheasant.

Enough for two people.

PARTRIDGES BRAISED *in* WHITE WINE

Perdrix à l'auvergnate

125g/4oz salt pork or unsmoked streaky bacon, 60g/2oz butter, 4 partridges, 5 tablespoons brandy, 8 tablespoons white wine, 4 tablespoons clear veal or other meat or game stock, a little bouquet of bay leaf, parsley, thyme and a crushed clove of garlic.

If salt pork is being used, steep it for 1 hour in water. Cut it in small cubes. Put it with 30g/1oz of the butter in an earthenware or other heavy pan just large enough to hold the four birds. When the fat from the pork or bacon runs, put in the birds, breast downwards. (If they have been trussed for roasting, take out the wooden skewer before cooking them; it only makes the birds more difficult to fit into the pot and is a nuisance when it comes to serving them.) After 2 or 3 minutes pour in the warmed brandy; set light to it. Shake the pan so that the flames spread. When these die down, put in the white wine, warmed if you are cooking in an earthenware pan. Let it bubble a minute; add the stock and the bouquet. Cover the pan with paper or foil and a well-fitting lid. Transfer to a slow oven, 160°C/gas 3, and cook for 1½–1¾ hours. Pour off all the liquid into a wide pan, and keep the birds hot in the serving dish. Reduce the liquid by fast boiling to about half its original volume. Off the fire, add the remaining butter and shake the pan until it has melted and given the sauce a slightly glazed appearance. Pour it over the partridges. Serve at the same time a purée of brown lentils or of celeriac and potatoes.

Enough for four people.

PIGEONS *with* PEAS

Piccioni coi piselli

A couple of chicken livers, added during the last 5 minutes of cooking, make a good addition to this excellent way of cooking pigeons.

1 onion, 30g/1oz butter, 60g/2oz cooked tongue, 60g/2oz ham or bacon, 2 pigeons, salt and pepper, basil, 125ml/4fl oz white wine, 125ml/4fl oz stock, 500g/1lb shelled green peas.

Brown the onion in the melted butter, add the tongue and the ham cut into squares, then the pigeons. Brown them all over. Season with salt, pepper, and basil. Pour the wine over the pigeons, and when it has bubbled a little pour in the stock. Cover the pan and simmer steadily for 1½ hours. Put in the peas and cook until they are tender (about 20 minutes). See that the seasoning is right.

Enough for two people.

PARA NAVIDAD

It is the last day of October. Here in the south-eastern corner of Spain the afternoon is hazy and the sun is warm, although not quite what it was a week ago. Then we were eating out-of-doors at midday, and were baked even in our cotton sweaters. The colours of the land are still those of late summer – roan, silver, lilac and ochre. In the soft light the formation of the rock and the ancient terracing of the hills become clearly visible. In the summer the sun on the limestone-white soil dazzles the eyes, and the greens of June obscure the shapes of the ravines and craggy outcroppings. Now there are signs of autumn on the leaves of some of the almond trees. They have turned a frail, transparent auburn, and this morning when I awoke I devoured two of the very first tangerines of the season. In the dawn their scent was piercing and their taste was sharp. During the night it had rained – not much, nothing like enough to affect the parched soil – but all the same there was a sheen on the rose bricks and grey stones of the courtyard. The immense old terra-cotta oil jar in the centre was freshly washed, and over the mountains a half-rainbow gave a pretty performance as we drank our breakfast coffee.

At midday we picked small figs, dusty purple and pale jade green. On the skins is a bloom not to be seen on midsummer figs. The taste, too, is quite different. The flesh is a clear garnet red, less rich and more subtle than that of the main-crop fruit, which is of the vernal variety, brilliant green. Some of the figs have split open and are half dried by the sun. In the north we can never taste fruit like this, fruit midway between fresh and dried. It has the same poignancy as the black Valencia grapes still hanging in heavy bunches on the vines. These, too, are in the process of transforming themselves – from fresh grapes to raisins on the stalk as we know them. Here the bunches have been tied up in cotton bags. The two ancients who tend the almond trees (this is Valencia almond country, and it has been a bad season. If the rain fails, next year's crop may prove to be another disaster) and who have known the estate of La Alfarella all their lives, were hoping that the grapes could be cut late and hung in the storeroom until Christmas. Their plans have been foiled by the wasps. This year there has been a fearsome plague of the persistent and destructive brutes. They have bitten their way through the protecting cotton, sucked out the juice of the fruit, and left nothing but husks. Here and there where a bunch has escaped the marauders, we have cut one and brought it back to the house in a basket with the green lemons and some of the wild thyme that has an almost overpowering scent, one that seems to be peculiar to Spanish thyme. It is perhaps fanciful, but it seems to have undertones of aniseed, chamomile, hyssop, lavender.

My English host, who has re-created this property of La Alfarella out of a ruin and is bringing its land back to life after twenty years of neglect, is at the cooking pots. He seizes on the green lemons and grates the skins of two of them into the meat mixture he is stirring up. He throws in a little of the sun-dried thyme and makes us a beguiling dish of *albóndigas*, little rissoles fried

in olive oil. He fries them skilfully and they emerge with a caramel-brown and gold coating reflecting the glaze of the shallow earthenware *sartén*, the frying dish in which they have been cooked and brought to the table. All the cooking here is done in the local earthenware pots. Even the water is boiled in them. They are very thick and sturdy, unglazed on the outside, and are used directly over the Butagaz flame, or sometimes on the wood fire in the open hearth. As yet there is no oven. That is one of next year's projects.

Surprisingly, in an isolated farmhouse in a country believed by so many people to produce the worst and most repetitive food in Europe, our diet has a good deal of variety, and some of the produce is of a very high quality. I have never eaten such delicate and fine-grained pork meat, and the cured fillet, *lomo de cerdo*, is by any standard a luxury worth paying for. The chicken and the rabbit that go into the ritual paella cooked in a vast burnished iron pan (only for paella on a big scale and for the frying of tortillas are metal pans used) over a crackling fire are tender, possessed of their true flavours. We have had little red mullet and fresh *sardines a la plancha*, grilled on primitive round tin grill plates made sizzling hot on the fire. This is the utensil, common to France, Italy, Spain and Greece, that also produces the best toast in the world – brittle and black-barred with the marks of the grill.

To start our midday meal we have, invariably, a tomato and onion salad, a few slices of fresh white cheese, and a dish of olives. The tomatoes are the Mediterranean ridged variety of which I never tire. They are huge, sweet, fleshy, richly red. Here they cut out and discard the central wedge, almost as we core apples, then slice the tomatoes into rough sections. They need no dressing, nothing but salt. With the roughly cut raw onions, sweet as all the vegetables grown in this limestone and clay soil, they make a wonderfully refreshing salad. It has no catchy name. It is just *ensalada*, and it cannot be reproduced without these sweet Spanish onions and Mediterranean tomatoes.

In the summer, seventeen-year-old Juanita asked for empty wine bottles to take to her married sister in the village, who would, she explained, preserve the tomatoes for the winter by slicing them, packing them in bottles, and sealing them with olive oil. They would keep for a year or more, Juanita said. Had her sister a bottle we could try? No. There were only two of last year's vintage left. They were to be kept *para Navidad*, for Christmas.

Yesterday in the market there were fresh dates from Elche, the first of the season. They are rather small, treacle-sticky, and come in tortoiseshell-cat colours: black, acorn brown, peeled-chestnut beige; like the lengths of Barcelona corduroy I have bought in the village shop. Inevitably, we were told that the best dates would not be ready until *Navidad*. That applies to the oranges and the muscatel raisins; and presumably also to the little rosy copper medlars now on sale in the market. They are not yet ripe enough to eat, so I suppose they are to be kept, like Juanita's sister's tomatoes, and the yellow and green Elche melons stored in an *esparto* basket in the house, for *Navidad*. We nibble at the candied melon peel in sugar-frosted and lemon-ice-coloured wedges we have bought in the market, and we have already torn open the Christmas-wrapped *mazapan* (it bears the trade name of El Alce, 'the elk'; a sad-faced moose with tired hooves and snow on its antlers decorates the paper), which is of a kind I have not before encountered. It is not at all like marzipan. It is very white, in bricks, with a consistency reminiscent of frozen sherbet. It is made of almonds and egg whites, and studded with crystallized fruit. There is the new season's quince cheese, the *carne de membrillo*, which we ought to be keeping to take to England for *Navidad* presents, and with it there is also a peach cheese. How is it that one never hears mention of this beautiful and delicious clear amber sweetmeat?

There are many more Mediterranean treats, cheap treats of autumn, like the newly brined green olives that the people of all olive-growing countries rightly regard as a delicacy. In Rome, one late October, I remember buying new green olives from a woman who was selling them straight from the barrel she had set up at a street corner. That was twelve years ago. I have never forgotten the fresh flavour of the Roman green olives. The manzanilla variety we have bought here come from Andalucía. They are neither green nor black, but purple, rose, lavender and brown, picked at varying stages of maturity, and intended for quick home consumption rather than for export. It is the tasting of familiar products at their point of origin (before they are graded, classified, prinked up, and imprisoned in bottles, tins, jars and packets) that makes them memorable; forever changes their aspect.

By chance, saffron is another commodity that has acquired a new dimension. It was somewhere on the way up to Córdoba that we saw the first purple patches of autumn-flowering saffron crocuses in bloom. On our return we called on Mercedes, the second village girl who works at La Alfarella, to tell her that we were back. Her father was preparing saffron – picking the orange stigmas one by one from the iridescent mauve flowers heaped up in a shoe box by his side and spreading them carefully on a piece of brown paper to dry. The heap of discarded crocus petals made a splash of intense and pure colour, shining like a pool of quicksilver in the cavernous shadows of the village living room. Every night, during the six-odd weeks that the season lasts, he prepares a boxful of flowers, so his wife told us. The bundle of saffron that she took out of a battered tin, wrapped in a square of paper, and gave to us must represent a fortnight's work. It is last year's vintage because there is not yet enough of the new season's batch to make a respectable offering. It appears to have lost nothing of its penetrating, quite violently acrid-sweet and pungent scent. It is certainly a handsome present that Mercedes' mother has given us, a rare present, straight from the source, and appropriate for us to take home to England for *Navidad*.

An even better one is the rain. At last, now it is real rain that is falling. The ancients have stopped work for the day, and most of the population of the village is gathered in the café. The day the rain comes the village votes its own fiesta day.

from The Spectator, *27 November 1964*

SAUCES

In simple French household cookery, because they are made freshly and in small quantities, sauces are rather different in both conception and execution from those made by chefs. The first principle is that whenever possible the sauce for a given dish is composed of elements supplied by the main ingredient of that dish itself. That is to say, the trimmings of a joint, the giblets of a bird, the carcass and head of a fish are simmered to make a broth or bouillon which will eventually supply the basis of the sauce. When no such elements are present, as in the case of grilled meat or fish, eggs, vegetables, rice, pasta and so on, then there are the egg and butter sauces of which béarnaise and hollandaise are the two most obvious, and the vegetable purée sauces such as *soubise* (onion), tomato, mushroom. Then there are the sauces of which the juices of the meat or fish itself after it has cooked form the basis, with cream or wine or stock and a binding of egg yolks or flour and butter (*beurre manié*) being used to complete it.

Butter, cream, eggs, wine, olive oil, fresh herbs; these are the ingredients which make the sauces, whether intricate or primitive, for summer food. A few fresh herbs and a little butter or olive oil, or an egg and a lemon, or perhaps a cup of stock and a small amount of cream, well seasoned and carefully mixed, will make little sauces which will turn the salads, vegetables, meat and fish of every day into fresh and original dishes. Fresh butter mixed with chives or parsley or tarragon melting into the juices of a grilled steak is just as delicious in its way as a grand sauce of truffles and Madeira, and more fitting for the summertime. For grilled lamb chops, use mint instead of parsley. Vinaigrette sauces (oil, lemon, herbs) and mayonnaise give plenty of scope to an inventive cook. For example, for a chicken salad add a little grated horseradish to the mayonnaise, or pounded tuna fish and anchovy in the Italian way; blanched and pounded herbs stirred into a mayonnaise make the *sauce verte* which is so good with salmon trout, a beaten white of egg lightens a mayonnaise to serve with salmon.

The foundations of many Italian sauces are olive oil and wine, and they are given consistency with breadcrumbs, cheese, tomato purée, pounded herbs and spices. They are simpler to cook than French sauces, there are fewer traps for the unwary: and though they are not so impressive, Italian sauces lack neither variety nor originality, and some of them have great freshness of flavour. Tomato sauce is erroneously supposed to be the unique sauce of the country; it does, of course, play a large part in Italian cookery, but the good cooks use it in only very small quantities, and there are as many ways of making it as there are cooks in Italy. The principles are always the same, but the flavourings and the time taken to cook it determine its character. Perhaps the best are both Neapolitan; *alla marinara*, in which the tomatoes are barely cooked at all, and *alla pizzaiola*, richly flavoured with garlic and herbs.

Sugo usually, but not invariably, denotes a meat sauce. The best known is the Bolognese sauce called *ragù* in its native town; but there are plenty of other variations to choose from. The green sauces of Liguria; the basil and cheese pesto, the walnut and parsley sauce for pasta; the fennel, capers, parsley, olives and oil of the sauce for *cappon magro* are aromatic, garlicky, exuberant with all the smells of the Mediterranean.

BÉARNAISE SAUCE

Half a wine glass (4 or 5 tablespoons) white wine, 2 tablespoons tarragon vinegar, 2 shallots, black pepper, 125–150g/4–5oz butter, 3 or 4 egg yolks, salt, lemon juice, a few leaves of fresh tarragon.

Put the white wine, vinegar, chopped shallots and a little ground black pepper in a small pan and reduce it by fast boiling to about 2 tablespoons. Strain it and add a few drops of cold water. Put this essence in the top half of a double saucepan or in a bowl which will fit into the top of an ordinary saucepan. This underneath saucepan should be half full of warm water and put on to a gentle flame. To the liquid already in the top pan, add half the butter, cut into small pieces. Let it melt quickly, then add the rest, stirring all the time. Now add, gradually, the beaten egg yolks and stir very carefully until the sauce thickens. Add salt if necessary, which will depend on whether the butter used is salted or unsalted, and a few drops of lemon juice and a few of cold water. Take the sauce off the heat and stir in the chopped tarragon, and the sauce is ready. At no time should the water underneath the sauce boil and the sauce is not intended to be served hot, but tepid.

Mint instead of tarragon turns béarnaise into *paloise*, a modern variation, useful for serving with lamb and mutton.

If you should be obliged to make your béarnaise in advance the least risky way of reheating it is to put the bowl which contains it inside another one containing hot water and stir it for a few seconds, but not over a flame. Never mind if the sauce is not very hot; it is better to have it cool than curdled.

Enough for four people.

HOLLANDAISE SAUCE

Here we get to a vexed question. Purists claim that the one and only true hollandaise sauce should consist of nothing but butter, egg yolks and lemon juice. The truth is that the basic hollandaise is apt to be insipid and many cooks have discovered that the addition of a preliminary reduction of white wine or vinegar, as in a béarnaise, makes a better-flavoured sauce. A hollandaise sauce is served with asparagus, artichoke hearts, broccoli, poached salmon, sole and all white fish, chicken, and poached or *mollet* eggs.

In a small pan put 3 tablespoons of *wine vinegar* (I prefer to use white wine if I happen to have a bottle open) and 2 tablespoons of *cold water*. Reduce it by boiling to one scant tablespoon. Add half a tablespoon of *cold water*. Have ready beaten in a bowl 3 large *egg yolks* and, on a warmed plate, 175–200g/6–7oz of the finest *unsalted butter*, divided into 6 or 7 portions.

Into the top half of a double saucepan or into a china or glass bowl which will equally fit into the bottom half of the double saucepan which contains the hot water, put the cooled reduction of vinegar or wine. Add the yolks. Stir thoroughly. Set the whole apparatus over the heat. Add one portion of butter. Stir until it starts to thicken before adding the next portion, and so on until all is used up. Do not allow the water underneath the saucepan to boil and, if you see that the sauce is thickening too quickly, add a few drops of cold water. The finished sauce should coat the back of the spoon. Season with *salt* and a few drops of *lemon juice*.

If all precautions fail and the sauce disintegrates, put another egg yolk into a clean bowl. To this add your failed sauce a little at a time, replace it over the hot water and proceed with greater circumspection this time until it has once more thickened. I should add, perhaps, that this only works if the sauce has separated. If the eggs have got so hot that they have granulated, what you have is scrambled eggs.

These quantities will serve four to six people.

OLIVES
SALÉES
DU PAYS
À VENDRE
HUILE d'OLIVES
de LUCERAM Extra Vierge
OLIVES non traitées
OLEICULTEUR Producteur.

BÉCHAMEL SAUCE

There are two different versions of this universally known, rather dull but useful sauce. One is a *béchamel grasse*, made with a proportion of meat or chicken stock, the other *béchamel maigre*, in which milk is the only liquid used. The latter is the one more generally useful – in fact essential – to know, for it forms the basis of many others which are infinitely more interesting.

To make a small quantity of straightforward béchamel, first put 300ml/½ pint of *milk* to heat in a small saucepan and melt 45g/1½oz of *butter* in another suitably thick saucepan. As soon as the butter starts to foam, add, off the fire, 2 level tablespoons of sieved *plain flour*; stir it into the butter immediately. Now add a little of the warmed milk, stirring until a thick paste is formed. Return the saucepan to a low flame and gradually add the rest of the milk. Upon this initial operation depends the success of the sauce, for once the butter, flour and milk are amalgamated and smooth, your sauce is unlikely later to turn lumpy. Having seasoned the mixture with about half a teaspoon of *salt*, a scrap of grated *nutmeg* and a little freshly ground white *pepper*, turn the heat down and let your sauce gently, very gently, simmer for a minimum of 10 minutes, stirring all the time. Half the badly made white sauces one encounters are due to the fact that they are not sufficiently cooked, and so have a crude taste of flour. Also, they are very often made too thick and pasty. A good béchamel should be of a creamy consistency.

After 10 minutes, the saucepan containing the béchamel can be placed in another larger one containing water; this improvised bain-marie is a better system than cooking the sauce in the top half of a double saucepan, for by the bain-marie method the sauce is surrounded by heat instead of only cooking over heat, and therefore matures better and more completely.

* If you have to cook your béchamel in advance, cover the surface while the sauce is still hot with minuscule knobs of butter which, in melting, create a film which prevents the formation of a skin.
* Always reheat the sauce by the bain-marie system.
* If the béchamel is to be served straight, without further flavouring, allow a little extra milk and simmer in it for a few minutes a little piece of *onion*, a *bay leaf*, a sprig of *parsley*, a slice of carrot, all tied together for easy removal when the milk is added to the sauce.
* If, in spite of all precautions, the sauce has turned lumpy, press it through a fine sieve into a clean saucepan. A liquidizer also comes to the rescue here.

MAYONNAISE

The excellence of a mayonnaise depends upon the quality of the olive oil employed to make it. Use genuine olive oil, heavy but not too fruity, as a mayonnaise always accentuates the flavour of the oil. The more egg yolks used the less tricky the mayonnaise is to make, and the quicker. Lemon juice is better than vinegar to flavour mayonnaise, but in either case there should be very little, as the flavour of the oil and the eggs, not the acid of the lemon or vinegar, should predominate.

In France, a little mustard is usually stirred into the eggs before adding the oil; in Italy only eggs and olive oil are used, and sometimes lemon juice.

It is very difficult to give quantities, owing to the difference in weight of different olive oils, and also because mayonnaise is one of those sauces of which people will eat whatever quantity you put before them.

2 eggs, salt, about 200ml/⅓ pint olive oil, the juice of a quarter of a lemon or a teaspoon of tarragon or white wine vinegar.

Break the egg yolks into a mortar or heavy china bowl; if you have time, do this an hour before making the mayonnaise; the eggs will be easier to work; stir in a very little salt, and a teaspoon of mustard powder if you like it. Stir the eggs for a minute; they quickly acquire thickness; then start adding the oil, drop by drop, and pouring if possible from a small jug or bottle with a lip. Stir all the time, and in a minute or two the mixture will start to acquire the ointment-like appearance of mayonnaise. Add the oil a little faster now, and finally in a slow but steady stream; when half the oil is used up add a squeeze of lemon juice or a drop of vinegar, and go on adding the oil until all is used up; then add a little more lemon juice or vinegar. If the mayonnaise has curdled break another egg yolk into a clean basin, and add the curdled mixture a spoonful at a time. Well-made mayonnaise will keep, even in hot weather, for several days. If you make enough for two or three days, and it does separate, start again with another egg yolk, as if it had curdled.

An average amount for 4 people.

TUNA MAYONNAISE

Maionese tonnata

Excellent for all kinds of cold dishes, particularly chicken or hard-boiled eggs, for sandwiches, or for filling raw tomatoes for an hors d'œuvre.

Make a stiff mayonnaise with 2 *egg yolks*, a little *salt*, 125ml/4fl oz of *olive oil*, and a very little *lemon juice*.

Pound or put through a sieve about 60g/2oz of tinned *tuna fish in oil*. Incorporate the purée gradually into the mayonnaise.

GREEN SAUCE

Sauce verte

This is, I think, one of the great achievements of the simpler French cooking, but when I say simple I mean simple in conception rather than in execution, for it is hard work to make in any quantity, and so far as I know there is no short cut.

First prepare a very thick mayonnaise with 2 or even 3 *egg yolks*, 200–300ml/⅓–½ pint of best *olive oil*, and a few drops of *wine or tarragon vinegar*. The other ingredients are 10 fine *spinach leaves*, 10 sprigs of *watercress*, 4 of *tarragon*, 4 of *parsley*. Pick the leaves of the watercress, tarragon and parsley from the stalks. Put all these leaves with the spinach into boiling water for 2 or 3 minutes. Strain, squeeze them quite dry, pound them and put the resulting paste through a fine sieve. It should emerge a compact and dry purée. Stir it gradually into the mayonnaise but leave this final operation as late as possible before the sauce is to be served.

To the salmon of the summer months, lacking the exquisite curdy flesh of the early part of the year, *sauce verte* supplies the interest which might otherwise be lacking, but it need not be confined to fish. A starter of hard-boiled eggs with this green sauce is just that much grander than an ordinary egg mayonnaise. It never fails to please.

AÏOLI

Aïoli is one of the most famous and most beloved of all Provençal dishes. The magnificent shining golden ointment which is the sauce is often affectionately referred to as the 'butter of Provence'. With this wonderful sauce are served boiled salt cod, potatoes, beetroot, sweet peppers, either raw or cooked, carrots, a fine boiled fish such as a bream or mullet, hard-boiled eggs, sometimes little squid or octopus, French beans, globe artichokes, even little snails and perhaps a salad of chick peas.

The *aïoli garni* is, in fact, a Friday dish as well as one of the traditional Christmas Eve dishes; on non-fasting days the beef from the *pot-au-feu* or even a boiled chicken may form part of the dish: it then becomes *le grand aïoli*. It will be seen, then, that with all these different accompaniments, the *aïoli garni* is essentially a dish for a large family or a party of intimate friends, although personally I could quite well dispense with all the rest provided there were a large bowl of potatoes boiled in their skins and perhaps some raw peppers and celery to go with the *aïoli*. In a small country restaurant in Provence where I once asked, at short notice, if it were possible to produce an *aïoli garni* for dinner, it was too late for the patron to go out and buy anything specially, but he produced a handsome dish of ham accompanied by potatoes and the vegetables in season, with the *aïoli* in a bowl in the centre of the dish. It was an excellent demonstration of the sort of impromptu *aïoli* which can be produced with ingredients to hand.

Allow roughly 2 large cloves of *garlic* per person and, for eight people, 3 *egg yolks* and nearly 600ml/1 pint of very good-quality *olive oil* – failing Provençal olive oil, the best Italian or Spanish will do. Crush the peeled garlic in a mortar until it is reduced absolutely to pulp. Add the yolks and a pinch of salt. Stir with a wooden spoon. When the eggs and garlic are well amalgamated, start adding the oil, very slowly at first, drop by drop, until the *aïoli* begins to thicken. This takes longer than with a straightforward mayonnaise because the garlic has thinned the yolks to a certain extent. When about half the oil has been used, the *aïoli* should be a very thick mass, and the oil can now be added in a slow but steady stream. The sauce gets thicker and thicker, and this is as it should be; a good *aïoli* is practically solid. Add a very little *lemon juice* at the end, and serve the sauce either in the kitchen mortar in which you have made it or piled up in a small salad bowl. Should the *aïoli* separate through the oil having been added too fast, put a fresh yolk into another bowl and gradually add the curdled mixture to it. The *aïoli* then comes back to life.

Now as to the amount of garlic: you can, of course, use less but you are likely to find that the mass of eggs and oil is then too heavy and rich. A true *aïoli* is a remarkable mixture of the smooth mayonnaise combined with the powerful garlic flavour which tingles in your throat as you swallow it.

VERONESE MUSHROOM SAUCE

Salsa di funghi alla veronese

In a mixture of *butter* and *olive oil* fry a small chopped *onion*, a handful of chopped *parsley* and a little *garlic*. Sprinkle with *flour* and then stir in 250g/½lb *of mushrooms*, washed and sliced. Season with *salt* and *pepper*, and simmer until the mushrooms are cooked. The liquid which comes from the mushrooms should be sufficient to amalgamate with the flour and so make a slightly thickened little mushroom stew rather than a sauce. Before serving the sauce, which is excellent for pasta, for chicken, steak or veal, add a generous lump of *butter*.

WALNUT *and* HORSERADISH SAUCE

Sauce raifort aux noix

60g/2oz shelled and skinned walnuts, 150ml/¼ pint thick cream, 2 tablespoons freshly and finely grated horseradish, a teaspoon of sugar, a little salt, the juice of half a lemon.

To skin the walnuts, pour boiling water over them and rub off the skins as soon as they are cool enough to handle. It is a tedious operation but, having compared the sauce made with unskinned walnuts to the original version, there is no question but that the latter is very much finer. It is an example of how a short cut in cooking can be taken only to the detriment of the final result.

Having skinned the walnuts, then, chop them finely. Stir them very lightly into the cream and add the horseradish. Add the seasonings, and lastly the lemon juice.

TOMATO SAUCE
Salsa di pomidoro

Chop 1kg/2lb of ripe *tomatoes*. Put them into a saucepan with 1 small *onion*, 1 *carrot*, 1 piece of *celery*, and a little *parsley*, all finely chopped. Add *salt, ground black pepper* and a pinch of *sugar*. Simmer until the tomatoes have turned almost to a purée. Put the sauce through a sieve.

If a concentrated sauce is needed put the purée back in a saucepan and cook it again until the watery part of it has dried up. Before serving it with meat, fish, or any kind of pasta add chopped fresh *basil leaves*.

FRESH TOMATO SAUCE
Salsa di pomidoro crudo

Plunge 500g/1lb of very ripe *tomatoes* into boiling water and skin them. Chop them up, adding a little finely cut *onion*, *garlic*, *parsley* or *fresh basil*, and as much good *olive oil* as you care for. Make it an hour or two before it is to be served.

TOMATO, GARLIC *and* ORANGE SAUCE
Sauce catalane

From the Perpignan district, to the west of the Languedoc, where the cookery has a distinct Spanish influence, comes this sauce which in its native region goes particularly with partridges and with pork. But it is good with other things from chicken and mutton to fried eggs or slices of baked gammon. The bitter orange slices give a curious and interesting flavour to the sauce but do not let them cook in it more than 20 minutes or they will be too bitter.

Heat 2 tablespoons of *olive oil* in a sauté pan. Put in several whole cloves of *garlic* and add immediately about 500g/1lb of ripe, peeled *tomatoes*, roughly cut up. Season with a little *salt*, *pepper* and a lump of *sugar*, and cook for 10 minutes. Now add half a dozen slices of *Seville or bitter orange*, pips, but not rind, removed. Cook uncovered for another 20 minutes, until the sauce is thick. Remove the garlic before serving.

BANKETTING STUFFE

> The flowers we have this month are single anemones, stock gilliflowers, single wall-flowers, primroses, snowdrops, black hellebore, winter aconite, polyanthus; and in the hot-beds the narcissus and the hyacinth.

The Complete English Gardener, *Samuel Cooke, Gardener at Overton, in Wiltshire. London: Printed for J. Cooke, at Shakespear's-Head, in Pater-noster-Row. c.1780.*

That little list of December flowers in the garden at Overton in the eighteenth century reminds me of the delightful directions for garnishing a trifle by Esther Copley in her *Housekeeper's Guide* of 1834. The recipe is a long one, calling for all the ingredients usual at the period – Naples or sponge biscuits, ratafia drops or miniature macaroons, white wine, brandy, split almonds, jam, a pint of rich thick custard, a pint and a half of whipped cream, a scattering of non-pareils (we now call them hundreds and thousands). Having built up the edifice 'stick here and there a light delicate flower. Be careful to choose only such as are innocent: violets, heart's-ease, polyanthus, primrose, cowslip, geranium, myrtle, virburnum, jessamine, stock gilliflower, and small roses. These will afford variety, and some of them be in season at most times of the year.'

I wonder if the ladies of Overton used some of the innocent flowers, the aconite, the primroses, the polyanthus, grown by Samuel Cooke the gardener to decorate the creams and trifles and custards which surely figured among their desserts at the festive season. How ravishing those eighteenth-century tables must have looked when the crystallized fruit, the oranges and raisins, the spun sugar confections, the trays of syllabubs, the pyramids of jellies, the dishes of little almond cakes shaped into knots and rings and bows, the marchpanes spiked with candied fruit, the curd tarts and all the sweetmeats were spread. No doubt many such delicacies were made in their own stillrooms by the ladies of the household. Others were bought from professional confectioners. Long experience and a specialist's skill were needed – as indeed they still are – to produce the candied and crystallized flowers and fruit, the lemon and orange and citron peel, the sugared almonds, and the gilded marchpane sweetmeats in perfection.

A point which we don't now always grasp when reading of the meals of the seventeenth century is that in those days, the dessert of sweetmeats and marchpanes, fresh and candied fruits, little cakes and biscuits, was known as the bankett or banquet course, and laid out in a room quite apart from the dining hall where the main meal was served. Sometimes there was even a separate building for the banquet room, perhaps in the garden, after the manner of a summer house, or even on the roof. There the party would proceed after dinner, to find the tables spread with 'banketting stuffe' as the Elizabethans and early Jacobeans had called the dessert. There would be sweet and spiced wines, the candles would be lit, the musicians would play, and if the banquet room was large enough, there would be dancing.

It was from Italian sources that the English had first learned of the art of sugar confectionery, our early recipes being based on those given in a translation of the French version of an Italian work first published in 1557 by a certain Girolamo Ruscelli, otherwise known as Alexis of Piedmont. This was one of those *Books of Secretes* popular in the sixteenth century, the secrets being at that time mainly medical and cosmetic, and written more for the benefit of professional apothecaries, alchemists and physicians than for the amateur household practitioner. Given, however, the Elizabethan passion for novelty and for knowledge of every kind (the translation appeared in 1558, the year of Elizabeth's accession), it was inevitable that such publications should find their way into many educated households, and the 'secrets' be frequently copied out into the recipe books kept by almost every family cultivated enough to read and write.

So it was that the handful of confectionery recipes contained in *The Secretes of the Reverende Maister Alexis of Piedmont, translated out of Frenche into Englishe by Wyllyam Warde* in 1558, reappeared in several little household compilations which found their way into print later in the century. It was a period when sugar was fast replacing honey as the main sweetening and preserving agent for fruit. Everybody wanted to know how to manage sugar, which required different techniques from the old ones used for honey. Alexis of Piedmont dealt with both, which makes his confectionery recipes – there were only a dozen of them – particularly interesting to us, as no doubt also to his original readers.

There were directions for clarifying both honey and sugar, for candying citrons, for candying peaches after the Spanish fashion, for making a conserve or confiture of quinces. There were methods of conserving melon, pumpkin and marrow rinds in honey, and others for candying green walnuts with spices, cherries preserved in honey, and orange peels also in honey.

Most interesting of all perhaps, to the original readers of the book, were the instructions for making a 'paste of sugre, whereof a man maye make all maner of fruites, and other fyne thynges, with theyr forme, as platters, dishes, glasses, cuppes, and such like thynges, wherewith you may furnish a table; and when you have doen, eate them up. A pleasant thing for them that sit at table.' The recipe is a detailed one for a sugar paste stiffened with gum tragacanth, but still pliable enough to be shaped into 'what things you will' and 'with suche fine knackes as maye serve a table, taking heede that there stand no hote thing nigh unto it. At the end of the banket they may eat al and breake the platters, dishes, glasses, cuppes, and all thinges: for this paste is verie delicate and savourous.'

From such modest beginnings grew the art of the sugar confectioner, an art which in the Italy of the mid-seventeenth century had already soared to such ambitious heights that the most eminent artists, woodcarvers and sculptors were involved in the design and execution of the ornamental *trionfi*, the triumphs or centrepieces in sugar work made to adorn the feasts given by popes and prelates, princes and noblemen of Rome, Florence, Naples, Mantua, Milan. From Italy this extraordinary art form spread to France, to find its apotheosis in the extravaganza designed by Anthonin Carême, the nineteenth-century chef who is said to have declared that architecture was nothing more than an offshoot of the pastry cook's art.

from Petits Propos Culinaires 3, *November 1979*

SWEET DISHES *and* CAKES

Please do not look in this chapter for anything but the simplest of creams and cakes, ices and fruit dishes. Elaborate patisserie and confectionery require practical experience and knowledge of an art quite distinct from that of normal household cookery.

The sweet course in southern countries, and particularly in the eastern Mediterranean, frequently consists of very sweet little cakes and pastries, and bowls of fresh fruit. The cakes usually require quantities of eggs, sugar, honey, almonds, pistachio nuts, rosewater, sesame seeds and other *Arabian Nights* ingredients. Very often, little bowls of yoghurt are handed round and eaten with sugar and a conserve of quinces or little oranges, more like jam than our compote.

In summer in England there is nothing more delicious than fruit and cream, quite plain when strawberries and raspberries first come into season; later, when they get cheaper, made into fools, purées and pies. Gooseberry fool and gooseberry tart and summer pudding made with raspberries and redcurrants are among the best things of the English table. Water ices made simply from fruit juice and sugar make a refreshing end to a meal. In the early summer, before the berry season starts, lemons are comparatively cheap and make delicious creams and ices; so do the early imported apricots which are not yet ripe enough for dessert.

In winter in the south there are the succulent dried figs and raisins of Greece and Smyrna; tender little apricots dried with their stones in from Damascus, *loukoúmi* (Turkish Delight) to accompany sweet Turkish coffee. In Italy there is zabaglione, Sicilian cassata and elaborate ice creams. The Spaniards serve nougats and turróns and quince paste with the coffee; the little town of Apt in northern Provence produces delicious candied apricots and other fruits confits, and no one who has seen them will forget the gorgeous displays of crystallized fruits of every conceivable variety in the shops of Nice, Cannes and Genoa.

SUMMER PUDDING

Although nearly everybody knows of this wonderful pudding, authentic recipes for it are rare.

500g/1lb of *raspberries* and 125g/¼lb of *redcurrants* with about 125g/¼lb of *sugar*. No water. Cook them only 2 or 3 minutes, and leave to cool. Line a fairly deep round dish (a soufflé dish does very well) with slices of one-day-old *white bread* with the crust removed. The bread should be of the thickness usual for sandwiches. The dish must be completely lined, bottom and sides, with no space through which the juice can escape. Fill up with the fruit, but reserve some of the juice. Cover the fruit with a complete layer of bread. On top put a plate which fits exactly inside the dish, and on the plate put a 1–1.5kg/2–3lb weight. Leave overnight in a very cold larder or refrigerator. When ready to serve turn the pudding out on to a dish (not a completely flat one, or the juice will overflow) and pour over it the reserved juice.

Thick fresh cream is usually served with summer pudding, but it is almost more delicious without.

Enough for four people.

GOOSEBERRY FOOL

Although this is a traditional English sweet it is not often well made.

Put 500g/1lb of hard green *gooseberries* in a pan with 125g/¼lb of *sugar* (there is no need to top and tail them). Steam them until they are quite soft. Sieve them, and when the purée is cold stir in 150ml/¼ pint of thick *cream*. Add more sugar if the fool is too acid. Serve very cold.

Enough for four people.

RASPBERRY SHORTBREAD

500g/1lb raspberries, a little white sugar, 60g/2oz butter, 175g/6oz flour, 120g/3½oz muscovado sugar, ½ teaspoon ground ginger, 1 teaspoon baking powder.

Put the raspberries in a fairly large shallow pie dish, strew them with white sugar. Cut the butter into very small pieces and crumble it with the flour until it is thoroughly blended. Add the sugar, ginger and baking powder. Spread this mixture lightly over the raspberries, and smooth it out evenly, but do not press down. Bake in the centre of a medium oven at 180°C/gas 4, for 25 minutes. Can be served hot or cold and is excellent.

Enough for four people.

RASPBERRY *and* REDCURRANT MOUSSE

250g/½lb each of redcurrants and raspberries, 125–175g/4–6oz sugar, 2 egg whites.

Sieve the raspberries and redcurrants – add the sugar and then the stiffly whipped egg whites to the juice. Put into a saucepan over a low flame and whisk continually for about 3 minutes, until the mixture starts to thicken and rise like a soufflé. Pour into wine glasses and serve hot with cream, or into a tall dish in which there is just room for the mousse, and leave to cool. When cold some of the juice will separate and sink to the bottom but can be whipped up again before serving.

A nice sweet for children.

Enough for four people.

toute l'année

MELON STUFFED *with* WILD STRAWBERRIES

Melon aux fraises des bois

Cut a slice off the thick end of a Cantaloup, Charentais or Cavaillon *melon* and keep it aside. Remove the seeds and scoop out the flesh, taking care not to damage the skin. Cut the flesh into cubes and mix with 375–500g/¾–1lb of wild or wood *strawberries*. Add a little *sugar* and 2 or 3 tablespoons of *port*. Return the mixture to the melon, put back the top slice, surround the melon with plenty of cracked ice and leave for several hours before serving. Do not put it in the refrigerator, as the powerful aroma of melon penetrates all other foodstuffs.

An alternative filling to wild strawberries and port is a mixture of raspberries and Kirsch or Grand Marnier.

Enough for four people.

PEACHES *in* WHITE WINE

Pêches au vin blanc

The best *peaches* for this dish are the yellow-fleshed variety. Dip the fruit in boiling water so that the skins can easily be peeled off. Slice them straight into big wine glasses, sprinkle with *sugar* and pour a tablespoon or two of *white wine* into each glass. Don't prepare them too long ahead or the fruit will go mushy.

MELON
Maroc
EXTRA
Sucrée
3€,50 Pièce
6€,00 les 2

APPLES *with* LEMON *and* CINNAMON

A cool and fresh sweet dish to serve after a rich or heavy meat course. An alternative flavouring for those who do not care for cinnamon is a vanilla pod, cut in half and put in with the apples before cooking. The lemon slices are still included in the flavouring of the syrup.

Core, peel and slice some good eating *apples*, preferably Cox's. Put the cores and peel into a saucepan with a heaped dessertspoon of *sugar* and a slice of *lemon*, peel included, for each apple. Cover amply with water and cook to a syrup. This will take about 7 minutes of rapid boiling.

Put the sliced apples into a skillet, sauté pan, or frying pan. Over them strain the prepared syrup. Cover the pan and cook over moderate heat until the apples are soft but not broken up. Add more sugar if necessary.

Arrange the apples in a shallow serving dish, with a few lemon slices on the top – for decoration and for the scent. These apples can be eaten hot or cold.

An alternative method of cooking this dish, much easier when you are making a large quantity, is to arrange the sliced apples in an oven dish, pour the prepared syrup over them, cover the dish (with foil, if you have no lid) and cook in a moderate oven at 160°–180°C/gas 3–4, for 25–35 minutes. Serve the apples in the dish in which they have cooked, not forgetting the final sprinkling of *cinnamon*.

Allow 2 apples per person.

PEARS BAKED *in* RED WINE

Poires étuvées au vin rouge

A method of making the most cast iron of cooking pears very delicious. It is especially suitable for those households where there is a solid fuel cooker of the Aga or Esse type.

Peel the *pears*, leaving the stalks on. Put them in a tall ovenproof dish, or earthenware crock. Add about 90g/3oz of *sugar* per 500g/1lb of pears. Half cover with *red wine*. Fill to the top with water. Bake in a very slow oven for anything between 5 and 7 hours, until the pears are quite tender and the juice greatly reduced. From time to time, as the wine diminishes, turn the pears over.

A big dish of these pears, almost mahogany-coloured by the time they are ready, served cold in their remaining juice with cream or creamed rice separately, makes a lovely sweet. The best way to present them is to pile them up in a pyramid, stalks uppermost, in a shallow bowl or a *compotier* on a pedestal.

COFFEE ICE CREAM

Glace moka

A luxury ice cream, with a mild but true coffee flavour and a very fine texture.

First put 125g/¼lb of freshly roasted *coffee beans* in a marble mortar. Do not crush them but simply bruise them with the pestle, so that the beans are cracked rather than broken up. Put them in a saucepan with 600ml/1 pint of *single cream*, *3 egg yolks* well beaten, a strip of *lemon peel* and 90g/3oz of *pale brown sugar*. Cook this mixture over very gentle heat, stirring constantly until it thickens. Take from the heat and go on stirring until it is cool. Strain through a fine sieve. When this cream is quite cold and thick, into it fold 125ml/¼ pint of *double cream* lightly whipped with a tablespoon of *white sugar*. Freeze in an ice-cream machine or turn into a freezing tray, cover with foil, and place in the ice-making compartment of the refrigerator, which should already be turned to maximum freezing point. Freeze for 3 hours; after the first hour stir the ice cream, turning sides to middle. Turn out whole on to a flat dish and cut into four portions.

The coffee beans can be used again for a second batch of ice cream; and a less expensive basic mixture using 600ml/1 pint of *milk* and 5 *egg yolks* still makes a very excellent ice. Always use a light roast of coffee.

Enough for four people.

BLACKBERRY WATER ICE

125g/4oz sugar, 125ml/¼ pint water, if possible 2 or 3 sweet-scented geranium leaves, 500g/1lb blackberries.

Make a syrup by boiling the sugar and water together for 5 or 6 minutes, with 2 sweet-scented geranium leaves. When cool add the syrup to the sieved blackberries, and put into the freezing tray with a fresh sweet-scented geranium leaf on the top or use an ice-cream machine. If using trays cover with foil and freeze for 2½ hours. A tablespoon or two of rosewater makes a fair substitute for the sweet-scented geranium leaves.

Enough for four people.

SNOW CHEESE

This lovely sweet dish is not strictly a cream cheese, but the system on which its confection is based is very similar to the French *crémets*. Recipes for snow cheese occur in English cookery books certainly as far back as the mid-seventeenth century, and possibly earlier. My own recipe is based on one from an early Victorian manuscript.

350ml/¾ pint double cream, 125g/4oz caster sugar, 1 lemon, 2 egg whites.

Pour the cream into a large bowl; stir in the sugar, the grated peel of the lemon, and its strained juice. Have also ready a round sieve or a cheese mould standing over a plate and lined with a piece of muslin wrung out in cold water.

Whisk the cream mixture until it stands in peaks. Don't overdo it or it will turn to a grainy mess. Fold in the stiffly whipped egg whites. Turn into the lined sieve. Leave to drain overnight. Turn out on to a shallow dish.

Serve the snow cheese with plain wheaten biscuits or crisp ice wafers.

Enough for four people.

APPLES COOKED *in* BUTTER

Pommes au beurre

I have never very greatly appreciated cooked apple dishes, but from the French I learned two valuable lessons about them. First, choose hard sweet apples whenever possible instead of the sour cooking variety which are used for English apple dishes. And secondly, if the apples are to be eaten hot, cook them in butter instead of in water. The scent of apples cooking in butter is alone more than worth the small extra expense.

For 1kg/2lb, then, of peeled and cored *sweet apples*, evenly and rather thinly sliced, melt 60g/2oz of *butter* in a frying pan. Put in your apples, add 3 or 4 tablespoons of soft *white sugar* (vanilla-flavoured if you like) and cook gently until the apples are pale golden and transparent. Turn the slices over very gently, so as not to break them, and, if they are very closely packed, shake the pan rather than stir the apples. Serve them hot; and I doubt if many people will find cream necessary. The delicate butter taste is enough.

Enough for four people.

APRICOT COMPÔTE

Apricots are exquisite to eat raw when they are slightly over-ripe, sun-warmed and straight off the tree. Otherwise they gain by being cooked, and this compôte brings out their slightly smoky, delicious flavour.

Halve the apricots and take out the stones. Cook them gently with water half-way to covering them and about 125g/¼lb of *sugar* to 1kg/2lb of *apricots*. Watch them to see that they do not dissolve into a purée. Take the apricots out of the pan and put them into a dish. Reduce the remaining syrup until it is thick, then pour it over the apricots.

Serve cold. Cream is unnecessary; it would disguise the taste of the apricots.

TORRONE MOLLE

Torrone is the Italian name for all kinds of nougat. This sweet, literally 'soft nougat', is an ingenious invention, for it needs no cooking and can be successfully turned out by the least experienced of cooks. The combination of the plain biscuits with the chocolate mixture is reminiscent of that most admirable picnic food, a slab of bitter chocolate accompanied by a Petit Beurre biscuit. The *torrone* is infinitely better when prepared the day before it is to be eaten.

175g/6oz each of butter, cocoa, ground almonds, sugar, 1 whole egg and 1 yolk, and plain biscuits such as Petit Beurre or Osborne.

Work the butter and the cocoa together until you have a soft paste, then stir in the ground almonds. Melt the sugar in a saucepan with a little water over a gentle flame and add it to the cocoa mixture. Stir in the eggs, and finally the biscuits cut into almond-sized pieces. This last operation must be performed gently so that the biscuits do not crumble. Turn the whole mixture into an oiled rectangular loaf tin or a cake tin with a removable base and put it in the refrigerator or the coldest part of the larder. Turn it out on to a dish to serve.

Enough for six to eight people.

CHOCOLATE MOUSSE

30g/1oz plain or vanilla chocolate per person, 1 egg per person.

Melt the chocolate in a thick pan over a low flame with a tablespoon of water. A tablespoon of rum added will do no harm. Stir the chocolate until it is smooth. Separate the eggs and beat the yolks. Stir the melted chocolate into the yolks.

Whip the whites very stiffly and fold them over and over into the chocolate, so that they are perfectly blended, or the chocolate may sink to the bottom. Put the mousse into a soufflé dish so that the mixture just about comes to the top (nothing is sadder than a small amount of mousse hiding at the bottom of a huge glass bowl) and leave it in a cool place to set. Unless in a hurry, don't put it on ice, as this tends to make it too hard.

Instead of water, the chocolate can be melted in a tablespoon of black coffee.

CHOCOLATE CHINCHILLA

This is a splendid – and cheap – recipe for using up egg whites left from the making of mayonnaise, béarnaise or other egg yolk based sauces. It is also a dish which demonstrates the excellent combination of chocolate with cinnamon. This flavouring stems from the sixteenth century, when the Spaniards first shipped the product of the cocoa bean from South America to Spain. Chocolate, both drinking and eating versions, spiced with cinnamon is still sometimes to be found in Spain, and also I believe in Mexico, although almost everywhere else cinnamon has long been superseded by vanilla as the favourite aromatic for flavouring chocolate.

Cinnamon varies a good deal in strength. If it has been kept for a long time in your kitchen cupboard, you may find that one heaped teaspoon is not enough to flavour the chocolate.

60g/2oz unsweetened cocoa powder, 90g/3oz caster sugar, 1 heaped teaspoon ground cinnamon, 5–7 egg whites.

Mix together the cocoa, sugar and cinnamon. Whip the egg whites to a stiff snow. Tip the cocoa and sugar mixture on to the egg whites. Fold the two together, gently but thoroughly. A large metal spoon or a wide flexible spatula are the best implements to use for this operation.

Have ready a buttered ring mould, kugelhopf, or best of all a steamed pudding mould with a central funnel and clip-on lid. Austrian and German cooks use these moulds for all puddings and cakes in which there is a high content of whisked egg white. The central funnel helps enormously in the even distribution of heat throughout the mixture, which in a soufflé dish or plain mould tends to remain moist in the centre for some minutes after the rest of the pudding is cooked. Whatever mould is used for this recipe, the capacity should be approximately 1 litre/1¾ pints.

Having filled your mould with the prepared mixture, stand it, uncovered (for this particular recipe the lid of the mould is not necessary) in a baking tin with water to reach half-way up the dish or mould. Cook the chinchilla – which is really a kind of soufflé without egg yolks – in the centre of a moderate oven, 160°C/gas 3, for about 45 to 50 minutes. It will rise in a spectacular manner. But since it is to be eaten cold, it will sink in an even more spectacular fashion unless, when taken from the oven, it is left to cool in a warm place, protected from draughts and sudden changes of temperature. When cold, the pudding, although shrunk, will have become compact enough to turn out easily. It will have a good texture and a very rich dark colour.

Serve with fresh thin pouring cream to which has been added a little sherry, rum or brandy.

Enough for four to six people.

ST ÉMILION *au* CHOCOLAT

125g/¼lb butter, 125g/¼lb sugar, 1 teacup milk, 1 egg yolk, 250g/½lb chocolate, 12 to 16 macaroons, rum or brandy.

Cream the butter and the sugar until they are well amalgamated. Scald the milk and let it cool, then mix it with the egg yolk. Melt the chocolate, with a very little water, then stir in the milk and egg mixture, then the butter and sugar. Stir this cream carefully until it is absolutely smooth.

In a soufflé dish arrange a layer of macaroons, soaked in a little rum or brandy; over these pour a layer of the chocolate cream, then put another layer of macaroons and so on until the dish is full, finishing with macaroons. Leave the dish in a cold place for at least 12 hours.

Enough for four to six people.

CHOCOLATE CAKE

Gâteau au chocolat

This is a cake which can also be eaten as a pudding, and is neither expensive nor difficult to make.

125g/¼lb bitter chocolate, 90g/3oz butter, 2 tablespoons flour, 125g/¼lb caster sugar, 5 eggs.

Melt the chocolate in the oven; mix it with the softened butter, flour, sugar and beaten egg yolks. Fold in the stiffly beaten whites. Turn into a buttered 15-cm/6-inch cake tin or 750-ml/1¼-pint loaf tin and cook in a preheated moderate oven, at 180°C/gas 4, for 35 minutes. There will be a thin crust on top of the cake but if you test it with a skewer the inside will appear insufficiently cooked, which in fact is correct, as it gets firmer as it cools.

As soon as it is cool enough to handle, turn upside down on to a cake rack. When cool, the cake can either be covered with lightly whipped cream or iced with the following mixture. Break up 90g/3oz of *plain chocolate* and melt it on an ovenproof plate in the oven, with 1–2 tablespoons of *sugar* and 2 or 3 tablespoons of water. Stir it smooth; add 30g/1oz of *butter*. Let it cool, then with a palette knife cover the whole cake with the chocolate, smoothing it with a knife dipped in water. Leave it to set before serving.

The quantities given make a small cake, but it is somewhat solid and goes quite a long way.

COFFEE CAKE

Gâteau moka

This is the simplest sort of old-fashioned plain cake, saved from dryness by a coffee-cream filling, and admirable to serve with creams and ices.

To make the cake, beat 90g/3oz of *vanilla sugar* with 3 *egg yolks* until the mixture is very creamy. Add 90g/3oz of *flour* and then fold in the stiffly whipped *whites of the eggs*. Turn into a lightly buttered oblong cake tin (900-ml/1½-pint capacity) and bake in a moderate oven, 180°C/gas 4, for 30 minutes. Turn the cake out upside down on to a cake rack a few minutes after taking it from the oven.

To make the cream filling, work 90g/3oz of *butter* with 1 *egg yolk*; add 90g/3oz of sieved *icing sugar*; when the cream is smooth stir in a dessertspoon of very strong black *coffee* (nowadays the most convenient method is to use instant coffee powder mixed to a thin paste).

Slice the cake into three or four layers. Spread each liberally with the coffee cream and reshape the cake. Press lightly as you put each layer back, so that the slices will stick together. Leave for some hours before serving.

ORANGE *and* ALMOND CAKE

The juice of 3 oranges, grated rind of 1 orange, 60g/2oz fine breadcrumbs, 125g/4oz ground almonds, orange-flower water, 4 eggs, 125g/4oz sugar, ½ teaspoon salt, cream.

Mix together the orange juice, grated orange rind and breadcrumbs, add the ground almonds and, if available, a tablespoon of orange-flower water.

Beat the egg yolks with the sugar and salt until almost white. Add to the first mixture. Fold in the stiffly beaten egg whites. Pour into a square cake tin, buttered and sprinkled with breadcrumbs, and bake in a moderate oven at 180°C/gas 4 for about 40 minutes.

When cold turn the cake out and cover the top with whipped cream (about 150ml/¼ pint). Very good and light.

The BAKING *of an* ENGLISH LOAF

Any human being possessed of sufficient gumption to track down a source of fresh yeast – it isn't all that rare – and collected enough to remember to buy at the same time a pound or two of plain flour, get it home, take a mixing bowl and a measuring jug from the cupboard, and read a few simple instructions can make a decent loaf of bread.

And if you cannot, after two or three attempts, make a better loaf than any to be bought in an English shop – and that goes for health-food and whole-food and crank-food and home-spun shops generally, just as much as for chain bakeries and provision stores and small independent bakers – then I am prepared to eat my hat, your hat, and almost anything else put before me, always with the absolute exception of a loaf of English commercial bread.

Please do not jump to conclusions. It is not my intention to make even a slight attempt to persuade you into baking your own bread. I am simply going to tell you how to set about it if you feel you must, and I find it comical as well as shameful that in this day and age anybody should be forced into so archaic an activity.

No Frenchwoman, at least no French townswoman, would dream of baking her own bread. In France, fresh loaves are baked twice daily by every baker and bought twice daily by every householder. If and when the French bakery system breaks down, there is, as every schoolchild knows, a revolution. Had Marie Antoinette been a French princess rather than a Hapsburg from Vienna, she could never have said, or have been credited with saying, that the people of France could make do with cake instead of bread.

As recently as the summer of 1965, the people of Paris rose up in revolt against the annual August closing of some sixty per cent of the city's bakeries. To Parisians, it had become a major grievance to be obliged to walk perhaps as far as a kilometre to find a baker who kept his business open during the summer exodus to the sea and the country. The Government was obliged to step in and decree that the bakers (not, mind you, the shoemakers, the plumbers, the electricians and the laundries, just the bakers) must stagger their holidays. A baker, in other words, has a public responsibility and cannot with impunity desert his post.

In France, a meal without good bread and plenty of it is simply not a meal. For that matter, a meal without bread isn't a meal anywhere in Europe except in England. And I mean England. I do not mean Scotland or Ireland, where it is still possible to buy real bread.

A certain school of English patriot is much given to the expression of belief in the creed that we have in England the finest ingredients in Europe and that 'British cuisine at its best is the best in the world'. I find it amazing that any responsible person can presume to make such a claim when our basic necessities are so hard to come by, when a new-laid egg is as rare as a flawless ruby, when English butter is not nearly as well made as Dutch, Danish or Polish, when the best fresh vegetables available to Londoners and other city-dwellers are flown from Cyprus or Kenya or sent from Italy, Spain or Madeira, when our cheese is marketed by packaging factories, and when, manifestly, not one householder or one restaurateur in a thousand has grasped the elementary truth that the finest ingredients and the greatest cooking skills this side of Escoffier can combine to produce only a bleak and hollow sham of a meal, joyless and devoid of stimulus, if the customer or the guest is offered no more in the way of bread to go with his food than a skimpy little wedge of white winceyette placed with boarding-house gentility underneath a folded napkin upon a side-plate.

A good many readers of cookery articles must be bored to death with being told that one main dish, with a salad, cheese, and a loaf of crusty bread, makes an ample, balanced, nourishing, economical, easily cooked and satisfying family meal. Well, so it does, if you can get it; in fact, the bread and the cheese would be a perfectly good meal without the so-called main dish. And the bleak truth is that mighty few of us can lay hands on either the cheese or the bread unless we happen to live within walking distance of a specialist cheese shop and a bakery which is not only independent and bakes its own bread but bakes it well and produces it for sale at an hour when the ordinary householder can go out and buy it.

I repeat, I am not canvassing those who are prepared to put up with shop bread because they just have not the time or inclination to make it themselves; I am not preaching to those who buy shop bread because they actually like it; I am giving instructions purely as basic guidance to those who have already reached the conclusion that it is pretty ludicrous to spend three days planning menus to include shrimp-filled avocados, trout with almonds, fillet of beef in puff pastry, pineapple ice cream and no end of a palaver over the grinding and percolating of the coffee, if they cannot offer their guests a decent piece of bread. It should be added, in fairness, that in those households where home-made and well-made bread is on offer nobody needs to worry about all that prestige-type food. Have it by all means, if that's what you like, but if it's prestige you're after – or, to put it in a cruder way and since it isn't unknown to any of us occasionally to do the right things for the wrong reasons – what will most impress your friends and arouse the maximum envy in your rivals is the sight and the taste of fresh, authentic, un-cranky bread, with its slightly rough and open texture, plain unvarnished crust, and perceptibly salty bite.

This is the kind of bread which should be cut in good thick chunky slices straight from the loaf left upon the table for all to see and enjoy.

from Queen, *4 December 1968*

BREAD *and* YEAST BAKING

The ideal flours for English bread, and for all yeast doughs, are milled from hard wheat, whereas cake, short pastry and sauce flours are or should be soft-wheat flours. Hard flours have a high gluten content, which makes the dough more elastic and expansive. Soft flour tends to make rather flat bread. (French bread is mostly made from a softish flour because this is the type of wheat mainly grown in France. The French have adapted their bread techniques to their flour.) Nearly all the ordinary white flour on sale is soft household flour, but strong white bread flour can now be found on the shelves too.

Whole-wheat flour, stoneground, 100%, 90% or 85%, whole wheatmeal, can be bought from supermarkets, grocers and health-food stores. The first type, 100% wholemeal, is the whole grain of the wheat with nothing removed and nothing added. The 85% and 90% wheatmeal have husk and bran removed and make a lighter and finer loaf. Some wholefood addicts recommend these flours for pastry and sauces. I don't.

The difference between hard gluten flours and ordinary soft household flours becomes apparent as soon as you start handling the dough. The first almost immediately becomes springy and lithe, the latter tends to be sticky and puttyish, although it becomes harder with kneading.

Flours can be mixed. For example, a mixture of say 125g/4oz of 100% whole wheatmeal flour and 375g/12oz of ordinary soft household flour make a quite respectable pale brown loaf, although not such a good one as strong plain or bakers' white flour and 85% or 90% whole wheatmeal flour in the same proportions.

Some of the whole wheatmeal flours on sale in health-food and crank shops make a heavy and pudding-like loaf. For that matter, much of the bread sold in these shops is inexpertly made, dry, heavy, calculated to put all but nut-food nuts right off home-made bread for life. Into the bargain, so-called home-made health food is extortionately expensive.

A BASIC LOAF

This basic recipe is for one large loaf weighing 800–850g/28–30oz. It is made with a mixture of one part 100 per cent wholemeal and two parts strong plain white flour – or if you prefer it, all strong white. The tin should be of the size known as a 1kg/2lb loaf tin, 10cm/4–4½ inches in depth with a capacity of 1½–2 litres/3–3½ pints.

500g/1lb strong plain unbleached white flour and 125g/4oz 100 per cent wholemeal, 20g/¾oz rock salt or sea salt, 15g/½oz bakers' compressed yeast or 10g/¼oz dried yeast, approximately 350ml/12fl oz water at blood heat, and oil or fat for the tin.

Put the flour and salt into a bowl, mix well, cover the bowl with a heat resistant plate or dish, and put it in a very low oven for about 5 to 7 minutes so that the flour is warmed. But not too much so. Leave the plate or dish in the oven.

In the meantime, put the yeast in a cup, pour enough tepid water over to just cover it. By the time the flour is warmed the yeast will be soft enough to mix to a cream. If you are using dried yeast you can add a pinch of sugar to the warm water, although with modern yeasts sugar is not necessary. Give the yeast a good 10 minutes to return to active life.

Pour the creamed yeast into the centre of the flour. Add some of the tepid water and stir it round with the yeast, using a wooden spoon. Now pour in the rest of the water and mix the dough with your hands. If it is too sticky and wet to work, sprinkle in more flour, until you feel that the dough is becoming lithe and elastic. Work it for a minute or two, until it comes away easily from the sides of the bowl. Form it into a ball, sprinkle it with flour. Cover the bowl with a sheet of cling film and the dish or plate left warming in the oven. By this means both the bowl and the cover are warm, the dough itself generates its own warmth as the yeast works, and unless the weather is very cold it should not be necessary to find a special warm place to leave the dough to rise. If you have no suitable cover for the bowl, use just the sheet of cling film, which helps to generate the damp steamy atmosphere propitious to the dough.

In 1½–2 hours the dough will have expanded to more than twice its original volume. It will look puffy and spongy. Break it down by giving it a good punch with your fist. Then gather it up and slap it down hard in the bowl several times. Put the dough on a work surface, sprinkle it with flour and knead it by pushing it out and then folding it over on itself in a roughly three-cornered fashion. Repeat the process two or three times. The punching down and kneading, or knocking back as it is also called, redistributes the gas bubbles produced by the yeast, helps the gluten to develop and reinvigorates the yeast so that it will renew its work and form new air balloons. With such a small amount of dough, the knocking back and kneading process takes only 3 or 4 minutes. A larger batch obviously takes longer and is harder work, which can be done, if you like, with the dough hook of an electric mixer.

Have ready the warmed tin, greased with a little oil or fat.

Shape the dough, so that the folds are underneath, and put it into the tin. At this stage the amount of dough looks totally inadequate for the size of the tin. But cover it with a sheet of cling film or a damp cloth and leave it in a warm place. Almost immediately it will start coming back to life, and in about 45 minutes – sometimes less, sometimes more – it will have risen to the top of the tin. If the dough has been well kneaded, the second proving is usually quicker, and the volume achieved greater, than in the initial rising.

Bake the loaf in the centre of a good hot oven, 220–230°C/gas 7–8, for the first 15 minutes, reducing the heat to 200°C/gas 6 for the next 15. Shake the loaf from the tin, return it, on its side, to the oven, now reduced to about 180°C/gas 4, and leave it for a final 15–20 minutes. When it is sufficiently baked the loaf gives out a resonant sound when you tap the sides and the bottom crust with your knuckles.

Leave it to cool on a rack, or lying across the empty tin. Bread should never be put away until it has cooled completely. As soon as it is wrapped or is put into a crock, the crust goes soft, so if I am baking bread in the evening, say for lunch the following day, I leave it uncovered overnight and until it is time to cut it. In this way the crust still retains some crispness.

This type of bread is not good until it is quite cold, and in fact does not develop its full flavour until the day after it is baked.

POTATO BREAD

Usually associated with times of grain shortage, or with a need for strict economy in the kitchen, potato bread is also advocated by some nineteenth-century writers as being the best bread for toast. This is because a proportion of potato mixed with ordinary white flour makes a loaf which retains its moisture and is also very light. The tin I use for this loaf is a narrow straight-sided one, as for a sandwich loaf with a capacity of 1.5 litres/2½ pints. The exact dimensions are not important, the reason for the shape being that I find potato bread makes good sandwiches, as well as good toast, and is also very useful for fried bread.

To 500g/1lb white flour, the proportion of potato is 125g/¼lb, mashed very smoothly, completely dry, and used while warm. Other ingredients are 15g/½oz fresh yeast, 300ml/½ pint milk and water mixed, a minimum of 20g/¾oz salt.

Note: *If you use dried granular yeast, use a scant 7g/¼oz.*

Have the flour and salt ready in a bowl, the yeast creamed with a little water, and the milk and water warm in a jug. When your potatoes (two medium-sized ones will be ample) are cooked, peeled, sieved and weighed, mix them with the flour as if you were rubbing in fat, so that the two are very thoroughly amalgamated. Then add the yeast and the warm milk and water. Mix the dough as for ordinary bread. Leave until it is well risen, which will take rather longer than usual – anything up to 2 hours. Break it down, knead lightly, shape and put into a 1.5–1.8-litre/2½–3-pint tin. Cover it with a damp cloth and leave until the dough reaches the top of the tin.

Bake in a moderately hot oven, at 220°C/gas 7, for about 45 minutes, taking care not to let the crust get too browned or hard.

Notes

1. The covering with a damp cloth while the dough is rising for the second time is important. This dough tends to form a skin, which inhibits the loaf rising when put in the oven, and makes for a tough crust.

2. To cook potatoes to add to bread dough, I find the best way is to boil them in their skins, watch them carefully and, immediately they are cooked but before they start to disintegrate, pour off the water, cover the potatoes with a clean thick cloth, put the lid on the saucepan and leave them for a few minutes. This method produces the best results with our indifferent English potatoes. They will be easy to peel, and to sieve enough of them to make 125g/¼lb is very quick work, although it is obviously more economical of effort to cook enough potatoes at one go to make potato cakes or potatoes browned in a frying pan.

BOULA

NGERIE

RICE BREAD

This is excellent bread for keeping, since the rice remains moist, and the texture is beautifully light and honeycombed. It is also a loaf which is very easy to mix and to bake. The variety of rice used is not, I think, of great importance. I always have Italian round-grained and basmati long-grained rice in the house and have used both for bread. Those who habitually use only brown unpolished rice will know that it takes longer to cook and absorbs more water than white rice. Use a sandwich loaf tin of 1.8–2-litre/3–3½-pint capacity.

90g/3oz rice (about ½ a cup) uncooked weight, three times its volume of water for cooking it, and for the dough 500g/1lb strong plain flour, 15g/½oz fresh yeast, 15–20g/½–¾oz salt, about 300ml/½ pint water, and fat for the tin. (If you use a larger saucepan you need extra water.)

Note: *If you use dried granular yeast, use a scant 7g/¼oz.*

Put the rice in a thick saucepan of 1 litre/1¾ pint capacity, cover it with 1½ cups of water. Bring it to the boil, cover the saucepan, leave the rice to cook steadily until the water is absorbed and little holes have formed all over the surface of the rice.

While the rice is cooking, weigh out and prepare all the other ingredients. Cream the yeast with a little warm water. Put the salt in a measuring jug and dissolve it in 150ml/¼ pint of very hot water, then add cold water to make up the correct quantity.

When the rice is cooked, and while it is still very warm, amalgamate it, very thoroughly, with the flour. Now add the yeast, then the salted water, and mix the dough in the usual way. It will be rather soft. Cover it and leave it to rise for 1–1½ hours, until it is at least double in volume, and bubbly.

Probably the dough will be too soft to handle very much, so it may be necessary to dry it out a little by adding more flour before breaking it down and transferring it – very little kneading is necessary – to a warmed and well-greased tin. The dough should fill the tin by two-thirds. Cover it with a cloth or a sheet of polythene, leave it until it has risen above the top of the tin.

Bake the bread in the usual way, at 230°C/gas 8 for 15 minutes, then at 200°C/gas 6, for another 15 minutes, before turning the loaf out of its tin and returning it to the oven, on its side, for a final 15–20 minutes at the same temperature. If the crust shows signs of baking too hard and taking too much colour, cover the loaf with a large bowl or an inverted oval casserole.

STAFFORDSHIRE OATCAKES

My recipe is adapted slightly from the one supplied by Philip Oakes, writing in the *Sunday Times* in December 1974: it came originally, he said, from the *North Staffordshire Evening Sentinel*:

> On Saturday nights my mother used to send me out to buy the oatcakes for Sunday breakfast . . .
>
> The shop stood half-way down the hill, the bottom of its bow window level with my eyes. It was open for business at 7.30 but always I got there half an hour early to watch the oatcakes being made. Looming above me, his belly bulging in a striped apron, the oatcake man would test the heat of his bakestone – a black iron plate which sent the thermals shimmering to the ceiling – and from a tall white jug he would pour out 12 liquid pats of oatmeal which spat and bubbled on the metal.
>
> There was an instant, mouth-watering smell of toasted oatmeal as the mixture crisped at the edges. One by one, the oatcakes would be flipped over, then with both sides done they would be stacked in a tender, tottering pile beside the bakestone. I would buy 12 and bear them home, clasped to my chest like a hot and fragrant poultice.
>
> When I left the Potteries oatcakes disappeared from my life and the loss was insupportable. I searched everywhere but soon found that they were an intensely local delicacy, unheard of north of Leek, unimagined south of Banbury. Most shops think of oatcake as an oatmeal biscuit. But the oatcakes of my childhood were soft oatmeal pancakes, delicious with butter and honey, delectable with bacon and eggs.

To make sixteen to eighteen 15–18-cm/6–7-inch oatcakes or pancakes: *250g/½lb each fine oatmeal and plain bread flour (I use 85 per cent wheatmeal, but white will do), 2 teaspoons salt, 15g/½oz bakers' yeast, approximately 450ml/¾ pint each warm milk and water. A little fat will be needed for the frying pan.*

Note: *If you use dried granular yeast, use a scant 7g/¼oz.*

Put the oatmeal and the wheatmeal into a bowl with the salt. Cream the yeast with a little of the warm milk and water mixture. Stir it into the flours, add the rest of the liquid and with a wooden spoon beat the mixture into a batter. If it is too thick add a little more warm water. Cover the bowl and leave to rise for an hour or so.

Make the oatcakes as for pancakes. I like them very thin and curling a little at the edges. Oatcakes can be kept warm and soft in a folded cloth; and if you want to make them in advance and reheat them in the pan or in a slow oven, dampen the cloth so that they remain moist.

Enough for eight or nine people.

THICK PARMESAN BISCUITS

A little-known recipe from *The Cookery Book of Lady Clark of Tillypronie*, compiled from a treasure-house of notebooks left by Lady Clark and published in 1909, nine years after her death. As is inevitable in books compiled from cookery notebooks, Lady Clark's recipes are often sketchy. It is for the ideas, the historical aspect and the feeling of authenticity, the certainty that these recipes were actually used and the dishes successful – or they would not have been recorded – that the book is so valuable.

This recipe is an exceptionally good one. With the help of a friend, I once made a huge batch of them for an Anglo-Greek wedding party held in my London house. Smoked salmon and chicken sandwiches made with the home-baked bread of the house, and an immense pyramid of the delicate Greek shortbread cakes called *kourabiedes* made by the bridegroom's mother, Greek sugared almonds, and an English cake (bought) completed a quite notable although extremely simple wedding buffet.

60g/2oz each butter and grated Parmesan, 125g/¼lb plain flour, 1 egg yolk, salt, cayenne pepper.

Rub the butter into the flour, add the cheese, egg and seasonings. Moisten with a little water if necessary. Roll out the dough to the thickness of 1cm/½ inch. Cut into 2.5-cm/1-inch diameter rounds. Arrange on a baking sheet. Bake in the centre or lower centre of a very moderate oven, at 150°C/gas 2, for just on 20 minutes. Serve hot.

Lady Clark makes the point that it is the thickness of these biscuits that gives them their character. The Parmesan is also essential. English cheese will not do.

The biscuits can be stored in a tin and heated up when wanted.

Makes 12 biscuits.

The ITALIAN PIZZA *and the* FRENCH PISSALADIÈRE

In colloquial Italian the word 'pizza' denotes a pie of almost any kind, savoury or sweet, open or covered, and with a basis of any variety of pastry or of leavened dough, and to the English-speaking world a pizza means a flat, round, open pie with a filling of tomato and onion topped with melting cheese.

In short, the pizza which has travelled the world, reached almost every deep-freeze cabinet in Europe and America, become a mainstay of the take-away food counters, and is manufactured by the ton in the food-processing factories, was originally the Neapolitan interpretation of an ancient method of dealing with a piece of bread dough in a rough and ready fashion, strewing it with a few onions, a handful of salt sardines or anchovies, or a sprinkling of pork scrapple left from the rendering down of lard. To us the pizza may be indissolubly associated with the tomato, but it did of course exist long before tomatoes were cultivated in Europe. Something like it was familiar to the Greeks and to the Romans, probably the early Arabs had a version of it – they certainly have one now – and the Armenians claim that they invented it (perhaps they did); there are variations to be found in Spain where it is called *coca*, meaning a kind of cake, and in Provence where it was once known as *pissaladeira*, and has now all but merged with the universal pizza. In eastern France the quiche of Lorraine, almost as much a victim of current fashion and factory production as the pizza, was originally made on a basis of bread dough, and a quiche was not committed exclusively to a filling of bacon and cream and eggs. It could be, and often was, the basis for a spread of fresh plums or cherries, which baked to a delicious sticky, sugary mass. This brings it all nearer home, to our own lardy cakes and fruit-enriched doughs. For surely, anywhere there was leavened bread there was likely to be left-over dough, to be quickly made up and baked to provide something cheap and filling for children, for the poor, the hungry.

What seems extraordinary is that so many people in so many places can be induced into paying so high a price for something so simple and cheap to make at home and so difficult to reproduce in mass-market terms as the Neapolitan pizza. Even taking into consideration your own time and work plus the cost of the oven fuel, a home-made pizza is something of a bargain, making the mass-produced 'pizza pie' – many are made with a baking powder dough, not a yeast-leavened one, hence their incredible toughness – seem rather more of a confidence trick than most products of its kind. This is probably because being an alien import with an unfamiliar name it contains a built-in mystique. Equivalent prices for a hot cheese sandwich or a take-away portion of cottage pie would soon meet with resistance.

Now, it must be said that the authentic Neapolitan pizza was – and is – heavy-going, and lies uneasy on any but the most robust of stomachs. It became popular because it was cheap, and the original pizzeria, or pizza house, furnished with its own brick oven in which every pizza was baked to order, was a refuge – if rather a noisy one – where the hungry and hard-up could eat their hefty round of cheese-topped pizza and drink a glass or two of cheap wine for the equivalent of a few pence. As late as 1950 the pizzeria was an almost exclusively southern Italian institution. The beehive-shaped brick oven installed in the pizzeria was a conscious survival, or revival, of the ancient, traditional bread oven, and it was then rare to find a pizzeria north of Rome, whereas now there must be one or more in almost every town throughout the Italian peninsula.

Along the Mediterranean coast, west beyond Genoa and across the borders of Provence a different version of pizza was to be bought from the bakeries. It was baked and displayed for sale in huge rectangular iron oven trays from which the customers could buy slices at the same time as they bought their morning bread. On the Ligurian coast this pizza was known as a sardenara, because originally salted sardines were part of the top dressing, the basis of which was onion and tomato. In Provence between Nice and Marseilles the *pissaladeira*, very similar to the *sardenara*, owed its name to *pissala*, a brined and potted mixture of small-fry peculiar to the coasts of the County of Nice and of Provence. By the time I first encountered the *pissaladeira*, in the 1930s, anchovies had taken the place of the *pissala*, and there were basically two kinds of dressings for the bread dough, one mainly of onions stewed in olive oil, with black olives added, the other with tomatoes, anchovies and, again, black olives. A third, called *anchoïade*, was an anchovy and garlic mixture. This one is now nearly always made on a basis of ready cooked, fresh and thick bread slices, but is much nicer spread on the raw dough and then baked. None of these versions featured the cheese of the Neapolitan pizza.

These variations, then, are the ones upon which I base my own pizza mixtures: onion, tomato, anchovy, black olives, in varying proportions and not necessarily all at once, but always cooked in olive oil and flavoured with oregano, the wild marjoram of Italy. Sometimes, but not invariably, garlic goes into the mixture. I don't include any top dressing of chewy cheese. The pizza manufacturers, evidently believing it to be an essential selling point, use either processed Cheddar or a specially developed 'pizza Mozzarella'. Both seem to me quite pointless. The mass-market product would be better as well as cheaper without them.

The dough I use is what the Italians would call *casalinga*, a household dough rather than a baker's basic bread dough, which means it is made rather lighter, with an egg or two and olive oil – or butter if you prefer it – so that what it amounts to is a very modified form of brioche dough.

Once you have acquired the knack of making this dough – it was through the pizza that I first discovered how easy it is to work with yeast – it is no trouble whatever to make a pizza in any size or form you please.

One word of advice, though, as to the filling or dressing for the dough. A great many English people make the mistake of thinking that the more oddments added in the way of bits of sausage, bacon, mushrooms, prawns and anything else that comes to hand, the better the pizza will be. In fact the reverse is true. The black olives for example, can be eliminated but you can use a few extra anchovies. And tomato is not obligatory any more than is cheese. Just onions, if you like them, slowly, slowly stewed in olive oil, and with a final addition of anchovy fillets before the dough goes into the oven, make an excellent pizza. For those allergic to onions, a tomato filling without them is perfectly feasible. There is really no problem and not many rules. The idea is, basically, that what you spread on the dough sinks into it, amalgamates itself with, and becomes an integral part of, the bread as it bakes. A mass of bitty things won't do this. They will just stay on top of the dough, toughen and probably burn as the pizza cooks. It is insufficient understanding of the nature and behaviour of leavened dough which causes English cooks to attempt so many non-viable additions and substitutions. Or is it the English propensity for treating every basic dish, so long as it is a foreign one, as a dustbin for the reception of left-overs?

from English Bread and Yeast Cookery, *1977*

LIGURIAN PIZZA

Sardenara

This recipe is for a small pizza baked in a 18–20-cm/7–8-inch shallow tart tin with a removable base. For those unfamiliar with yeast-leavened dough and its workings, this is the easiest way to start, and the best way to ensure that a presentable pizza will be produced at the first attempt.

For the filling: *500g/1lb ripe tomatoes, or half and half fresh and Italian tinned tomatoes, 2 small onions, 2 cloves of garlic, salt, sugar, freshly ground pepper, dried oregano, olive oil, 60g/2oz tin of flat anchovy fillets in olive oil, 12 very small black olives with their stones removed.*

For the dough: *10g/¼oz fresh yeast, 2 tablespoons milk, 1 teaspoon salt, 125g/¼lb plain white flour/strong bread flour for preference, 1 whole egg, 2 tablespoons olive oil.*

Note: *If you use dried granular yeast, use 5g/⅛oz.*

To make the dough: put the yeast into a cup with the milk. Mix it to a cream. Put the flour into a bowl with the salt, warm it for 4 or 5 minutes – no longer – in a very low oven; add the yeast mixture, then the whole egg and the olive oil. Mix all well together, then with your hands work the dough rapidly until it is smooth. Form it into a ball. Shake a little extra flour over it. Cover the bowl. Put it in a warm place and leave for 1½–2 hours until the dough is well risen and very light.

To make the filling: pour boiling water over the tomatoes, leave them a couple of minutes, then slip off the skins. Chop the tomatoes roughly. Peel the onions, slice them into the thinnest possible rounds. Peel the garlic cloves. Crush them with the flat of a knife. Into a heavy 25-cm/10-inch frying pan or sauté pan put enough olive oil to cover the surface. Let the oil warm over low heat then put in the onions. They should stew gently, without frying, for about 7 minutes. Add the crushed garlic cloves, then the fresh tomatoes. With the pan uncovered, increase the heat, so that the water content of the tomatoes evaporates rapidly. Add seasonings of salt and a very little sugar. When the fresh tomatoes have reduced almost to a pulp add the tinned ones if you are using them. There is no need to chop them. Simply spoon them into the pan with some of their juice and crush them with a wooden spoon.

Cook for a further few minutes, until the sauce has again reduced. Taste for seasoning – not forgetting that the olives and anchovies will provide extra salt – and scatter in a scant teaspoon of oregano. The basis of the pizza filling is now ready. The olives and anchovies are added when the dough is spread with the tomato mixture and is all but ready to cook.

Brush the tart tin, or a round iron sheet with slightly raised rim, or an earthenware plate of similar shape and size, with olive oil. Break down the dough, which should have doubled in volume and feel puffy and soft, sprinkle it with flour so that it does not stick to your hands, reshape it into a ball which you put into the centre of the oiled tin. With your knuckles gently press out the dough until it fills the tin. Turn the oven on to fairly hot, 220–230°C/gas 7–8, and have a baking sheet ready on the centre shelf.

Now spread the dough with the warm tomato mixture, break the anchovy fillets into pieces and arrange them at random on the top. Season them with a little ground black pepper. Scatter the black olives among the pieces of anchovy, add a final extra sprinkling of oregano and olive oil.

Leave the prepared pizza on the top of the stove for about 10 minutes, until the oven is really hot and the dough has started to rise again. Now slip the tin into the oven, leave it for 15 minutes, then decrease the heat to 190°C/gas 5, and cook for another 10–15 minutes. Alternatively, leave the oven at the same temperature and simply move the pizza to a lower shelf. If the filling begins to look dry, cover it with a piece of oiled foil or greaseproof paper.

Serve your pizza hot, with the base of the tart tin still underneath it, the whole on a flat serving platter.

Enough for four people for a first dish.

A LARGE ROUND PIZZA *in the* MIDDLE EASTERN MANNER

The filling for this pizza is made with meat, spices, garlic and a good deal of tomato. In Armenian and Lebanese cooking the ground berries of a plant called sumac are much used as a spice and should go into the filling. Sumac can be found in some Middle Eastern shops. It is because, for most of us, the filling must be made without this spice that I call it 'in the Middle Eastern manner'. This is an excellent pizza, in some ways the best of all, and if you have lamb left from a joint it provides a splendid way of using it, and at very little cost.

For the dough: *10g/¼oz fresh yeast, approximately 10 tablespoons milk, 250g/½lb strong flour, 2 teaspoons salt, 1 whole large egg, 2 tablespoons olive oil. Extra olive oil will be needed for the dish.*

Note: *If you use dried granular yeast, use 5g/⅛oz.*

For the filling: *a small onion, olive oil, 175–250g/6–8oz cooked or raw minced lamb, 2 or 3 cloves of garlic, salt, seasonings of ground cinnamon, cumin, cloves, pepper and sumac (if available), 250g/8oz tin of peeled tomatoes, 1 teaspoon sugar, 1 teaspoon dried mint.*

To cook the filling, melt the chopped onion in olive oil. Add the meat and let it brown gently; put in the peeled and crushed garlic cloves, salt, a level teaspoon each of cinnamon and ground cumin, a half teaspoon of ground cloves, or of mixed sweet spice, and the same of freshly ground black pepper and sumac. Add the tomatoes from the tin, cover the pan and simmer gently until the juice has evaporated and the whole mixture is fairly thick. Taste it for seasoning. It should be really well spiced, so may need more pepper and perhaps extra cumin. A teaspoon or two of sugar may be needed, and a little dried mint can also be added.

Having mixed the dough (as on page 366) and left it to rise until very light and puffy, oil a large 30-cm/12-inch platter and spread the dough on it, taking it right up to the edges. Leave it, covered, for 15 minutes, until it has returned to life. Spread the warm filling over it. There should not be too thick a layer. Again leave the prepared pizza for 10–15 minutes before putting it into the oven at 220°C/gas 7 for 15 minutes, and another 15 at 190–200°C/gas 5–6, or alternatively at the original temperature but on a lower shelf. In either case it is a good idea to cover the pizza with a piece of oiled greaseproof paper at half time, as the filling should not dry out.

Enough for seven to ten people for a first dish.

PROVENÇAL ONION PIE

Pissaladière

Pissaladière is not so common nowadays as it was before the war, when it could be bought hot from the oven in the early morning at every street corner in the old quarters of Marseille and Toulon. Not so long ago, however, having spotted some in a bakery in Avignon, I went in and asked for '*une tranche de Pissaladière*'. The shopkeeper did not know what I meant. 'What, then, is that?' I asked. '*Ça, Madame, c'est du Pizza Provençal,*' was the surprising reply. Odd how that Neapolitan pizza has captured people's imaginations, even in Provence, where they have their own traditional version of it, the great difference being that the Provençal variety is made without the top dressing of chewy cheese characteristic of the Neapolitan pizza.

For the dough: *45g/1½oz butter, 150g/5oz plain flour, salt, 1 egg, 15g/½oz fresh yeast, a little water.*

Note: *If you use dried granular yeast, use 7g/¼oz.*

For the filling: *olive oil, 625g/1¼lb onions, 2 tomatoes, pepper, salt, a dozen anchovy fillets, a dozen small, stoned black olives.*

Cut the butter in little pieces and rub it into the flour. Add a good pinch of salt. Make a well in the centre; put in the egg and the yeast dissolved in about 2 tablespoons of barely tepid water. Mix and knead until the dough comes away clean from the sides of the bowl. Shape into a ball, make a deep cross-cut on the top, put on a floured plate, cover with a floured cloth and leave in a warm place to rise for 2 hours.

Heat 3 or 4 tablespoons of olive oil in a heavy frying pan. Put in the thinly sliced onions and cook them very gently, with the cover on the pan, until they are quite soft and pale golden. They must not fry or turn brown. Add the skinned tomatoes and the seasonings (plus garlic if you like). Continue cooking until tomatoes and onions are amalgamated, and the water from the tomatoes evaporated.

When the dough has risen, sprinkle it with flour and break it down again. Knead once more into a ball, which you place in the centre of an oiled, 20-cm/8-inch tart tin. With your knuckles press it gently but quickly outwards until it is spread right over the tin and all round the sides. Put in the filling. Make a criss-cross pattern all over the top with the anchovies, then fill in with the olives. Leave to rise another 15 minutes. Bake in the centre of a preheated oven, with the tin standing on a baking sheet, at 200°C/gas 6, for 20 minutes, then turn down to 180°C/gas 4, and cook another 20 minutes.

Enough for four people as a first dish.

BOOKS *by* ELIZABETH DAVID

A Book of Mediterranean Food

First published by John Lehmann 1950. Revised editions 1955, 1958, 1965, 1988.
New introduction 1991
Copyright © The Estate of Elizabeth David 1950, 1955, 1958, 1965, 1988, 1991

French Country Cooking

First published by John Lehmann 1951. Revised editions 1958, 1966
Copyright © The Estate of Elizabeth David 1951, 1958, 1966

Italian Food

First published by Macdonald and Co 1954. Revised editions 1963, 1969, 1977, 1987
Copyright © The Estate of Elizabeth David 1954, 1963, 1969, 1977, 1987

Summer Cooking

First published by Museum Press 1955. Revised edition 1965
Copyright © The Estate of Elizabeth David 1955, 1965

French Provincial Cooking

First published by Michael Joseph Ltd 1960. Revised editions 1965, 1967, 1970
Copyright © The Estate of Elizabeth David 1960, 1965, 1967, 1970

Spices, Salt and Aromatics in the English Kitchen

First published by Penguin Books 1970. Revised editions 1973, 1975
Copyright © The Estate of Elizabeth David 1970, 1973, 1975

English Bread and Yeast Cookery

First published by Allen Lane 1977
Copyright © The Estate of Elizabeth David 1977

An Omelette and a Glass of Wine

First published by Jill Norman at Robert Hale Ltd 1984
Copyright © The Estate of Elizabeth David 1984

Harvest of the Cold Months

First published by Michael Joseph Ltd 1994
Copyright © The Estate of Elizabeth David 1994

Elizabeth David's Christmas

First published by Michael Joseph Ltd 2003. Reissued 2005
Copyright © The Estate of Elizabeth David and Jill Norman 2003

French country cooking
a Penguin Handbook
Elizabeth David
ELIZABETH DAVID
October
BY ELIZABETH DAVID
FRENCH COUNTRY COOKING
by Elizabeth David
Mediterranean Food
Elizabeth David
Mediterranean FOOD
by Elizabeth David
A BOOK OF MEDITERRANEAN FOOD
A PENGUIN HANDBOOK BY ELIZABETH DAVID
DECORATIONS BY JOHN MINTON
French Provincial

INDEX

A

aïoli 302, 303
  grilled red mullet with *aïoli* and *sauce rouille* 178, 179
almonds
  orange and almond cake 342, 343
  torrone molle 330, 331
anitra in agrodolce 278, 279
apples
  apples cooked in butter 329
  apples with lemon and cinnamon 320, 321
  pheasant with cream, Calvados and apple 283
apricot compôte 329
Armenian mushrooms 141
artichokes
  Jerusalem artichoke soup 58, 59
  Venetian artichokes 124, 125
aubergines
  aubergine chutney 31
  aubergine purée 31
  lamb and aubergine stew 236, 237
  Persian lamb with aubergines 240, 241
  Provençal aubergine mousse 127
  Turkish aubergines 126

B

bacon
  bacon omelette 77
  broad beans with bacon 130, 131
  quiche Lorraine 88, 89
  scallops with white wine and bacon 194
baked bream 180, 181
baked eggs 82, 83
baked salmon trout 186, 187
bar à la marseillaise 182, 183
Barbados baked and glazed gammon 254, 255
basil 42
  trenette with pesto 114, 115
beans
  best end of neck of lamb with haricot beans 238–9
  broad beans with bacon 130, 131
  broad beans with egg and lemon 130
  broad beans with yoghurt 130
  haricot beans 134
  slow-cooked beans 132, 133
  see also lentils
béarnaise sauce 294
béchamel sauce 298
beef
  beef and wine stew with black olives 218, 219
  beef with red wine, onions and mushrooms 216–17
  courgette moussaka 242, 243
  oxtail stewed with white grapes 224, 225
  paupiettes of beef 220, 221
  Provençal beef and wine stew 210–211, 212
  spiced beef loaf 222, 223
  Sussex stewed steak 214
  tagliatelle with Bolognese sauce 100, 101
  see also veal
best end of neck of lamb with haricot beans 238–9
biscuits: thick Parmesan biscuits 360, 361
blackberry water ice 325
bœuf à la bourguignonne 216–17
bœuf à la gardiane 218, 219
Bolognese sauce: tagliatelle with Bolognese sauce 100, 101
braised meat roll 228, 229
braised shin of veal 226, 227
brandy
  langouste in tomato and brandy sauce 202
  mutton stewed with brandy and garlic 232, 233
  pheasant with cream, Calvados and apple 283
bread 344–5, 349
  a basic loaf 350–51
  potato bread 352, 353
  rice bread 356, 357
  see also yeast baking
bream: baked bream 180, 181
broad beans
  with bacon 130, 131
  with egg and lemon 130
  with yoghurt 130
butter
  apples cooked in butter 329
  chicken baked with green pepper and cinnamon butter 272
  chicory braised in butter 138

C

cakes 311
  chocolate cake 338, 339

coffee cake 340, 341
orange and almond cake 342, 343
calamari in umido 203
Calvados: pheasant with cream, Calvados and apple 283
carciofi alla veneziana 124, 125
carré d'agneau aux haricots à la bretonne 238–9
carrottes Vichy 136, 137
Cavaillon 118–21
chatchouka 86, 87
cheese
green gnocchi 116, 117
penne with mascarpone 102, 103
potato pie 150
snow cheese 326, 327
spinach pie 152, 153
thick Parmesan biscuits 360, 361
tomatoes baked with Gruyère 140, 141
chestnuts: roast pheasant with chestnut sauce 284, 285
chicken
chicken baked with green pepper and cinnamon butter 270, 271
chicken baked with Italian spice and olive oil 268
chicken liver pâté 32, 33
chicken pot-roasted with fennel and ham 266, 267
chicken risotto 164
chicken with tarragon 260, 261
sautéd chicken with olives and tomatoes 262, 263
chicory braised in butter 138
chocolate
chocolate cake 338, 339
chocolate chinchilla 334
chocolate mousse 332, 333
St Émilion au chocolat 336, 337
torrone molle 330, 331
chutney: aubergine chutney 31
cider: grilled pork chops with cider sauce 248
cinnamon
apples with lemon and cinnamon 320, 321
chicken baked with green pepper and cinnamon butter 270, 271
chocolate chinchilla 334
clams
fisherman's clams 192
spaghetti with clams 110, 111
coffee
coffee cake 340, 341
coffee ice cream 324, 325
compôte: apricot compôte 329
coriander mushrooms 26, 27
côtes de porc vallée d'auge 248
courgettes
courgette moussaka 242, 243
courgette and tomato soup 60, 61
tian of courgettes 74–5

D

daube de bœuf provençale 210–211, 212
desserts *see* sweet dishes
duck
duck in sour-sweet sauce 278, 279
duck with figs 274, 275
Welsh salt duck 276

E

eggs 71
aïoli 302, 303
baked eggs 82, 83
béarnaise sauce 294
broad beans with egg and lemon 130
chatchouka 86, 87
chocolate chinchilla 334
green sauce 300
hollandaise sauce 295
leek and cream pie 92, 93
macaroni carbonara 106, 107
mayonnaise 299
omelettes 76–7
onion tart 90, 91
pipérade 85
poached eggs 84
quiche Lorraine 88, 89
quick kedgeree 168, 169
Spanish omelette 80–81
tian of courgettes 74–5
tian with spinach and potatoes 72, 73
tuna mayonnaise 300
Egypt 18–20
endives au beurre 138
épaule d'agneau boulangère 234, 235
escalopes of veal with vermouth and cream sauce 229

F

faisin à la cauchoise 283
fasœil al fùrn 132, 133
fasoūlia 134
fennel 42, 44
  chicken pot-roasted with fennel and ham 266, 267
fettuccine: with fresh tomato sauce 104, 105
figs: duck with figs 274, 275
filetti di tacchino al marsala 280, 281
fillets of sole with cream and onion sauce 188, 189
fish 172–5, 177
  baked bream 180, 181
  baked salmon trout 186, 187
  fillets of sole with cream and onion sauce 188, 189
  grey mullet with olives and white wine 181
  grilled red mullet with *aïoli* and *sauce rouille* 178, 179
  quick kedgeree 168, 169
  sea bass with mushrooms and potatoes 182, 183
  tuna mayonnaise 300
  turbot with cream and herb sauce 190, 191
  see also shellfish
fisherman's clams 192
fistuqia 130
flan de poireaux à la berrichonne 92, 93
France
  Cavaillon market 118–21
  dishes for collectors 204–7
  French fare 66–9
  pissaladière 362–3
  Vichy 137
fresh green pea soup 50, 51
fresh tomato sauce 305

G

game birds 259
  partridges braised in white wine 286
  pheasant with cream, Calvados and apple 283
  pigeons with peas 287
  roast pheasant with chestnut sauce 284, 285
gammon: Barbados baked and glazed gammon 254, 255
garlic
  aïoli 302, 303
  grilled red mullet with *aïoli* and *sauce rouille* 178, 179
  mutton stewed with brandy and garlic 232, 233
  spaghetti with oil and garlic 112
  spaghetti with oil, garlic and chilli 112, 113
  tomato, garlic and orange sauce 305
gâteau au chocolat 338, 339
gâteau moka 340, 341
gazpacho 48, 49
globe artichokes: Venetian artichokes 124, 125
gnocchi: green gnocchi 116, 117
gooseberry fool 312
grapes: oxtail stewed with white grapes 224, 225
gratin dauphinois 148, 149
green gnocchi 116, 117
green peas
  fresh green pea soup 50, 51
  green peas and ham 145
  pigeons with peas 287
  risotto with green peas 162, 163
green pepper berries: chicken baked with green pepper and cinnamon butter 270, 271
green peppers
  chatchouka 86, 87
  Piedmontese peppers 24, 25
green sauce 300
grey mullet with olives and white wine 181
grilled pork chops with cider sauce 248
grilled red mullet with *aïoli* and *sauce rouille* 178, 179
Gruyère cheese
  spinach pie 152, 153
  tomatoes baked with Gruyère 140, 141

H

haddock: quick kedgeree 168, 169
ham
  Barbados baked and glazed gammon 254, 255
  chicken pot-roasted with fennel and ham 266, 267
  green peas and ham 145
  macaroni carbonara 106, 107
  potato pie 150
haricot beans 134
  best end of neck of lamb with haricot beans 238–9
  slow-cooked beans 132, 133
herbs 42–5
  omelette with herbs 77
  pork chops baked with aromatic herbs 248, 249
  turbot with cream and herb sauce 190, 191
  vegetable and herb soup 52, 53
  see also individual herbs
hollandaise sauce 295
horseradish: walnut and horseradish sauce 304

I

ice cream
blackberry water ice 325
coffee ice cream 324, 325
Italy
fish markets 172–5
Ligurian pizza 366–7
pizza 362–3

J

Jerusalem artichoke soup 58, 59

K

kedgeree 168, 169
khichri 170, 171
kitchens 156–7

L

lamb
best end of neck of lamb with haricot beans 238–9
courgette moussaka 242, 243
lamb and aubergine stew 236, 237
mutton stewed with brandy and garlic 232, 233
Persian lamb with aubergines 240, 241
shoulder of lamb baked with potatoes 234, 235
langouste in tomato and brandy sauce 202
leeks
leek and cream pie 92, 93
Provençal leeks 138, 139
vegetable and herb soup 52, 53
lemons
apples with lemon and cinnamon 320, 321
broad beans with egg and lemon 130
lentils
khichri 170, 171
spiced lentil soup 62, 63
Ligurian pizza 366–7
liver
chicken liver pâté 32, 33
pork and liver pâté 34, 35
tagliatelle with Bolognese sauce 100, 101
lobster Courchamps 201

M

macaroni carbonara 106, 107
maiale al latte 246, 247
maqlub of aubergines 240, 241
marjoram 44, 45
marsala: turkey breasts with marsala 280, 281
mascarpone: penne with mascarpone 102, 103
mayonnaise 299
green sauce 300
tuna mayonnaise 300
meat 209
braised meat roll 228, 229
see also lamb, pork, beef
melon stuffed with wild strawberries 318
milk
béchamel sauce 298
pork cooked in milk 246, 247
potatoes cooked in milk 146
minestra di pomodoro 51
mint 42
moules au riz à la basquaise 195
moules marinière 196, 197
moussaka: courgette moussaka 242, 243
mousse
chocolate mousse 332, 333
raspberry and redcurrant mousse 315
mulet aux olives et au vin blanc 181
mushrooms
Armenian mushrooms 141
coriander mushrooms 26, 27
mushroom soup 54, 55
sea bass with mushrooms and potatoes 182, 183
Veronese mushroom sauce 304
mussels
moules marinière 196, 197
mussel soup 64, 65
mussels with spiced rice 195
ragoût of shellfish 198, 199
mutton stewed with brandy and garlic 232, 233

N

noisettes de porc aux pruneaux 204–7, 250–51, 252
nougat: *torrone molle* 330, 331

O

oatcakes: Staffordshire oatcakes 358, 359
œufs en cocotte 82, 83
olive oil
aïoli 302, 303
chicken baked with Italian spice and olive oil 269
mayonnaise 299
spaghetti with oil and garlic 112
spaghetti with oil, garlic and chilli 112, 113

olives
beef and wine stew with black olives 218, 219
grey mullet with olives and white wine 181
Provençal leeks 138, 139
sautéd chicken with olives and tomatoes 262, 263
omelettes 76–7
bacon omelette 77
with herbs 77
Spanish omelette 80–81
tomato omelette 77
onions
fillets of sole with cream and onion sauce 188, 189
onion tart 90, 91
pipérade 85
Provençal onion pie 370, 371
oranges
orange and almond cake 342, 343
pork baked with wine and oranges 244, 245
tomato, garlic and orange sauce 305
oregano 44, 45
ossi buchi milanese 226, 227
oxtail stewed with white grapes 224, 225

P

pancetta: slow-cooked beans 132, 133
papeton d'aubergines 127
Parmesan: thick Parmesan biscuits 360, 361
partridges braised in white wine 286
pasta 94–5, 99
fettuccine with fresh tomato sauce 104, 105
green gnocchi 116, 117
macaroni carbonara 106, 107
penne with mascarpone 102, 103
spaghetti with clams 110, 111
spaghetti with oil and garlic 112
spaghetti with oil, garlic and chilli 112, 113
tagliatelle with Bolognese sauce 100, 101
trenette with pesto 114, 115
pastry
leek and cream pie 92, 93
onion tart 90, 91
quiche Lorraine 88, 89
spinach pie 152, 153
pâtés
chicken liver pâté 32, 33
pork and liver pâté 34, 35
pork and spinach terrine 38, 39
rillettes 36, 37
paupiettes of beef 220, 221
peaches in white wine 318
pears baked in red wine 322, 323
peas
fresh green pea soup 50, 51
green peas and ham 145
pigeons with peas 287
risotto with green peas 162, 163
pêches au vin blanc 318
penne with mascarpone 102, 103
peperonata 144, 145
peperoni alla Piemontese 24, 25
pepper: chicken baked with green pepper and cinnamon butter 272
peppers
chatchouka 86, 87
Piedmontese peppers 24, 25
pipérade 85
spaghetti with oil, garlic and chilli 112, 113
sweet pepper and tomato stew 144, 145
perdrix à l'auvergnate 286
Périgord potatoes 146
Persian lamb with aubergines 240, 241
pesto: trenette with pesto 114, 115
pheasant
pheasant with cream, Calvados and apple 283
roast pheasant with chestnut sauce 284, 285
piccioni coi piselli 287
Piedmontese peppers 24, 25
pies
leek and cream pie 92, 93
potato pie 150
Provençal onion pie 370, 371
spinach pie 152, 153
pigeons with peas 287
pilaff rice 166–7
pipérade 85
piselli al prosciutto 145
pissaladière 362–3, 370, 371
pizza 362–4
a large round pizza in the Middle Eastern manner 368, 369
Ligurian pizza 366–7
poached eggs 84
poireaux à la provençale 138, 139
poires étuvées au vin rouge 322, 323
polpettone 228, 229
pommes au beurre 329

pommes de terre à la échirlète 146
pork
grilled pork chops with cider sauce 248
pork baked with wine and oranges 244, 245
pork chops baked with aromatic herbs 248, 249
pork cooked in milk 246, 247
pork and liver pâté 34, 35
pork noisettes with a prune and cream sauce 204–7, 250–51, 252
pork and spinach terrine 38, 39
rillettes 36, 37
slow-cooked beans 132, 133
see also bacon; ham; pancetta
potage aux champignons à la bressane 54, 55
potage de topinambours à la provençale 58, 59
potatoes
gratin dauphinois 148, 149
Périgord potatoes 146
potato bread 352, 353
potato pie 150
potatoes cooked in milk 146
potatoes in a paper bag 150, 151
sea bass with mushrooms and potatoes 182, 183
shoulder of lamb baked with potatoes 234, 235
Spanish omelette 80–81
tian with spinach and potatoes 72, 73
poulet à l'estragon 260, 261
poulet sauté aux olives de Provence 262, 263
poultry 259
see also chicken; duck; turkey
prawns: ragoût of shellfish 198, 199
Provençal aubergine mousse 127
Provençal beef and wine stew 210–211, 212
Provençal leeks 138, 139
Provençal onion pie 370, 371
Provençal tomato salad 28, 29
prunes: pork noisettes with a prune and cream sauce 204–7, 250–51, 252
puddings *see* sweet dishes
purée léontine 52, 53

Q

queue de bœuf des vignerons 224, 225
quiche Lorraine 88, 89

R

ragoût of shellfish 198, 199
ragù 100, 101
raspberries
raspberry and redcurrant mousse 315
raspberry shortbread 314, 315
summer pudding 312, 313
red mullet: grilled red mullet with *aïoli* and *sauce rouille* 178, 179
red peppers
grilled red mullet with *aïoli* and *sauce rouille* 178, 179
Piedmontese peppers 24, 25
pipérade 85
spaghetti with oil, garlic and chilli 112, 113
sweet pepper and tomato stew 144, 145
redcurrants
raspberry and redcurrant mousse 315
summer pudding 312, 313
rice 159
chicken risotto 164
khichri 170, 171
Milanese risotto 160
mussels with spiced rice 195
Persian lamb with aubergines 240, 241
pilaff rice 166–7
quick kedgeree 168, 169
rice bread 356, 357
risotto with green peas 162, 163
ricotta: green gnocchi 116, 117
rillettes 36, 37
risi e bisi 162, 163
risotto
chicken risotto 164
with green peas 162, 163
Milanese risotto 160
roast pheasant with chestnut sauce 284, 285
rosemary 42, 44, 45
rougets à la provençale 178, 179

S

sage 44, 45
St Émilion au chocolat 336, 337
salads: Provençal tomato salad 28, 29
salmon trout: baked salmon trout 186, 187
salsa di funghi alla veronese 304
salsa di pomidoro 305
salsa di pomidoro crudo 305
salt: Welsh salt duck 276
sardenara 366–7
sauces 293
aïoli 302, 303
béarnaise sauce 294

béchamel sauce 298
fettuccine with fresh tomato sauce 104, 105
fresh tomato sauce 305
green sauce 300
grilled red mullet with aïoli and *sauce rouille* 178, 179
hollandaise sauce 295
mayonnaise 299
roast pheasant with chestnut sauce 284, 285
tagliatelle with Bolognese sauce 100, 101
tomato, garlic and orange sauce 305
tomato sauce 305
tuna mayonnaise 300
turbot with cream and herb sauce 190, 191
Veronese mushroom sauce 304
walnut and horseradish sauce 304
sautéd chicken with olives and tomatoes 262, 263
scallops
ragoût of shellfish 198, 199
scallops with white wine and bacon 194
scampi: ragoût of shellfish 198, 199
sea bass with mushrooms and potatoes 182, 183
shellfish
fisherman's clams 192
langouste in tomato and brandy sauce 202
lobster Courchamps 201
moules marinière 196, 197
mussel soup 64, 65
mussels with spiced rice 195
ragoût of shellfish 198, 199
scallops with white wine and bacon 194
slow-cooked squid 203
spaghetti with clams 110, 111
shortbread: raspberry shortbread 314, 315
shoulder of lamb baked with potatoes 234, 235
slow-cooked beans 132, 133
slow-cooked squid 203
snow cheese 326, 327
sole: fillets of sole with cream and onion sauce 188, 189
soupe menerboise 60, 61
soups 47
courgette and tomato soup 60, 61
fresh green pea soup 50, 51
gazpacho 48, 49
Jerusalem artichoke soup 58, 59
mushroom soup 54, 55
mussel soup 64, 65
spiced lentil soup 62, 63
tomato soup 51
vegetable and herb soup 52, 53
spaghetti
with clams 110, 111
with oil and garlic 112
with oil, garlic and chilli 112, 113
Spain 288–91
spanakopittá 152, 153
Spanish omelette 80–81
spiced beef loaf 222, 223
spiced lentil soup 62, 63
spices
chicken baked with Italian spice and olive oil 269
mussels with spiced rice 195
see also individual spices
spinach
green gnocchi 116, 117
pork and spinach terrine 38, 39
spinach pie 152, 153
spinach with sultanas 154, 155
tian with spinach and potatoes 72, 73
squid: slow-cooked squid 203
Staffordshire oatcakes 358, 359
starters and light dishes 23
aubergine chutney 31
aubergine purée 31
chicken liver pâté 32, 33
coriander mushrooms 26, 27
Piedmontese peppers 24, 25
pork and liver pâté 34, 35
pork and spinach terrine 38, 39
Provençal tomato salad 28, 29
rillettes 36, 37
tomatoes with cream 28
strawberries: melon stuffed with wild strawberries 318
sugar confectionery 306–9
sultanas: with sultanas 154, 155
summer pudding 312, 313
Sussex stewed steak 214
sweet dishes 311
apples cooked in butter 329
apples with lemon and cinnamon 320, 321
apricot compôte 329
blackberry water ice 325
chocolate chinchilla 334
chocolate mousse 332, 333

coffee ice cream 324, 325
gooseberry fool 312
melon stuffed with wild strawberries 318
peaches in white wine 318
pears baked in red wine 322, 323
raspberry and redcurrant mousse 315
raspberry shortbread 314, 315
St Émilion au chocolat 336, 337
snow cheese 326, 327
summer pudding 312, 313
torrone molle 330, 331
see also cakes
sweet pepper and tomato stew 144, 145

T

tagliatelle with Bolognese sauce 100, 101
tarragon 45
chicken with tarragon 260, 261
tarts: onion tart 90, 91
terrine de campagne 34, 35
thick Parmesan biscuits 360, 361
thyme 44, 45
tian
of courgettes 74–5
with spinach and potatoes 72, 73
tomatoes
chatchouka 86, 87
courgette and tomato soup 60, 61
fettuccine with fresh tomato sauce 104, 105
fresh tomato sauce 305
gazpacho 48, 49
langouste in tomato and brandy sauce 202
pipérade 85
Provençal leeks 138, 139
Provençal tomato salad 28, 29
sautéd chicken with olives and tomatoes 262, 263
sweet pepper and tomato stew 144, 145
tomato, garlic and orange sauce 305
tomato omelette 77
tomato sauce 305
tomato soup 51
tomatoes baked with Gruyère 140, 141
tomatoes with cream 28
torrone molle 330, 331
tortilla 80–81
tranches de mouton à la poitevine 232, 233
trenette with pesto 114, 115
trout: baked salmon trout 186, 187
truite saumonée au four 186, 187
tuna mayonnaise 300
turbot with cream and herb sauce 190, 191
turkey: turkey breasts with marsala 280, 281
Turkish aubergines 126

V

veal
braised shin of veal 226, 227
escalopes of veal with vermouth and cream sauce 229
vegetables 123
vegetable and herb soup 52, 53
see also individual vegetables
Venetian artichokes 124, 125
Veronese mushroom sauce 304
Vichy 137
vongole alla marinara 192

W

walnut and horseradish sauce 304
Welsh salt duck 276
wine 256–7
beef and wine stew with black olives 218, 219
beef with red wine, onions and mushrooms 216–17
grey mullet with olives and white wine 181
partridges braised in white wine 286
peaches in white wine 318
pears baked in red wine 322, 323
pork baked with wine and oranges 244, 245
Provençal beef and wine stew 210–211, 212
scallops with white wine and bacon 194
turkey breasts with marsala 280, 281

Y

yeast baking
a large round pizza in the Middle Eastern manner 368, 369
Ligurian pizza 366–7
pizza and *pissaladière* 362–4
Provençal onion pie 370, 371
Staffordshire oatcakes 358, 359
see also bread
yellow peppers: Piedmontese peppers 24, 25
yoghurt: broad beans with yoghurt 130

Z

zuppa di cozze 64, 65